Best Behaviour

$\mathscr{B}$EST $\mathscr{B}$EHAVIOUR

A Complete Guide to Manners in the 1990s

NIGEL REES

BLOOMSBURY

This edition published in 1992 by
Bloomsbury Publishing Limited
2 Soho Square, London W1V 5DE

The moral right of the author has been asserted.

A copy of the CIP entry for this book is available from the British Library.

ISBN 0 7475 1208 6

10 9 8 7 6 5 4 3 2 1

Designed by Geoff Green
Typeset by Hewer Text Composition Services, Edinburgh
Printed in England by Clays Ltd, St Ives Plc

$\mathscr{C}$ONTENTS

Introduction		vii
1	Eating In	1
2	Eating Out	23
3	Family Life	43
4	Guests and Hosts	64
5	Marriage and Divorce	95
6	Neighbourliness	117
7	Public Behaviour	143
8	Relationships and Sex	167
9	Service and the Customer	182
10	Social Life	196
11	Speaking	225
12	Special Occasions	254
13	Titles and Addressing	274
14	Travel and Tipping	306
15	Working Life	321
16	Written Communication	338
Index		355

$\mathcal{I}$NTRODUCTION

I was once told of a Franciscan monk who, when travelling by train, encountered a group of yobbos. They were obviously rather taken with his monk's habit, his sandals, and possibly even his haircut. One of them said to him, rather rudely, "'Ere, what are you supposed to be, then?' The monk, with aplomb, replied, 'I'm supposed to be polite. What are *you* supposed to be?'

We are all supposed to be polite. Even in yobbo circles, which are held to be ever-widening these days, there is probably a dim memory of once having been told that good manners are what people are supposed to have, even if it has never been quite clear to yobbos why this should be.

Barely a month passes without some horrendous example of churlish manners being featured in the papers. Not so long ago there was the pregnant mother in Bristol who, when she asked a supermarket checkout girl for help with packing her purchases, was told: 'No, we're not in America, you know.' It appears also that barely a month passes without someone editorializing along the lines of, 'Whatever happened to common courtesy?' or 'What makes the British so beastly?' – usually in the adopted tones of a retired colonel from Godalming.

Yet, it is because of such concerns – which I believe are perfectly genuine – that I have found myself pondering two basic questions – which, like so many of the questions about manners I explore in this book, are very difficult to answer conclusively. First of all, have manners *really* worsened? (How, after all, could you measure such a shift?) And, secondly, in the more codified area of manners – which one may call 'etiquette' – how much of it really stands up to examination today?

A personal view

I do not consider myself to be a particularly well-mannered person. Indeed, there are some close to me who have greeted with amusement the idea of my pontificating on manners at all. In mitigation, I would plead that I am extremely well-behaved in queues – in fact, I could claim to be almost a world-class queuer – and I do not think that anyone would possibly class me as a yobbo, not with any degree of seriousness.

Yet I can be impatient and irritable, particularly when behind the wheel of a car, and, when it comes to those codified rules of etiquette, I am more than a little subversive. If I see nothing wrong, from a practical point of view, in shovelling my peas, putting my elbows on the table, or in ignoring the bores I find next to me at dinner table, then I do so.

Another relevant fact to disclose may be that I am in my late forties, and as the years go by one does tend to become rather less tolerant of other people's manners and rather more neglectful of one's own.

'Good manners always mean our own manners.'
G.K. Chesterton, *All Things Considered* (1908)

'I don't mind if you don't like my manners. I don't like 'em myself. They're pretty bad. I grieve over them long winter evenings.'
Humphrey Bogart as 'Philip Marlowe' in *The Big Sleep* (film 1946, from Raymond Chandler's novel)

Have manners really worsened?

It seems generally to be assumed that manners, social behaviour, call them what you will, *have* got worse, and the assumption is not only made by those people who are old enough to have valid points of reference.

I am not so sure. There have always been people who have fallen below the accepted level of behaviour at any particular time. There have always been yobbos and louts, though the names used to describe them have come and gone. There have always been pushy, rude people even within the confines of 'polite society'. Nothing very much changes in human behaviour, though there may be ups and downs, to be sure.

What people mean, when they say that manners have got worse, is that either the rules of behaviour have become laxer or that they are observed less. Uncouth people have probably always eaten food in the street. The brash (or the brave, depending on your point of view) may always have allowed themselves to express various degrees of sexual affection to members of the opposite (or even the same) sex while in public places. What may have changed is the extent to which the rest of society has decided to turn a blind eye to this kind of behaviour and to say nothing. It is also possible that because bad behaviour is now commonly available to the gaze of all in fictional and nonfictional television programmes, we are more aware of it, and in the comfort of our own homes. The foulness of the accompanying language these days makes the behaviour all the more noticeable. Society's perception is then that manners have got worse.

Manners are continuously, if slowly changing phenomena. They come and go. They decline and gradually reassert themselves. And, as I say, our perceptions of them shift. But no, though they may change, I do not think that they are actually *worse* – especially when it is only possible to view them subjectively and to measure any changes in them with the shakiest of data.

Whenever manners are discussed, one of the striking things is that there is very little consensus. To be sure, if you ask what sort of manners annoy people these days, they will frequently come up with the same areas of complaint – young people not saying 'please' and 'thank you', unhelpful shop assistants, bad table manners, litter, male chauvinist piggery. Above all, they mention transport-related manners. Transport does seem to bring out the worst in people – whether it's pushing pointlessly to get on a bus or train or, above all, when people sit behind a steering wheel.

However, although most people will say that, yes, manners are worse than they were, there are also individuals who assert that, on the other hand, some young people are a good deal better-mannered than their parents ever were. Or, as if it were some compensation, that many people are nowadays often better-mannered towards animals and the environment – kinder, in fact, to green issues than pink people.

'The gentle mind by gentle deeds is known.
For a man by nothing is so well bewray'd,
As by his manners.'
  Edmund Spenser, *The Faerie Queene* **(1589)**

'Good manners is the art of making those people easy with whom we converse. Whoever makes the fewest persons uneasy is the best bred in the company.'
  Jonathan Swift, *A Treatise on Good Manners and Good Breeding* **(c 1720)**

'You may observe that I am wellbred to a degree of needless scrupulosity.'
  Dr Samuel Johnson (1709–84)

'There is one rule relative to behaviour that ought to regulate every other; and it is simply to cherish such an habitual respect for mankind as may prevent us from disgusting a fellow-creature for the sake of a present indulgence.'
Mary Wollstonecraft, *A Vindication of the Rights of Woman* (1792)

'Manners are of more importance than laws. Upon them, in a great measure, the laws depend. The law touches us but here and there, and now and then. Manners are what vex or soothe, corrupt or purify, exalt or debase, barbarize or refine us, by a constant, steady, uniform, insensible operation, like that of the air we breathe in.'
Edmund Burke, *Letters on a Regicide Peace* (1797)

'Politeness is like an air cushion: there is nothing inside, but it softens the shocks of life.'
Arthur Schopenhauer (1788–1860)

Links to economic and political change

To put it another way, if manners are worse – or merely different – is it possible to identify a cause? It is, surely, quite likely that the get-rich-quick philosophy of the late 1980s, seemingly encouraged by government, gave rise to the kind of conspicuous spending and high-profile lack of consideration for others less well off than themselves, that characterized the successful young business types of that period. Government sets a tone for society. Politicians generally – particularly through their knock-about verbal brawls in parliament (now televised) – set a bad example. One way or another, some of this must rub off on the governed.

When times are hard, when unemployment is rife, it is

expecting rather a lot of the hard-pressed to display exquisite manners. If they are hungry, or have to exist within an increasingly brutal and inefficient social framework, it would be no surprise if they neglected to put good manners high on their order of priorities.

Changes in formalized manners – the rules of etiquette – take time, however, to come through. It is almost a definition of manners that they don't change quickly or in response to pressure or fashion or trends. Nevertheless, whatever is the 'done thing' or 'correct form' at any one time, can be put under pressure by the arrival of new types of social behaviour. It is one aim of this book to show how economic pressures and social trends have brought about identifiable changes in behaviour.

'It is almost a definition of a gentleman to say that he is one who never inflicts pain.'
Cardinal Newman, *The Idea of a University* (1852)

'A gentleman never offers a warm seat to a lady.'
Victorian etiquette book

'No gentleman ever has any money'; 'No gentleman ever takes exercise'; 'A gentleman never looks out of the window.'
Oscar Wilde (1854–1900)

'No gentleman ever weighs over two hundred pounds.'
Thomas B. Reed to David B. Henderson in the (US) House lobby (*c* 1895)

'No gentleman goes on a bus.'
Henry Cecil Wyld, Merton Professor of English Language and Literature at Oxford University (1920–45)

'Gentlemen do not take soup at luncheon.'
Lord Curzon to the Bursar of Balliol College, Oxford, when presented with a specimen menu for a visit by Queen Mary (1921)

'Gentlemen never wear brown in London'.
Lord Curzon (again) to a fellow member of Cabinet about a colleague's clothes

Terms of reference

Is there a difference between 'manners' and 'behaviour', 'etiquette' and 'correct form'? The terms tend to be used interchangeably; I have already done so, and will continue to, but it is worthwhile making the distinction between *manners*, meaning social behaviour of an acceptable standard, which it hardly needs to be argued is something worth having, and *etiquette*, which is a code of correct form for people who feel the need for such a thing. Questions about manners often shade over into questions of ethics and morality; etiquette questions, never.

I like neither the word 'etiquette', nor most of what it stands for. It is an artificial set of rules and regulations, often arbitrary and without obvious point. It is rather like a religion for some people, but without any justifiable claim to be divinely inspired. Etiquette is not holy writ. It is not even temporal law. It is merely what has emerged from custom, aided and abetted by self-appointed authorities, would-be oracles making their pronouncements like dowager duchesses in dimly lit rooms.

'I would not enter on my list of friends
(Though graced with polished manners and fine
sense,
Yet wanting sensibility) the man
Who needlessly sets foot upon a worm.'
                    William Cowper, *The Task* (1785)

'All the pretences of etiquette seemed naturally to
drop away, leaving nothing but the forms dictated
and preserved by true manliness and true womanli-
ness.'
        Dinah Maria Mulock, *John Halifax, Gentleman* (1856)

'Manners are the happy ways of doing things; each
once a stroke of genius or of love, now repeated and
hardened into usage.'
        **Ralph Waldo Emerson, 'Behaviour', *The Conduct of Life*
        (1860)**

'Manners are especially the need of the plain. The
pretty can get away with anything.'
        Evelyn Waugh, quoted in the *Observer* (1962)

Social divisiveness

The chief argument against manners – and, more
particularly, etiquette – is that they often appear to be
operated chiefly as a way of excluding those who do not
understand them. In other words, they sort the sheep
from the goats; rather than engendering courtesy and
wellbeing, they are socially divisive. People always trot
out the phrase about manners that they 'oil the wheels
of social intercourse', which is all very well if you know
what sort of oil to use. So, mixing the metaphors, are
they a lubricant or an exclusion zone? The answer, even

in these superficially egalitarian times, must be that they are, or can be, both.

'Savages we call them because their manners differ from ours.'
Benjamin Franklin (1706–90)

'Manners and money make a gentleman.'
Thomas Fuller, *Gnomologia* (1732)

'The principle of politeness is the same among all nations, but the ceremonials which etiquette imposes differ according to the taste and habits of various countries . . . But still the polite of every country have about the same manners.'
Arthur Martine, *Handbook of Etiquette and Guide to True Politeness* (New York, 1866)

It can be argued, too, that by having strict codes of what is correct form and the done thing, we restrict behaviour unnecessarily and unimaginatively. There is something to be said for that. Unconventional behaviour is not necessarily wrong. What this book probably says is that it is all right to behave unconventionally, or to depart from the norm, provided you know what it is that you are departing from and provided you know that you are doing it. Hence, this book spells out what is the norm, points out the variations, contradictions and customary departures from that position, and then advises you to make up your own mind what to do. To put it another way, if it is not mentioned in this book, it probably does not matter.

Double dealing

When people have talked to me about manners, it has been pretty obvious that they know what is meant by good manners – what they should aspire to – even if they don't necessarily believe in using those manners themselves. Which is another way of saying that people are often twofaced.

We pay lip-service to the importance of manners, but don't always employ them. We say we disapprove of swearing, for example, but we do it just the same. And we advance reasons why manners are good for us, but can use those same reasons to disguise what we are really up to and why we resort, in some cases, to archaic and arbitrary codes of conduct.

'Great politeness usually means "I want something".'
Chinese proverb

'Manners make often fortunes.'
English proverb, collected 1670

'Civility costs nothing and buys everything.'
Lady Mary Wortley Montagu (1689–1762)

'Where etiquette prevents me from doing things disagreeable to myself, I am a perfect martinet.'
The Rev. Sydney Smith (1771–1845)

'The great secret is not having bad manners or good manners or any other particular sort of manners, but having the same manners for all human souls.'
George Bernard Shaw (1856–1950)

'Politeness is one-half good nature and the other half good lying.'
Mary Wilson Little (?1880–??)

'Etiquette is knowing how to yawn with your mouth closed.'
Herbert V. Prochnow (*b* 1897)

'Etiquette is what you are doing and saying when people are looking and listening. What you are thinking is your business.'
Virginia Cary Hudson, *O Ye Jigs & Juleps* (1962)

Useful rules

If manners are less codified these days, does that make life easier or more confusing? Having already expressed dislike of formalized codes of conduct, it seems only right that I should state the principal argument for manners in general. As they are necessary, for example, on the hunting field, to stop the whole thing turning into a rout, so they are necessary in social life, in the workplace, and even in the bedroom, as a way of giving order, structure and possibly meaning to our behaviour.

But is life really easier if you have a code of manners – when trying to conform to a code of manners can make things more difficult? The balance of opinion would seem to be that life is made easier by having such a code, if only because you then know what you are entitled to diverge from. That, however, depends on the code being clear, and from time to time in this book I intend to have a little fun pointing out the discrepancies in other etiquette manuals – discrepancies which can only serve to disconcert the credulous.

Types of manners

Is there a difference between manners for form's sake and manners that stem from a genuine consideration for others? In his ironic reworking of the Ten Commandments, 'The Latest Decalogue' (1862), Arthur Hugh Clough included the couplet:

> Honour thy parents; that is all
> From whom advancement may befall,

and it has to be conceded that there is more than an element of calculation in the manners of many people. They are courteous because they know it will get them somewhere. This is the less acceptable face of manners, but it is interesting how often social advancement, if not economic gain, is held up as a good reason for being well-mannered. In exhorting businesses to improve relations with their customers, campaigners point to the tangible economic gains involved.

So be it, if that approach is necessary, but the ideal must remain the disinterested one – typified by the distinction said to have been made by Lord David Cecil (1902–86) between manners of mere politeness and manners of the heart.

To encourage the others

Should you attempt to change other people's manners? In 1986, The Rev. Ian Gregory, a Congregational Minister from Staffordshire in his late fifties, founded what is rather quaintly known as The Polite Society. He says that the idea came to him when he met a couple who had returned to England after many years working in Malaysia and who commented on the conspicuous lack of courtesy and consideration they now encountered. According to Mr Gregory's *Good Manners Guide* which, among other things, points readers in the direction of service-providers who aren't likely to spit at them, The Polite Society was established as 'a resounding volley against the vulgarian hordes'.

The book was written in 1989, when not only yobbos but yuppies were at their loudest and most disagreeable. But the 'caring 1990s', which may have replaced the 'grab-what-you-can late 1980s', are not being particularly well-mannered towards Mr Gregory's Polite Society. It has had difficulty in finding sponsors for its activities, and has threatened to suspend its activities, though it is still just about ticking over, as I write.

The existence of The Polite Society – despite those who laugh at the very idea of it – is a reminder that manners are worthwhile and worth going on about. The comicality stems, I would be the first to admit, from the prospect of predominantly middle-class worriers bleating over what may seem to other eyes as being utterly 'nice' and 'wet' concerns. If such worriers find people behaving loutishly in the street, do they attempt to persuade them to behave otherwise? Probably, they do not, as that would only invite trouble. The thought of these pundits arguing their points with some reluctantly-detained yobbo on a street corner is deliciously comic. On the other hand, in the office or home, there may be opportunity to persuade people against their grosser natures if some kind of tangible benefit can be held out for more considerate behaviour.

If manners missionaries are not going to deal with breaches of manners head on, then is there anything to be said for the kind of formalized manners training which is all the rage these days in the service-providing industries? I would vote for a determined rejection of any attempt to produce good manners in people simply by spraying it on. No one wants synthetic manners, surface etiquette or junk civility. For the arguments pro and con, see Chapter 9 SERVICE AND THE CUSTOMER and Chapter 15 WORKING LIFE.

Towards better behaviour

What kind of book is this? Etiquette manuals used to be given titles like *Manners and Tone of Good Society*, or, *Solecisms To Be Avoided* and used to be written, anonymously, by 'A Member of the Aristocracy' or similar, like the one with that title first published in 1880 which ran through many editions. The traditional type of etiquette book tends to be concerned with such arcane matters as the correct way of addressing a divorced Earl's wife's brother or how best to dispose of cherry stones when dining at Buckingham Palace.

Best Behaviour is designed to deal with more everyday problems of behaviour in the modern age. In fact, given that we live in years when assertiveness and aggression have demolished many traditional courtesies and politenesses, for much of the time the book does not merely advise people how to behave, but advises them how they should behave in the light of bad behaviour by others.

This is a genuine guide, then, designed to help people with late-twentieth-century social dilemmas. For the most part, it is not prescriptive in tone – often concluding that there is no answer to some social dilemmas, but recommends what might be 'the done thing' according to circumstances. It may also be more challenging and pragmatic in its evaluation of traditional social conduct than similar guides.

Above all, it is a guide rather than a handbook, it is a primer rather than a manual. Unlike similar books in the field, it does not set out to give a complete set of instructions as to how, for example, to organize a wedding or run your own business. Its purpose is to explore those aspects of social life where doubt enters in, where there is uncertainty, and where conduct is not only open to debate but negotiable. It does not pretend, therefore, to be a complete 'How to . . .' guide to what you should do in every conceivable situation you might find yourself.

As I have already indicated, manners, by their very nature, don't change much; they are a constant. If they do change, then they change with almost imperceptible slowness. What I hope is happening, though, is that people are being less prone to accept manners at their face value, are questioning them, being pragmatic about them, and, if necessary, discarding them but I hope for the right reasons.

'[Manners are] a contrivance of wise men to keep fools at a distance.'
Anonymous, quoted by R.W. Emerson (1860)

'*Dumby:* Awful manners young Hopper has!
'*Cecil Graham:* Ah! Hopper is one of Nature's gentlemen, the worst type of gentleman I know.'
Oscar Wilde, *Lady Windermere's Fan* (1892)

The quotations displayed in the text come from many sources and their chief purpose is to entertain, but they underline the truth that concern about manners has been with us down the ages and does not seem to change. What does change is the etiquette of dealing with the problems.

Acknowledgements

The book *Best Behaviour* shares its theme and its title with a series of six programmes that I wrote and presented for BBC Radio 4 in the autumn of 1991. Though it is not a 'book of the programme' in the customary sense, I am nonetheless indebted to Anne Sloman, Editor, Special Current Affairs Programmes, BBC Radio, for sponsoring that original series. The producer was Sallie Davies, to whom I am grateful, especially, for making me clarify my thoughts on a number of manners and etiquette issues. She also arranged for me to compare notes on the subject with a fascinatingly wide range of people. In particular, I was pleased to be given an opportunity to hear the views of: Una-Mary Parker, a former Social Editor of

The Tatler; Moyra Bremner, author of *Enquire Within Upon Modern Etiquette*; Lynne Brennan, co-author of *The Complete Book of Business Etiquette*; Ann Dickson; Dr Adrian Furnham, University College, London; The Rev. Ian Gregory of The Polite Society; Chris Tame and Marjorie Brady of FOREST (Freedom Organization for the Right to Enjoy Smoking Tobacco); Stephen Hitchcock, Director of the Institute of Customer Care; Philip Mellor and Kay Galvin of Dun & Bradstreet Limited; and Stephen Bull, restaurateur.

For the radio series, the BBC commissioned an opinion poll from Public Attitude Surveys Ltd of High Wycombe. PAS interviewed a nationally representative quota sample of 3,685 adults (aged fifteen and over) during April and May 1991, at 152 sampling points throughout the United Kingdom. My thanks are due to Barry Lee, Managing Director of PAS Ltd, for giving me permission to reflect some of the findings of that poll in this book.

Finally, I have to thank various friends and correspondents who have given me the benefit of their advice and views. Most would prefer to remain anonymous, but I am allowed to mention Donald Hickling, Richard Tyson and my wife, Sue, whose daily task it is to keep me up to scratch on so many behavioural matters. Kathy Rooney, Nicky Thompson, Kate Newman and Tracey Smith at Bloomsbury Publishing have been as courteous, charming and enthusiastic as ever, even when dealing with the appalling bias of a predominantly heterosexual, middle-class, Anglican and male author. Hence, however:

Author's note

Masculine and feminine nouns and pronouns are used throughout *Best Behaviour* on the basis of appropriate-

ness to the context and, it is to be hoped, overall
equality. The reader may substitute the masculine for
the feminine, and vice versa, as he or she desires.

NIGEL REES
London, 1992

Chapter 1

$\mathscr{E}$ATING IN

Is it always necessary to abide by formal table etiquette? Impeccably well-mannered people would, presumably, not eat peas off their knives or place their elbows on the table, even if they were dining on their own. For most of us, though, there are, understandably, grades of manners. If we are eating at home, within the family, informality is only to be expected and it would be ridiculous to insist on the manners appropriate for dining at a state banquet in Windsor Castle.

The basic rule, as when eating out, is to suit your table manners to the company. Children dining with their parents should approximate to their parents' manners (if they have any); if you are eating at home with one other person, adapt your manners accordingly; if you are with company, as host or hostess, you should set an example. It would be unmannerly to draw attention to your guests' lack of manners and so, within reason, you should go along with them and not make a point of being different.

(See also Chapter 2 EATING OUT; 'Children' in Chapter 3 FAMILY LIFE; and 'Dinner parties' in Chapter 4 GUESTS AND HOSTS.)

Do table manners still matter?

From the PAS survey, it is quite clear that lip-service is still being paid to the importance of table manners. 70%

1

of the sample said they thought that table manners were *very* important. 25% thought they were *quite* important; and a mere 3% thought they were *not* important at all.

The problem with table manners is that though it can be argued, in most cases, that there is some reason for them, or there may have been once, they often appear to be an arbitrary code, chiefly designed to show up the ignorance of the uninitiated. Surely port tastes exactly the same, whether you pass it clockwise or anticlockwise? And why are you not supposed to dunk your biscuits in your tea? Such rules, more often than not, seem to be the sort of thing parents and people in authority insist on for the sole reason that the rules are there.

However, the new liberalism of the table makes the traditional etiquette seem like some arcane religious rite of little relevance to the majority of ordinary folk. But if we are not so bothered today about whether we pick up the correct knife and fork, or the right-shaped wine glass, and if we chop up our asparagus rather than eat it with our fingers, as we are supposed to do, some behaviour at the table is still regarded as pretty repellent. Slurping tea or soup, talking with the mouth full, chewing with the mouth open, taking the head down to the food rather than bringing the food up to the mouth, gesticulating with knife and fork, stretching across the table, grabbing food for oneself before others, and any behaviour calculated to put other people off their food, are all such obvious examples of bad manners that the finer points of etiquette barely come into the argument.

It is a fact, though, that people with repellent table manners are mostly conscious of what they are doing — or not doing. On very special occasions, they are quite capable of getting it right. This is a useful thing to remember also when the time comes for loved ones with a penchant for licking their plates or belching audibly at table to be brought into line and encouraged to set an example to growing children.

'Being set at the table, scratch not thy self, and take
thou heed as much as thou canst to spit, cough, and
to blow thy nose; but if it be needful, do it
dextrously without much noise, turning thy face
sideling.'
Francis Hawkins, *Youth's Behaviour* (17th century)

'Bad manners simply indicate that you care a good
deal more for the food than for the society at the
table.'
Gelett Burgess (1866–1951)

'On the Continent people have good food, in
England people have good table manners.'
George Mikes, *How To Be An Alien* (1946)

'Bad table manners, my dear Gigi, have broken up
more households than infidelity.'
Alan Jay Lerner, *Gigi* (1958 film script from Colette's novel)

Why are manners worse today, if indeed they are? The
PAS survey shows that in an average week, almost five
out of ten people sit down *around a table* to eat a meal
with family or friends, every day or more often. But a
substantial 21% of people *never* do this. That is, they
never participate in meals as a communal activity (where
the behaviour of fellow eaters would have some bearing
on their enjoyment of the food-consuming process).

The chief cause is not hard to find. Television can
determine not only the timing of a meal but also draw
people away from eating at table completely. All this has
a knock-on effect on table etiquette. Eating out in fast
food restaurants (where often you may have to eat with
your hands) and the increasing use of disposable plates
and plastic cutlery, has contributed to the malaise, if
indeed that is how it should be considered.

Eating at a table is the very basis of table manners. It

encourages those living together under the same roof to communicate and teaches children, in particular, the value of meal-sharing and discipline. Hence, the importance of bringing up children to appreciate that 'getting down' from table before the end of a meal, or before everyone else has finished eating, is a symbolic act.

Laying the table

The degree of care taken in laying the table will depend on the circumstances. 'Eating in' covers everything from a snack on the kitchen table to a semi-formal meal for guests at the dining table (dealt with more fully under 'Dinner parties' in Chapter 4 GUESTS AND HOSTS.) Some questions worth pondering:

Bottles. On the table? Milk bottles never (though milk cartons just about, informally, in the kitchen); ketchup bottles and mustard jars, up to a point. It is sensible to stand such containers on saucers, so that any spoon used for doling out the sauce can be rested on it rather than left in the jar. Elaborate holders for sauce bottles seem as unnecessary and work-making as those prim holders for jamjars, which merely serve to cover up the label, as though it was not quite nice for people to see it.

Drinking straight from bottles is quite out of the question. When I was young I think I was horrified into submission on this point by being told stories of people getting their tongues stuck in the bottle mouth – though I can't say I have ever actually encountered anyone to whom this has happened.

Candles. Their use is always to be encouraged, at anything beyond the most informal occasions – and even then. Candles are conducive to a mellow, intimate atmosphere. They are not just romantic. They evoke the age-old tradition of shared meals and good fellowship.

White candles are best, in my opinion, and the lower the holder, the longer the candle required.

Coasters. These should probably not be used at the dinner table. Even splendid silver ones are more of an ornament than anything useful. Elsewhere, it has to be said that there is something rather genteel about coasters wherever they stand whether they are pleasant little things bearing pictures on them or beer mats with advertising slogans on them. It is quite natural to want to protect your polished wood furniture or to prevent discoloration of your tablecloths, but the old view of coasters as fiddly things, a species of Victorian clutter, just won't go away.

Condiments. Salt, pepper and other flavourings may be sprinkled directly over food and do not need to be placed at the side of the plate (except for mustard, etc.). There is naturally no alternative to this method if a pepper-mill is being used. Some would hold that it is insulting to the cook if you sprinkle salt and pepper before tasting food, or even *after* tasting it. Indeed, a certain celebrity French chef in Lancashire not only kept condiments off his tables but would personally deliver a large bag of salt to customers if they asked for any. If salt and pepper *are* available, then you may put some on the side of the plate after the food is served and can then add it on more discreetly from this position.

Cruet-stands have always been impossibly genteel and remain so.

Cutlery. This should be laid out so that the eater can start on the outside and work in, according to the course. Forks are on the left of the placing, spoons and knives on the right. At a more formal meal, if there has been some mistake in the laying, follow the host or hostess. Pudding spoons should almost invariably be accompanied by a fork, even if this may seem a little superfluous. The fork can be used to guide the pudding on to the spoon. In less formal situations, the pudding spoon and fork may be placed at the top of the place setting – spoon bowl towards the left, fork prongs towards the right. Or, better still, they can be left out of the original setting and brought in with the pudding itself.

Finger-bowls. The source of many a joke – the inept drink the lemon-flavoured water by mistake, etc. Finger-bowls should always be supplied when the fingers have to be used for eating (prawns, fruit, and so on). At the end, dip your fingers in the water and wipe them on your napkin.

Glasses. There is no particular order in which to arrange glasses, though they should be grouped in a logical fashion to the upper right of the place setting. One way is to have the water glass where it can be used first, then the first wine glass a little to the right of it, and so on. In other words, from the inside to the outside, the reverse of the order for using cutlery. By and large, though, people will be quite happy to pick up the appropriate glass from wherever it is positioned.

Which glass to use? Generally speaking, red wine should be served in a broad, goblet-type glass, white wine in a slenderer glass, water in a tumbler. Champagne once used to be served, popularly, in a wide-brimmed, flat 'coupe' glass but now, like other sparkling wines, is often served in a 'flute' glass to keep in the aroma and bubbles.

Napkins. (If you want to call them 'serviettes' have a look first under 'U and Non-U language' in Chapter 11 SPEAKING.) Placed to the left of the table setting, sometimes on the side plate, sometimes folded into a shape, napkins should be donned as soon as you sit down. In a restaurant, a waiter may bestow it as soon as you sit – otherwise, wait a little, perhaps until after the orders have been taken, then don the napkin so that it is in position when the first food arrives.

Normally, the napkin is placed across your lap and is not tucked into your belt or collar (but see *Spaghetti* under 'How are we eating this?', below). At the end of a meal it is left crumpled up on the table – unless within the family circle and rings are provided so that the napkin may be used again. (See also under 'Dinner parties' in Chapter 4 GUESTS AND HOSTS.)

The signal to start

It is very rude of people to start eating straight away – whether in private or in company – as soon as they have served themselves or been served, and before anybody else has been. On the other hand, even at a meal for two, the chances are that food will start going cold. Some authorities say quite clearly that you may start to eat as soon as you are served. A gentle compromise should wisely be struck – namely, that everyone should get a move on with serving and with making sure that everyone else has been served – before starting.

A host or hostess should encourage people to start eating, but their guests should wait for this signal. At larger, more formal dinners, it would be pointless to wait until everyone was served – the food would be stone cold by the time it was eaten. As soon as the Grace has been said (if it is to be said), and you have been served, it is permissible to begin, though you may wish to encourage those on either side of you to join you, so as not to feel to remarkable yourself.

What order should you eat in? The order in which dishes are served – though there may be debate as to whether the cheese should be served before the pudding, in the French fashion, or after. This is purely a matter of choice.

Knife and forking it

There is no escaping it, this is the class-divider and the culture-divider. Those who do eat with knife and fork simultaneously (the 'correct' British way), hold the knife so that the handle goes into the palm of the hand rather than resting on the thumb. They hold the fork with the curve facing down, again with with the handle tucked into the palm.

Then they refrain from putting anything on the knife directly into the mouth – from the days when knives were so sharp that they might have cut your tongue – and they always put food on the top of the downward-facing curve of the fork. They do not use the fork as a shovel.

But then, there is a lot to be said for eating some dishes with fork only, and using it as kind of shovel. This is the American method. Meat and difficult foods are first cut with knife and fork, then the knife is laid down on the plate and the fork employed on its own from then on.

There is no logical objection to this alternative method. However, the American habit of leaving knife and fork haphazardly on the plate at the conclusion of eating, rather than lining them up neatly, side by side, handles towards the bottom of the plate, both looks ugly and does not make it clear (to a waiter or anyone else) that eating has actually finished.

How are we eating this?

The testing part of any formal meal comes when certain types of dish are laid before the quaking diner. People know they *shouldn't* do certain things like shovelling, holding food with the fingers, and using the wrong cutlery, even if they don't know what they *should* do. The awareness of pitfalls, if not the etiquette to deal with them, gets passed on from generation to generation.

This is all very silly. If you are confronted with food which you don't normally eat or which obviously presents some kind of difficulty, there really is no harm in asking, 'How are we eating this?' or, at least, in waiting until someone else gives a lead. Observing the host or hostess and fellow eaters is the only sensible way to proceed when there is any uncertainty. 'I saw, I imitated, I survived!' exclaims a character in Mrs Gaskell's novel *Cranford* (see below), and her approach is to be commended.

Artichokes. Pull out the leaves, starting on the outside, using your finger and thumb, dipping the leaves in any sauce provided. Stack the parts of the leaves you have been unable to eat on the side of your plate. If you like, the centre of the artichoke may be cut into small pieces using the small knife and fork that should be provided.

Asparagus. A Victorian guide to etiquette (in 1880) was confidently instructing its readers that 'the points should be cut off asparagus and then eaten with a knife and fork'. There is no reason why this should not still be done, but the practice is to eat with the fingers. First dip the asparagus tip in the butter and then, however dangerously, convey the food to the mouth and chew it down as far as you like – probably stopping when the vegetable gets a little hard.

Avocados. Any sauce or filling goes in the hollow left by the removal of the stone. Hold the pear with the fingers and spoon out the flesh. (There is no need to refer to 'avocado pears' in full.)

Bananas. 'Ladies,' according to one decorous hostess, 'should not eat bananas'. One can see that there might be a hint of eroticism in the procedure, but if ladies – or any one else – do eat bananas in any reasonably formal surroundings, the fruit should not be chomped while still in the skin. The skin should be completely removed and then sliced with a knife and eaten with a fork. For some reason, I have always felt inclined not only to remove the 'strings' from the sides of the banana but also to clip off the top and the bottom. Is this to save me from some terrible fate? I simply don't know.

Bones. Fish bones should be removed using your knife and fork, or just possibly with your fingers. Bones of larger birds are not eaten with the fingers except in films of the life of King Henry VIII (in which they are also discarded, when nibbled clean, over the shoulder). Small game birds (and frog's legs) may be tackled first with knife and fork and then with the fingers. (Fingers come into their own more when eating out of doors, at barbecues and picnics, for example.)

Bread. With French bread, break off rather than cut pieces of a reasonable size. With rolls, always break them, never cut, then apply butter with a knife if so desired. With some dishes, ready-buttered bread is supplied, sometimes with the crust removed. These pieces can be slippery and may be folded before eating as they cannot be broken into bits.

Caviare. Butter any toast you are given, squeeze lemon on the caviare, and use a knife to put the caviare on to the toast, a mouthful at a time.

Cheese. Butter (if you will) the biscuit or bread, place small piece of cheese thereon, a mouthful at a time, and consume.

Corn on the cob. A notoriously difficult dish to eat stylishly and an impossible one to eat without getting into a mess. Small daggers are sometimes supplied which you jam into each end of the cob and use to turn it as you nibble methodically. You would certainly never attack this dish with knife and fork.

Someone said of an ageing actor's infatuation with his young mistress, 'I couldn't imagine what he saw in her, until I watched her eating corn on the cob one day at the Caprice'. Clearly, the process *can* add to the gaiety of nations.

Fish. Special silver fish knives and forks were introduced by the middle classes in Victorian times because steel cutlery was supposed to affect the flavour. The risk of silver polish doing the same appears to have been overlooked. Even before this, apparently, fish was eaten with a fork and a crust of bread. Nowadays, fish knives are frowned upon as in John Betjeman's 1954 poem cataloguing gentility, 'Phone for the fish-knives, Norman'.

Whatever implement is used, any skin should be gently removed using the knife (and eaten, if you choose); then the 'meat' should be consumed in small pieces, any bones being removed first and placed on the side of the plate.

There is a school of thought that says you should never fillet a fish before eating it. If you do, you will probably need a separate plate on which to place the bones.

Fruit. Often considered to be some kind of manners test. The basic rule is that you eat the fruit according to the tools you are supplied with. If with a knife and fork, then you use them. If only with a knife, you do the preliminary quartering and peeling making use of the knife, if appropriate, and then resort to the fingers. If you are given no tools, you eat the whole thing with your fingers. Stones and pips should be removed from the mouth with the fingers – or with a spoon if that is provided – and deposited on the side of the plate.

Grapefruit. Only a sadist would serve grapefruit in its original state without the necessary tools for the job.

Serving grapefruit segments smacks mildly of cheating, however. A curved grapefruit knife enables the eater to detach the edible portions of the fruit – if they have not been loosened already – but even so a certain amount of hacking and hewing with a spoon may be necessary. Hard to eat sveltely.

Gravy. Generally speaking, it is quite in order to spoon up any gravy or sauce, should you be able to acquire the spoon to do so. Use pieces of bread roll to do the same, in continental fashion, though large-scale operations to demolish left-over soup are probably best avoided.

Jelly. Eaten with a spoon and fork, and with care. Never, needless to say, with just a fork.

Kebabs. Kebabs should be served on the skewer. The diner then picks up the skewer in one hand and guides the meat and vegetables off the skewer into a line on to the plate, where they are then eaten using a knife and fork.

Lobster. Use a knife and fork to eat the flesh. For the claws, a special fork should be provided.

Melon. Served in a segment, to which ginger may be added, if you are adventurous. Then cut down to the hard part with a knife or spoon, and hew out a small segment at a time.

Mussels. Hold the shell in one hand and remove the edible bit with a fork. Using the empty half of the shell to winkle out the mussel is tricky and messy, but quite common on the Continent. If the shell has not opened, or been opened, during the cooking, do not attempt to prise it open with a knife, because the mussel is not fit to eat. Where the mussels have been cooked in a sauce, it is quite in order to finish off by drinking this with a soup spoon or mopping up with bread. Empty shells should be placed on a separate dish or, however perilously, around the main dish. Finger-bowls are obligatory.

Oysters. Fortunately, you are seldom expected to open these for yourself and they will be served in the half-shell. Use a fork to extract the oyster while holding the shell with your other hand.

Paté. Using a knife, place a small portion on the toast or bread provided, a mouthful at a time.

Peas. The way you eat peas has long been a key test of table manners. In the Gilbert and Sullivan opera *Ruddigore* (1887), Rose Maybud opines, 'The man who bites his bread [rather than breaks off a small piece first], or eats peas with a knife, I look upon as a lost creature.' Of course, balancing peas on a knife is about as unforgivable a sin in the grown-up world as would be drawing pictures in your tapioca with jam. You are supposed to mush the peas against the outer curve of the fork and convey them to your mouth in that fashion. Using the concave curve of the fork as a shovel is frowned upon – I am inclined to say 'Alas' – as it seems a reasonably sensible procedure. But you can probably get away with it almost anywhere these days.

'Fingers were made before forks, and hands before knives.'
Old saying included in Jonathan Swift, *Polite Conversation* (1738)

'When the ducks and green peas came, we looked at each other in dismay; we had only two-pronged black-handled forks. It is true that the steel was as bright as silver; but what were we to do? Miss Matty picked up her peas, one by one, on the point of the prongs . . . Miss Pole sighed over her delicate

young peas as she left them on one side of her plate
untasted, for they *would* drop between the prongs. I
looked at my host: the peas were going wholesale
into his capacious mouth, shovelled up by his large
round-ended knife. I saw, I imitated, I survived! My
friends, in spite of my precedent, could not muster
up courage enough to do an ungenteel thing; and, if
Mr Holbrook had not been so heartily hungry, he
would probably have seen that the good peas went
away almost untouched.'

Elizabeth Gaskell, *Cranford* (1851–3)

'"Have you ever seen Spode eat asparagus?"
'"No."
'"Revolting. It alters one's whole conception of Man
as Nature's last word".'

P.G. Wodehouse, *The Code of the Woosters* (1938)

'[How to eat like a child.] Spinach: divide into little
piles. Rearrange again into new piles. After five or
six manouevres, sit back and say you are full.'

Delia Ephron, in the *New York Times* (1983)

Peaches. Do you use a knife and fork or just squelch in
with your fingers? A bit of both, methinks.

Prawns. These are labour-intensive but more often than
not justify the effort. Reconcile yourself to the mess. Pull
off the head first, then gently ease away the tendrils and
gelatinous bits, revealing the prawn proper. However
boring it may be, it makes sense to do all this stripping
and preparation first before starting to eat the prawns.
Do this eating with knife and fork, with fork alone, or
with your fingers, according to circumstances.

Sardines. Remove the head and backbone, first. You can
quite safely eat everything else without worrying about
the smaller bones.

Sauce. See *Gravy*, above.

Seafood. Crab, lobster and most other types of shellfish can be very messy to eat. Thank heaven for 'dressed crab' from which the hard labour has been extracted. If you have to crack the shell, then the correct tools will have been supplied – also for scooping out the meat. On my honeymoon, I had a chicken and seafood 'speciality of the house' in a restaurant in the South of France. It required the wearing of a baby's plastic bib to catch the fallout. It was also quite exhausting. Eating any seafood tends to be.

Smoked salmon. Eat with a knife and fork; any buttered bread supplied is consumed separately.

Snails. These can only be eaten using the special grips provided, as they are probably too hot to hold with the fingers. The meat is teased out with a fork or small pin-like implement. The empty shell is then placed back in the special serving tray – like an egg-holder – that should have been provided.

Soup. The spoon is lowered into the soup and allowed to fill; the soup is not scooped up. The spoon is then lifted to the mouth, held parallel to the edge of the table, and sipped – not sucked. As the amount of soup in the bowl decreases, the bowl is tilted away from the eater and the spoon encouraged to fill that way. Hot soup is never cooled by blowing. Merely pausing on the journey between bowl and mouth should aid the cooling process. Sip gingerly if you are not sure, of course. The soup spoon should be lifted out of the bowl when you have finished eating and placed on the side of the plate beneath.

Spaghetti. It is most unlikely that daunting strings of pasta would ever be presented for consumption at a dinner where elegant behaviour was expected, so one can assume that a certain amount of amateurishness is allowed with this dish. There is more than one method of eating spaghetti. Either try to collect not too many strands with your fork alone, dip in any sauce, and convey to the mouth, never mind if there are straggly bits. Your napkin should be deployed brazenly, like Pavarotti's handkerchief, to protect yourself and wipe away any sauce, not to sit primly on your lap doing nothing.

Alternatively, you can guide the strands with the fork held in your right hand to the bowl of a spoon held in your left hand. Twist the fork round a few times to make a small parcel for conveying to the mouth. This is rather laborious, however.

Never use a knife to cut the spaghetti to acceptable lengths. This is laborious, too – and smacks of cheating.

Spare ribs. Again, only a peculiarly sadistic host or hostess would serve spare ribs at a dinner party as they really require you to get down on the floor with the dog. This is barbecue fare, principally, but should it ever appear at the dinner table, fingers would be used. Afterwards, finger-bowls, if not hot baths, tooth picks and dental floss, would be essential.

Whitebait. You eat the lot, heads, tails and all. Try not to think about it.

Eating manners

Some general points can be remembered or ignored according to circumstance.

Dressing at table. It may seem unduly demanding but at anything more than a meal round the kitchen table, some minimum level of dress is required. For a man to eat at table without wearing a tie or a jacket could indicate that he is unconscious of the fact that there is more to a meal than eating – it is a social occasion and should not be regarded as a pig regards going to the trough.

Elbows off the table. Almost everybody is aware that there is such a thing as table manners, but from what one sees and hears, people quite obviously pick and choose which manners they are going to employ themselves. It is significant that 'no elbows on the table' is not only the best-known rule of the table but the most frequently flouted one.

There is a reason for the rule. It is that having your elbows on the table is bad body language. You block out the people sitting on either side of you. This is certainly the case at formal dinners – and that is obviously where the rule comes from – but you could argue that talking to the person opposite to you, with your elbows on the table, certainly in a less formal setting, is *good* body language – because it focuses your attention on the person, or persons, directly in front of you.

Plate-fingering. This is a habit mostly confined to former food-guide inspectors and is not to be encouraged. The Finger Test is designed to establish whether or not the plates have been warmed up specially (or, indeed, whether they have just been extracted from the dish washer, which amounts to the same thing). Rather too much importance is nowadays attached by the British to having hot plates, possibly because they still haven't forgotten the cold winters of the late 1940s and the way food used to be served at school. The French, on the other hand, do not bother about the warmth of the plate. They concentrate on serving the food hot.

Portion control. It stands to reason that, if you are serving yourself, you should not hog a certain dish just because it is your favourite. Make sure that everyone else can have their fair share. The wonderful instruction 'FHB' – for 'Family Hold Back' – was invented to prevent guests being left wanting by members of the family pleasing themselves first.

Serving yourself. It is not considered correct to use your own cutlery to serve yourself out of communal bowls and dishes. Use the serving cutlery that should be provided.

Wine snobbery

A great deal too much fuss is still made over which wine should be drunk with what dish, though it has to be said that when the matching up is right it adds greatly to the pleasure of the meal. Broadly speaking, you can begin by ruling out sweet wines. These, if drunk at all, go with puddings. I speak with some feeling on this matter having been brought up in a family where Sauternes was drunk with everything.

This leaves us with dry white wines and red. White wines can be drunk with almost everything and, for this reason, they are a very good choice when people at one table are eating a variety of foods and where one type of wine is to be drunk throughout a meal. Admittedly, drinking a white wine with beef or game might seem a little odd, but it can work perfectly well. On the other hand, drinking a red wine with fish would be chancy, though again it need not be ruled out.

Champagne is a very versatile wine and can be drunk at almost any point during the course of a meal, though it would be wasted as an accompaniment to red meat or spicy foods.

Anyone who buys any sort of wine to accompany an Indian meal is wasting money. Beers are best, or simply water. Which reminds me, beers should not be ruled out as an accompaniment to a dinner-party meal. Some of the specialist brews are as interesting and subtle as wines.

White wines should be served chilled, though ice buckets are not called for outside of restaurants. Domestic wine coolers (like Thermos flasks) are believed by some to work. Red wine should be opened to breathe for a while before drinking. A young wine needs longer than an older one, possibly several hours. That is why some wines taste much better when the bottle is finished off the following day.

A word about champagne (or, to put it cautiously, champagne-method or champagne-style wine)

Champagne has always had an image of high-living and celebration, if not of frivolity. In Britain, especially as a result of the boom years of the 1980s, it has steadily increased in popularity despite the expense. Above all, a bottle of champagne makes a very good gift – the word says 'fun' almost audibly – and a very useful gift, too. Champagne can be drunk with almost everything, at any stage in the meal, and all it needs to be is served chilled. The only problem is how to open the bottle . . .

Indeed, champagne is now so widely consumed on every conveivable occasion, that it behoves me to say something about this serious matter. Of course, part of the charm of drinking champagne is the initial popping of the cork, but removing the cork can be rather a nerve-wracking experience for everyone. You don't know whether the cork is going to allow itself to be eased out quietly – possibly with a little or a lot of holding down by yourself – or whether it is going to shoot off and hit the ceiling or, as has happened, blind someone.

So, having first removed the foil and the wire guard, what is the way forward? Obviously, you would never use a corkscrew (the very thought . . .)

but neither should you force off the cork with your thumbs, as you might get more than you bargained for. The thing to do is simply to twist the bottle with one hand while holding a napkin or tea-towel over the cork with the other. The napkin will be very useful for mopping up any spillage should you wish to allow a 'pop' to be heard; it also protects your hands if you prefer to go for a soundless removal.

I once heard it said that a champagne cork should be removed not with a 'pop' or a 'splat' but with a gentle sound, 'like the sigh of satisfied woman'. Without wishing to get too deeply drawn into discussing the rights and wrongs of this worldly view – which is not one I necessarily subscribe to – I should explain that this view was expressed by a character in a play. He was champagne importer, if I remember correctly. But, every time I have opened a bottle of champagne since, I have recalled it, and struggled accordingly to lessen the impending explosion, with eyes tightly closed, any amount of arm wrenching, tea-towels to the fore, and what not.

Have I ever managed to recapture the sigh of a satisfied woman when opening a bottle of champagne? To put it bluntly, do satisfied women actually sigh? These questions are no longer of the slightest moment to me, however, as Toad-like I have lately discovered a much more exciting game with champagne bottles.

Staying at a country hotel in Ireland and sitting in the lounge minding our own business, my wife and I became aware of the activities of a group of young French people, among our fellow guests. They ordered a bottle of champagne and then requested that a knife be brought from the kitchen. So, indeed, it was – a longish carving knife. One of their number then proceeded to point the champagne bottle at the fireplace. With a deft slashing motion, he used the carving knife to chop the neck off the bottle. As you might expect, this then shot into the fireplace with a sound totally *unlike* the sigh of any woman I have ever heard being satisfied.

The young French persons then proceeded to drink the champagne and did not, apparently, have to remove any fragments of glass from between their teeth. Subsequently, in France itself, I came across a newspaper photograph of a champion golfer removing a champagne cork by breaking the neck of the bottle with an iron. The caption spoke of him 'sabring' it, as though this was a totally natural thing to do.

I have made this digression, but only to draw attention to the basic problem. Unless you are always doing it, removing a champagne cork is no easy matter. Imagine how much more difficult it is if you have been presented with a magnum (the equivalent of two normal bottles), a jeroboam or double magnum (four bottles), a rehoboam (six bottles), a Methuselah (eight bottles) or a Nebuchad-nezzar (twenty bottles). These should only be opened for parties because the considerable amount of champagne contained in such large bottles needs to be drunk straight away: there is no way in which the bottle can be sealed again. The force of the cork coming out is something akin to a bullet from a supergun, and I have yet to discover a way of removing one with without soaking everybody in sight. It should probably only be done out of doors, then you still have a problem lifting the bottle and pouring out the champagne . . .

Special champagne cork removers are now available but – odd isn't it? – they remove all danger and adventure from the proceedings.

Afternoon tea

No meal is more delightful and no meal is more fraught with petty restrictions. A considerate host or hostess will make sure you have a little table on which to put your cup and saucer and your plate. Otherwise, you will have a tricky balancing act on your hands. Doilies are considered genteel. Cake knives are in order but not, for some reason, cake forks. (Actually, the reason seems to be that if a cake can be cut with a knife but cannot be eaten without a fork, it should not be served.) Sugar must be in lumps. Tea strainers are in order. Jam should not be served from the jar, and certainly not from a jamjar within a plastic holder. On the other hand, you could just do what you like.

As for 'milk in first', this is quite one of the most ridiculous and, of course, snobbish aspects of etiquette: the traditional division of the world into those who put milk in to a cup before pouring out the tea and those who put it in afterwards. The acronym 'MIF' has been applied to those suspected of committing the solecism of putting the milk in first.

Is there any logic to this? The lower classes may have wanted to avoid breaking their best china by pouring hot tea in first. Adding the milk afterwards may give a little more scope for judging the desired amount. But neither of these reasons justifies all the fuss. Do what comes naturally and, if you suspect that those you are having tea with *may* care about these things, make a little joke about it and ascertain what they think is the correct way to proceed. Refrain, however, from saying you will take the tea, 'As it comes . . .'

Tea cups should be raised to the mouth from the saucer. Little fingers should on no account be crooked.

Chapter 2

$\mathscr{E}$ATING OUT

Where there are lapses in restaurant manners, on both sides, they can be quite dramatic. Is there a reason why people get so agitated when they are dining out? Somehow it has crept into the folklore that restaurateurs are out to get their customers and that, therefore, the diners are obliged to go to any lengths to stand up for their rights. Consequently, too many people go into restaurants in a combative frame of mind, expecting to be defrauded and messed about. But restaurants are no worse than most other places in producing challenges to people's virility or femininity.

I was amused to hear from chef/proprietor Stephen Bull about the man who complained about the amount of salt that had been applied to his duck. 'Every time I take a bite,' he said, 'I have to take a sip of wine – which must be very good for your wine bill . . .' Unfortunately, Stephen Bull, through a spyhole in his kitchen wall, had earlier observed the diner adding liberal doses of salt to his duck with every mouthful.

It is ridiculous when diners attempt to use restaurants as a forum for working off their personal inadequacies and frustrations. And yet, there are occasions when complaints are justified . . .

(See also Chapter 1 EATING IN; Chapter 4 GUESTS AND HOSTS; and 'Eating/snacking in the street' in Chapter 7 PUBLIC BEHAVIOUR.)

Sins of restaurateurs

The most noticeable sin of restaurateurs is too much asking, 'Is everything all right, sir?' – even if through the head waiter. I once went to a restaurant where the (extremely nervous) proprietor came round and asked us this every two minutes. It wasn't, and we didn't trouble him again. Not that he really wanted to know, of course. As in Latin, his was a *num* question, a construction anticipating the answer 'Yes'.

The provision of canned music in restaurants, though often deplored, has a useful purpose. Clearly, if it drowns your conversation, or is allowed to continue with the tape wowing or the loudspeaker distorting, it should be stopped. But if there are, say, only two tables occupied in a 60–seater restaurant, music is a positive relief if it prevents you from having to listen to everything the other diners say to each other. As soon as the music has served its purpose in getting everyone chattering loudly, and when the restaurant fills up, it should be turned off.

Sins of waiters

The chief sin of waiters, of course, is that they ignore you. One wonders quite how one is supposed to draw the attention of those waiters who would appear to have been schooled in the art of sailing through a restaurant wearing blinkers, whose eye one can never catch, and whose attention can only be seized by jumping on them bodily. Then there is their habit of laying tables for future customers while ignoring the needs of present ones. Most curious of all is the reluctance to bring you the bill when it is asked for. In which case, quite the best thing to do is simply to get up and start walking out of the restaurant. The bill always comes then.

Another vexing sin of waiters is for them not to grasp

who is the host. The wine should be offered for tasting
to that person (of whatever sex), and the bill should be
presented to the same. It is also extremely tedious if a
waiter tops up glasses after every sip, presumably
having been told to do this in order to precipitate the
ordering of another bottle. It is very difficult for a
customer to stop this practice without appearing prickly.
If, however, the opposite should be the case – a
reluctance to pour out wine – it is quite in order for the
host to pour out wine for the guests, even if the bottle
has been parked some way away in an ice bucket.

Because they have been put up to it, some waiters also
try to get you to commit yourself to a pudding when you
give your initial order. This is understandable if it is
because the pudding needs special preparation or long
cooking time. Even so, at the start of a meal, most of us
have no idea whether we will be wanting a pudding at
all. If you suspect that you are only being asked for your
pudding order at this early stage for the convenience of
the chef, don't go along with it. Unfortunately, the
waiter will still be in a position to make you wait
inordinately long for your pudding when you do order it.

The chief sin of waiters in Britain is not to be content
with their lot. A writer in the *Economist* once pointed
out, a trifle incredulously, 'In America, they call waiters
"sir"!' Indeed they sometimes do, but what I have
observed is that waiters in the United States are, by and
large, content with their lot. They may be a pain with
their 'performing' of the menu or their overly attentive
service (in expectation of a generous tip, see 'Service
charges' below), but they are apparently happy in the
knowledge that they are doing a worthwhile job. Too
often, in Britain, one gets the impression that they feel
they are slumming and, but for a quite unjustified act of
fate, they would be by rights in the proprietor's or
customer's shoes. This communicates itself to the diners
and is, of course, of absolutely no concern to them.

Some waiters have the wretched habit of attempting to

clear away the dishes of people who have finished eating before others at the table have done so. They should be quietly advised to wait. On the whole, though, I like waiters and waitresses. They *can* make all the difference between a pleasant and an unpleasant meal.

'"And mind you go first to the ladies," put in Miss Matilda. "Always go to the ladies before gentlemen when you are waiting."
'"I'll do it as you tell me ma'am," said Martha, "but I like the lads best".'
> Elizabeth Gaskell, *Cranford* (1851–3)

'*Diner*: I'd complain about the service if I could find a waiter to complain to.'
> Caption to cartoon, Mel Calman, *How to Survive Abroad* (1971)

Sins of head waiters

The principles upon which head-waiters seat diners is largely unfathomable, except that in an emptyish Italian restaurant you are likely to be put next to another occupied table rather than given the freedom of space at some distance from other diners. Is this to make you feel cosy, close to human warmth? Whatever the case, here is your golden chance to request another table to the one you are being offered. It would take a fair amount of gall for the head waiter to claim that all the others were reserved. Object if you feel up to it, too, especially if the signs are that the next table may have a different code to yours on smoking.

Another curious seating practice, again particularly in Italian restaurants, is for women diners at two-seater tables to be sat with their backs to the wall. It may mean that the woman has a very good view of the restaurant whereas the man, who may have to bear the brunt of signalling to waiters, is awkwardly placed to do so. I suppose the reasoning is that the man is better placed to sign the bill – or have any food spilled on him and waiters crash into him – if he is on the 'outside' of the table. The seat against the wall is often comfier, too. But I suspect this is just something that restaurants do without thinking. Where a woman is paying the bill, I look forward to seeing the man put with his back to the wall.

Sins of diners

Where table manners are fully on display and open to public scrutiny, they are also open to the scrutiny of waiters and managers, and don't they have stories to tell . . . Probably the worst sin diners can commit is to snap their fingers at a waiter, in order to get attention. Getting a waiter's attention can be notoriously difficult, but this is not the way to do it – and is quite likely to precipitate something akin to the French Revolution if persisted with. The best thing is to cry 'Waiter!', 'Excuse me!' or signal your needs by a wave. Miming that you require the bill is something I do myself and always feel rather ashamed about, though it works in any language.

'If I tell a footman to bring me a glass of wine, in a rough, insulting manner, I should expect that, in obeying me, he would contrive to spill some of it upon me, and I am sure I should deserve it.'
4th Earl of Chesterfield (1694–1773)

A small sin is when the host diner remorselessly thanks the waiter every time he brings something to the table, tops up the wine, offers bread, or whatever. This is not necessary. A slight inclination of the head is more than sufficient acknowledgement most of the time.

Dress

In the 1970s or thereabouts, it seemed as though restaurants made rather a thing about male diners wearing a tie. Incidents were reported of famous (and other) diners either being turned away because they did not sport the requisite neck gear or being forced to wear a tie from the selection the head waiter had to hand. Even in very formal restaurants such confrontations now seem less of an event. It is possible that the message has been put over to the more casual of diners that they are not there just to eat but to be part of the ambience and decor. Or possibly waiters and owners are less fussy. It is reasonable, however, to expect that diners should be sensitive to the status a restaurant assumes for itself. If they want to eat wearing any old clothes, they should go to an old clothes restaurant.

Ordering

It is a sensible restaurateur who only offers a short menu and a very sensible restaurateur who offers no choice at all (provided that there are always back-up dishes for vegetarians and diners with specific dietary requirements). If a waiter hands you a menu card the size of a broadsheet newspaper, you can be forgiven for not wanting to bother with any of it and for wondering just how many of the dishes would be properly cooked. (In such cases, the dishes of the day would be the safest option.)

Some restaurants still offer unpriced menus to guests – a double-edged gesture as it means that if you do not wish to embarrass your host by ordering the most expensive dishes, you are operating in the dark. If you do find yourself in this position, remember that the more exotic forms of fresh fish particularly are often very expensive. Give a host the opportunity to make suggestions as to what you should have as this will enable them to steer you away from anything they are not prepared to pay for.

There is no proper procedure for making orders, though the host can either funnel the orders through to the waiter or, better still, prompt the guests one by one, to give their orders direct to the waiter. 'Ladies first' is an agreeable way of doing things but, especially at a large table, it might be better to go round the table in order, regardless of sex. People may like to order their starters first and then their main courses, although they can give both orders together. The waiter should be able to cope. Again, the host should gently try to standardize the procedure.

Be amazed, if you like, but beware waiters who attempt to carry all the orders in their heads. Be amazed, and slightly sniffy, about waiters who simply use a bar-code reading device on the menu (which transmits the order directly to the kitchen).

If the host conveys the guests' orders to the waiter, there will always be guests who choose that moment to change their minds – even if they decide to wait until the waiter has disappeared into the kitchen. The host should remain smiling and courteous as always through-out this ritual.

When dining *à deux*, it can seem unbelievably formal for a man to say to the waiter, 'The lady would like to have so-and-so . . .' 'My wife/my friend would like the sole . . .' can also sound artificial, if not patronizing. How much better then for the host diner to say to the other, 'Now what would you like for your main course . . ?' and allow the waiter to eavesdrop on the order, as it were.

Campaigners for the printing of menus in English (who should be supported) may insist on ordering dishes in English rather than by what it says on the menu (by saying 'The chicken' rather than '*poulet*' or '*coq au vin*', for example). But they should make sure they point to the right dish on the menu at the same time, just in case there is more than one of that type concealed under an exotic foreign name. Some foreign dishes, of course, are only known by their native names and there is no English equivalent.

Wine snobbery

This is a pain, but largely unavoidable. If the person who is ordering wants to consult at length with the wine waiter and then to make a fuss about the bottle that has been fetched – on grounds of fussiness rather than drinkability – a guest can only groan inwardly. A great deal of unnecessary palaver is often made about choosing the right wine. The rules about red for meat, white for fish, etc., are just waiting to be broken. By and large, restaurant mark-ups are so exorbitant that it is hopeless looking for a bargain, and much better to plump for the house wine, usually the cheapest on the menu. When was the last time you had an undrinkable house wine?

It is probably a myth that the second cheapest wine on the menu is the one the restaurant is trying to get rid of, but ask about it carefully just to be on the safe side. Wine waiters are not all to be distrusted. When asked to, they will quite often recommend interesting wines and not always the most expensive ones. If you do accept their recommendation (and it is more than likely that you will) and they comment, 'A very wise choice, monsieur, if I may say so', resist the urge to throw something at them.

Tasting the wine

It is amazing how many diners seem to think that they are being offered a taste of the wine they have chosen in order that they can pronounce on its quality. 'Yes, that is very good,' they say, doing an impression of an expert wine taster, often leaning their head slightly to one side as if they were *listening* to the wine . . . Not at all; the wine is offered for tasting so that the person (of whichever sex) who has ordered it can merely check that it is drinkable. In the extremely unlikely event of the wine being 'corked', they will have absolutely no difficulty in recognizing the fact: it will be like putting the nose in a sewer. This can be done simply be sniffing. On the other hand, if the wine is a white or rosé and ought to be served chilled, the only way to check the temperature is to sip it (without draining the glass).

One of the worst sins of waiters is automatically to offer wine for tasting to the man at a table, even if a woman has ordered the bottle (the waiter should be capable of remembering this). A waiter who makes this basic and extremely annoying mistake, should be directed to offer the wine to the right person.

Second bottles of the same wine are not always offered for tasting, the assumption being that they come from the same case and will be in the same condition. House wines do not need to be tasted and, indeed, will probably be brought to the table already opened. Champagne is not offered for tasting, either.

Serving

Food should be served at the diner's left-hand side and dishes removed from the right when finished with. Similarly, wine should be poured at the right-hand side. This is easy to remember because that is the side of the plate on which the glasses are always placed. Indeed, the reason for these rules is that by serving food at the left, you avoid knocking the wine glasses over and, by serving wine at the right, you don't need to stretch across the diner.

A good deal of latitude is given on these rules when a table is of difficult access. Sense suggests that these operations are best performed from whichever side is most convenient, without any conclusions being drawn.

Dining out on one's own

This can be pleasurable – which is why I often find myself dining on trains, even when I am not hungry. To have oneself pampered, even by British Rail stewards, is almost as soothing as having your hair cut or being given a massage. In a restaurant on dry land, it can also be very amusing, as a solo diner, to observe your fellow diners and to half-hear their conversations.

However, particularly in hotels, dining on one's own can present problems, especially for women. It is probably the case nowadays that a woman is capable of being allowed to sit at a restaurant table on her own without being suspected of being at least an oddity or at worst on the game. She should, of course, be left alone to enjoy her meal as she would wish. And she should not be put at a table hidden out of sight as though she presented some terrible threat to other people in the restaurant.

Men dining on their own are not treated like pariahs to quite the same extent, but are all too often parked by the squeaking kitchen door, or at a table no couple would be expected to eat at. Reading a book or a paper may enable the solo eater to fend off odd looks from other diners, but is not, unhappily, the best solution. The best approach for both sexes in this situation is to be super assertive. If all else fails, take your custom elsewhere – and that does not mean settling for a lonely room service meal in your hotel.

Waiters and restaurateurs should go out of their way to make sure that solitary diners are looked after and

valued every bit as much as those dining in a group –
without unduly fussing over them.

Inedible and unwanted food

If you are dining out in another person's home or in a
restaurant and you find the food inedible or in too great
a quantity, what should you do? Leave it on the side of
the plate, don't pick at it, and assume that nobody will
be so bad mannered as to draw attention to the fact. If
they do, you should not blame the food, but politely
claim that you do not feel like it 'just now'. This may
make your inquirer think you have some subtle medical
condition and that further discussion would be quite
uncalled for. In a restaurant, there may be cause to send
the food back, if you feel brave enough (see 'Complaining', below).

If you find the food indebile once it has reached your
mouth, one form of proper procedure I have been told
about is ludicrously elaborate. You are supposed to
place the food in your napkin and put the napkin under
your seat. You are then supposed to summon a waiter,
explain the position, and ask him to remove the
offending parcel. This is also very hard work and it
would be entirely understandable if you decided not to
go through with it, simply leaving the unwanted food on
the side of your plate, hidden if possible under something else.

Should you get food stuck between your teeth and
can't bear it, there is nothing that can reasonably be
done at the table. Restaurants, particularly of Mediterranean origin, often supply toothpicks, but these are
difficult to use discreetly unless you operate them
behind your hand. Should you have the sort of front
teeth which always manage to trap pieces of unsightly
spinach, take frequent opportunities to suck the offending matter off with your tongue, though it is imperative

to hold your hand in front of your mouth as you do so. Using pocket mirrors or, heaven forbid, reflections in your knife, to check the state of your teeth, is definitely not done.

What should you do if the person sitting opposite to you ends up with bits of food festooned about their mouth? Some of us are all too prone to flick the offending morsels off with our napkins. This is unforgivable and smacks of giving lick-wipes to children. A miming gesture with the napkin will probably produce a much happier result. It is clearly thoughtful, however, to draw a person's attention to this state of affairs.

Mutual tasting

Sometimes the urge to taste an obviously delicious dish which your dining partner has ordered (and for which you may be paying) is overwhelming. Of course, you will only take a taste with their agreement, but there is absolutely nothing wrong with this procedure, even in the most formal of restaurants. The food may be passed across on a side plate; an extra plate and cutlery can be obtained from a waiter to do this with. Alternatively, the eater's plate may be offered across to the taster, who can then use his or her own fork.

Complaining

Should you complain in a restaurant – if complaining might make your guests feel uncomfortable? Or, in other words, when you have cause for complaint, should you do it – even though it may embarrass the people you are eating with?

It is interesting that the British often wait until the *end* of a meal before registering a complaint. Simmering isn't just restricted to the kitchen. Resentment is allowed to build up until the bill comes. Indeed, it is often said that, in this country, we are not good complainers. We would rather not spoil the atmosphere of a dinner by making a fuss. But according to the chefs and restaurant managers I have talked to, first, they genuinely like to know if anything has gone wrong, and secondly, they would rather be told as soon as the diner becomes aware of the problem, the evidence is still to hand, and there is something that can be done about it. The worst thing is for diners to grin and bear it and then complain, having destroyed the evidence.

There is no clear advice. Yes, you should complain, if it doesn't make you feel wretched doing so. Yes, you should grin and bear it, if causing a scene would spoil the occasion for your guests. Declining to give a tip, or writing rude comments on the credit card slip, are silent, possibly preferable, ways of making your point but they will not get to the root of the problem.

Smoking in restaurants

Speaking as a card-carrying non-smoker, this is very much a concern of mine. If I am in a restaurant having a meal and someone at the next table lights up a cigarette, the smoke gets up my nose, both literally and metaphorically. Would I do anything about it? Well, actually I would dither.

I am not alone. In the PAS survey, only one in ten people in this situation said they would ask the smoker to desist. Half the sample, five out of every ten people, said they would simply grin and bear it. And I wouldn't have been surprised if even more people had said that. Which, if nothing else, may mean that there is a vast pool of resentment against bad-mannered smokers in this country. No wonder that smokers, with their backs to the wall, have acquired their own preservation society. It is known by the acronym FOREST, which stands for Freedom Organization for the Right to Enjoy Smoking Tobacco.

You can only get the management to stop other diners from smoking if they are doing so in a designated no-smoking area. So it is obviously best to find out whether such an area exists in the restaurant you have chosen to go to. Some restaurants do have them, others – chiefly Italian – most certainly do not. In the United States, almost all restaurants have clearly defined smoking and non-smoking areas, and you are asked which you prefer, when booking your table.

Smokers may be a minority these days but whenever I go to a restaurant they appear to be the majority – as if they have come from far and wide just to sit together and annoy me. But it would still have to be very bad interference with my enjoyment of the meal for me to make a complaint. The other day, however, I was quite bowled over when a smoker, who had already lit up, cheerily said, 'I hope this isn't bothering you?' It was a very winning gesture and quite unanswerable in the affirmative.

If there was a simple rule that all smokers followed and which would avoid so much aggravation, it would be: ask before lighting up, don't smoke when others are eating, and stop if asked.

(See also *Guests who smoke* under 'Dinner parties' in Chapter 4 GUESTS AND HOSTS and 'Smoking in company' in Chapter 6 NEIGHBOURLINESS.)

Restaurant conversations

Can I put in a plea for the banning of one particular type of restaurant conversation? That is the type when one of a couple chooses to take the other out to a restaurant in order to break the news that they are splitting up. I suppose people do this because they think it will soften the blow and perhaps lessen the chances of embarrassing reaction.

Unfortunately, what it usually means is that everyone else in the restaurant gets to share in the fallout. As with any row between diners, it spoils things for other people, and should not be inflicted on anyone.

Eavesdropping

Occasionally you may be seated at a restaurant table in a way that makes it quite impossible to ignore what is being said at an adjoining table. Sometimes this is just annoying; at others – particularly when dining alone – it can be richly entertaining.

I was dining alone in a restaurant and sitting near two elderly ex-colonial types during the great period of 'butter' jokes following the opening of the film *Last Tango in Paris* in 1973. The man admitted having seen the film and the woman, in all innocence, pressed him to explain all the fuss about the butter. 'Oh, it's nothing very much,' he replied, dismissively. 'Do tell,' she insisted. 'Well, they got very *excited* about the butter,' he explained diplomatically. 'But why?' the woman pressed on, gaily. 'Did he *throw* it at her?'

One cannot be blamed for letting oneself overhear this sort of thing and one cannot be expected to block one's ears to it. On another occasion, my wife and I were forced to listen as a man of advancing years at the table next to us told his female companion that she had 'the most kissable teeth in London'. (They didn't look as if they were, but the line seemed to have the desired effect, which just goes to show.)

However, there is one rule about this sort of thing. Should you overhear someone making an error of fact or asking a question no one at the table can answer, on no account should you proffer the information or make a correction.

'You will forbear to interrupt a person who is
telling a story, even though he is making historical
mistakes in dates and facts. If he makes mistakes it
is his own fault, and it is not your business to
mortify him by attempting to correct his blunders in
presence of those with whom he is ambitious to
stand well.'

Arthur Martine, *Hand-book of Etiquette and Guide to True
Politeness* (New York, 1866)

Splitting the bill

Most restaurants are happy to split the bill equally
between the number of credit cards that are placed on
the plate with it. Each card-holder is then presented with
a separate bill for signature but is well advised to agree
on a common level of tip with the others. Other combina-
tions of credit cards and cash are also quite in order –
just ask.

Any haggling along the lines of, 'Well, you had a more
expensive main course/more to drink than me' is inappropriate in this context. Indeed, in *any* context. Shared
eating requires a sharing of the communal cost.

It should be established *before* the meal if the participants are 'going Dutch'. If, at the bill stage, one party
wants to be generous – and some people have almost a
compulsion to do this – then it is ungracious of those
who are about to be treated to put up too stubborn a
front. They should concede, 'Well, you must let *me* take
you out for a meal soon,' and do so.

Even so, compulsive bill-payers can be hard to keep up
with. If you wish to make sure that the bill is brought to
you, you can arrange this beforehand with the head
waiter. Or, you can nip off during coffee and look after
the matter. Or you can arrange for the bill to be sent on
to you.

What should you do if you are meant to be taking someone out for a meal and find you have (genuinely) left all your money behind? Be mortified, is the first thing. So many people pull this trick intentionally (especially when inviting you to join them for a drink in a pub) that there really ought to be a special name for it ('robbery' might do). It is highly unlikely that the restaurant will extend you credit, so the guest must pay. You must then get a cheque to your guest in absolutely the fastest way possible. On no account should you let the guest end up paying for the meal.

Service charges

Much confusion – and resentment – is spread by the imposition of service charges by restaurants. Leaving aside the question of why it is necessary for a *separate* charge to be made for service, when serving is the whole point of a restaurant, the matter is complicated by the various methods adopted by different establishments. Some impose a service charge (which, theoretically, the customer may ignore); some helpfully introduce a voluntary charge (figuring that you are too inebriated at the bill-paying stage to calculate the 15% or so they think is appropriate); some leave it entirely to the customer. There have been mutterings that legislation should be introduced to standardize the procedure but these, to date, have come to nothing.

As to the precise percentage you are expected to leave as a tip, between 10% and 15% is normal in the UK. Starting at 10% makes it easier to calculate, but then add a bit more, taking it up to a roundish number.

There is the question, however – 10% of *what*? If a service charge has not been included, your bill total will nevertheless include VAT on food and wine, calculated at the current rate. When this is 17.5% or more, you might well wince at giving a tip based not just on the value of your meal and the service but on the tax as well. Regrettable though it may seem, it seems to be expected that your tip (as ever, voluntary, totally unexpected, and your own decision entirely) should be based on the total of the bill *including* tax.

Two things complicate what ought to be a straightforward matter: the VAT and paying by credit card. If a restaurant imposes the service charge itself, then VAT is payable on that, too. But on credit card slips, many restaurants still leave the total blank or 'open', even if the total includes the service charge. The point of this is to trap the unwary into adding a further tip.

When challenged on the matter, such establishments will say that they like to make it easier for exceptional service to be rewarded, over and above the service charge. Or, as it was put to me in one of my (up till then) favourite restaurants when I asked to be reminded whether service was included or not: 'Yes, sir, the service *is* included – but not the tip.'

Boring though it may be to do so, the only thing is *always* to ask, 'Is service included?' By the bill-paying stage, inebriated or not, you are likely to have forgotten what it stated on the menu about a service charge. If a service charge is included when the credit-card slip is presented for signing, do not be cowed into adding anything extra. I can even recall a waiter in a swanky Indian restaurant in London trying to talk up the imposed service charge, on the grounds that he did not get enough of it.

Such methods must always be resisted. Equally, the 'open' credit-card slip ploy must always be fought. Some irate diners attempt to hit back. They write in the 'total' line a sum which is 15% (or whatever) of the actual total and wait to see if the restaurant spots that.

In the United States, such guerilla tactics get you nowhere. 15% plus for service is standard and as good as mandatory. I was staying in California and resisted the meal-long performance put on by a waitress in the hotel restaurant, obviously with the sole purpose of wringing the best possible tip out of me. Foolishly allowing myself to think that all this could be dealt with when I came to pay my hotel bill at the end of my stay, I was amazed to be rung up in my room at the end of the evening by the restaurant manageress pointing out that I hadn't left a tip . . . It shouldn't be called the Land of the Free at all.

Some restaurants encourage you to give tips in cash and to keep them separate from the payment for the meal, if that is being done with plastic money. This seems reasonable, if only because it is more likely to go direct to the staff rather than have to be filtered out later from credit card payments.

Do not be forced into giving a greater tip than you would wish simply because you do not have the requisite cash. If necessary the waiter should be asked to break down a note into smaller parts. Similarly, if change is being brought after payment in full by cash, the waiter should bring a sufficient range of denominations so that a tip can be extracted from it. Having written all this, I am reminded that tipping can be a pleasurable activity, especially when it is to reward genuinely good and helpful service. Greasing the palms of head waiters in the old style always seemed a regrettable thing to do, but then, Sir Walter Scott happily admitted to overtipping waiters in order to make them smile and look genial. He presumably was not disappointed.

(See also Chapter 14 TRAVEL AND TIPPING.)

Doggie bagging

The American custom of allowing diners to take away unfinished food, supposedly so that they can feed it to their dogs, has not caught on in the UK in a big way. On the other hand, I have witnessed the request for a piece of left-over tart to be taken away being dealt with very deftly in a smart British restaurant. What's more, it was handed to the diner in a box, deftly done up with a piece of ribbon.

On the whole, though, what you cannot eat (or drink) in a restaurant at the time of the meal should be left behind. The attitude, 'Well, I've paid for it, so I might as well have it,' is hardly dignified. You go to a restaurant to eat out in a restaurant, not just to consume food.

Chapter 3

$\mathcal{F}$AMILY LIFE

For a number of years the Commercial Union insurance company has been using the slogan, 'We won't make a drama out of a crisis.' Families, alas, often seem hell-bent on making a crisis out of what should only be a good old-fashioned drama. Consideration for others begins at home. Before examining manners and etiquette in the wider world of social and public life, let us consider them in the familiar battleground.

Embarrassments

Your best friends won't tell you – though your family possibly will. Bad enough though they are to deal with in public, life's little embarrassments can still prove intractable at home. I'm talking here about BO, burping, belching, rumbling stomachs, farting, slips showing, flies undone.

Should you draw attention to them, if they involve other people? Should you apologize for them if they involve you? Yes, you should help other people with these indelicacies, though you will have to tread carefully and spare their feelings. No, you shouldn't apologize for your own failings in these areas, though in some cases, a brief, matter-of-fact apology can quickly cover your embarrassment.

If reason were needed for this otherwise unmannerly reticence, remember the (albeit apocryphal) story of the

Queen and General Gowon. In the early 1970s, Gowon, at that time President of Nigeria, came to London on a state visit. As the two were being driven along the Mall in a horse-drawn carriage, one of the Royal horses gave vent to a very audible fart. 'I do apologize,' said the Queen to her guest. 'Oh,' said Gowon, 'I thought it was one of the horses . . .'

'Never pick your nose or your ear save with your elbow.'

Chinese proverb

'Oh! that halitosis. It's so thick – a greyhound couldn't jump it.' ⌒
Sir Cecil Beaton on the halitosis of Professor Tancred Borenius

---

Belching, burping, rumbling stomachs. In private, a quick – even mumbled – apology on the perpetrator's part is all that is needed. Not to apologize, in the hope that people with you won't have noticed, is foolish. But other people should not draw attention to any such shortcomings – and certainly not with any Pooterish remarks like, 'Foggy on the river tonight, eh?'

In the 1960s, Katharine Whitehorn, in her book *Whitehorn's Social Survival*, recommended – quite how seriously I know not – that offenders should employ diversionary techniques. If there was nothing they could do to head off rude noises, she said, they should try to move away from the group, saying 'I must find an ashtray' or 'Just look at that squirrel!'. Try to create diversionary noises, she added, 'Snap a handbag, scrape a foot'. I fear she was having us on.

Clothing disorders. It is very helpful if other people quietly and promptly draw attention to disarranged clothing – flies undone, slips or labels showing, shirt hanging out, skirts caught in tights. Unfortunately, it takes a brave person to do this as gratitude is rarely forthcoming. No one finds it easy to accept that they have been unknowingly negligent; no finds it easy to accept the correction from another.

Farting. When the inevitable happens, as with belching, etc., I don't think anyone would countenance the Whitehorn avoidance techniques these days. Nor – given the Gowon story above – should they embrace the new openness about personal matters. Look what happened to that poor old actor, the late Sir Rex Harrison. Famously prone to farting, even before he was an old man, in his later years he became equally famous for his ill-advised attempts to disguise what he had done. Evidently, when he broke wind on stage, there was no mistaking the fact. It was about as inaudible as a stage whisper. Fellow cast members would instantly begin to titter and eventually ended up crying with uncontrollable laughter as Sir Rex indulged in increasingly hammy stage coughing which only served further to identify himself as the culprit. The ultimate indignity, caused by this unwise course of action, was that a substantial portion of the fellow's obituary in the *Independent* was devoted to his unfortunate failing.

Depending on which edition you read, the 13th-century song or poem 'Sumer is icumen in' does or does not incorporate this interesting information about what happens in the countryside at that time of year:

> Ewe bleateth after lamb,
> Cow loweth after calf,
> Bullock starteth, buck farteth,
> Merry sing cuckoo!

And, in an anonymous 10th-century Irish poem – here translated from the Gaelic – we learn:

> There's a woman in the country
> – I do not mention her name –
> who breaks wind
> like a stone from a sling.

These are rare mentions of what is by and large a still unmentionable phenomenon. The fart barrier remains largely unbroken; the shame of it all remains. Some people even suffer from *flatus retentus*, a medically recognized condition brought about by their reluctance to perform what is, after all, a perfectly natural and proper function. Perhaps it will always remain unacceptable in company, but may we be spared, please, the one or two intrepid pioneers of the acceptable fart? These are people who would appear to want those upon whom they inflict this behaviour to treat it as a normal turn of events; so they fart quite freely in company while their less mature friends sit boggle-eyed with embarrassment. I suppose this is a development of the 'better out than in' school of belching, but somehow I doubt that modern manners will ever embrace unwanted flatulence.

Halitosis. Bad breath is, if anything, an even worse problem than farting because it is not the slightest bit funny. Like BO ('Body odour', that great euphemism of 1930s soap advertising), one wonders how aware of it offenders are. Do they notice that you are turning your head away from them to gasp for air? Do their partners cease to notice it after a period of time and prolonged exposure? It is all a great mystery. There are things that can be done to ease the condition – proper dental care, attention to diet, mouth fresheners – but can you actually *mention* the problem to the people who have it?

No, that is an impossible thing to expect anybody to do, though conceivably offenders might eventually get the message if sufferers visibly keep their distance. Frankly, I am at a loss to know what to suggest. Twenty years on, I still cringe at the memory of a girlfriend I had who, though splendid in many ways, had a pronounced armpit problem. I said nothing, grinned and bore it, for a while at least. On reflection, I probably should have bought some expensive scent and introduced it to the relevant part of her person, rather like someone serving a writ. That way, she might not have got the message but the problem would have been alleviated.

Actor Michael Caine, indeed, suggests a similar method for heading off the bad breath problem in advance. When about to play a love scene before the cameras, he says he produces a mouth spray and shows it to his romantic partner. While she has her mouth open to ask what it is, he presses the button . . .

Children

This is not a Dr Spock child-rearing manual, so it will tread modestly into this area. Sending children off to bed if they misbehave either in public or in private is a punishment not much used nowadays. Sending out of the room is still practised, though as with sending to bed, this is a measure that probably gives more relief than punishment to children – particularly if they have their own TV and computer games to play with elsewhere.

The days when any child was expected to be seen and not heard are similarly not the ones we are living through now. But, yes, of course, children should behave. They shouldn't show off, dominate the conversation, make a noise, or generally make life intolerable for grown-ups, especially visitors to the home. Such behaviour has always been intolerable but in modern life it has been exacerbated by parents who, with a shaky grasp of psychological theory, are unsure about correcting the child, and don't.

Much bad behaviour among children stems from being denied their need to be the focus of attention and from being forced to be present with adults when they cannot participate. To this day, I can recall the agonies I went through as a child while my mother conducted long conversations with people she met when we went out shopping. Children should not be forced to remain in a situation where they can do nothing. Fortunately, round-the-clock television, videos and the widespread availability of computer games now means that a child can quite easily be relocated elsewhere, away from adult company, with some hope that he or she will be content. Although some would argue that brain-rot results from this method, it can hardly be worse than the frustration and boredom caused by making the child stay.

Although it is reasonable to expect that a child stays at the table until others have finished eating (see Chapter 1 EATING IN), it also asking rather much, and tempting fate, to insist that the child linger only to listen to adult conversation.

Children's questions. Annoying questions of the 'Mummy, why is snow white?' variety can cheerfully be left unanswered, but genuine questions to which the parent or adult can find out the answer should be dealt with in due course. This is known as education. I once asked my mother to tell me the facts of life and was fobbed off with, 'I'll tell you when you know how to keep a secret' (I'm still waiting). Embarrassing questions posed in public places – 'What's that dog doing to that other dog?' – should be deferred to a more appropriate time, if not ignored entirely. Not all of us have the invention of Sir Noël Coward who, on being asked by a five-year-old girl what two dogs were doing together, replied, 'The doggie in front has suddenly gone blind, and the other one has very kindly offered to push him all the way to St Dunstan's.'

Big Ears Is Listening To You. It is unwise to assume that children are deaf or do not understand what is being talked about. They have a sixth sense that tells them when parents are upset or are saying things that children are not supposed to hear. They will happily replay to you, at a later date, what you may foolishly have allowed them to hear.

Other people's children. Other people's children can be a delight. When they are not, it is ill-advised to discipline them on their home territory, unless you or your possessions are being assaulted. In your own home, you are entitled to go a little further in protecting your person and possessions from visiting children. You may hope to involve the children's parents in this process rather than take the law into your own hands. Simply grinning and bearing it does no one any good.

A difficult question arises outside their home, as to whether children are expected to behave according to their parents' standards, or whether they should conform to those of relatives, friends or strangers being visited. The clashing of rival codes can be problematic, though it is only reasonable that the children should behave as any guest should, if they are visiting someone else's home, and should be encouraged to this end. If someone else's child hits yours or adopts a dog-in-the-manger attitude over sharing toys, there is no very good alternative to explaining, simply, why you think they should behave otherwise. Who knows? it might be the first time anyone has bothered to do this for them.

When children meet the rest of the world on neutral ground – in places for eating or entertainment, say – they should be encouraged to match their manners to the surrounding norm, without sinking to anyone else's level, however.

Doting parents. An additional hazard of child-rearing arises when parents are so enamoured with the wit and wisdom of their offspring that they write it all down in leather-bound volumes to prevent it being forgotten. This has been known, I assure you. This is not a practice that any sane parent should follow. But, if parents have to do it, then on no account should the book be shown to anyone else.

If doting parents try to involve their offspring in grown-up occasions – parties, formal meals, and so on – resist with all your might, arrange a parallel event with your own offspring, or give in gracefully, just this once.

'A doting father once proposed to Dr Johnson that his two sons should, alternately, repeat Gray's "Elegy", that he might judge which had the happiest cadence. "No," said the doctor, beseechingly, "pray, sir, let the dears both speak it at once; more noise by that means will be made, but it will be the sooner over".'

quoted in *Etiquette for Ladies* (1837)

'All the universal experience of the ages, showing that imperceptibly children do grow from the cradle to manhood, did not exist for the countess. Her son's progress towards manhood at each of its stages had seemed as extraordinary as though there had never been millions and millions of human beings who had gone through the same process.'

Count Leo N. Tolstoy (1828–1910)

'[*Eve to Cain*] They tell me too of their last-born: the clever thing the darling child said yesterday, and how much more wonderful or witty or quaint it is than any child that ever was before. And I have to pretend to be surprised, delighted, interested; though the last child is like the first, and has said and done nothing that did not delight Adam and me when you and Abel said it. For you were the first children in the world, and filled it with such wonder and delight as no couple can ever again feel while the world lasts.'

Bernard Shaw, *Back to Methuselah* (1921)

The au pair

Treating an au pair like a member of the family would seem to be the only acceptable approach, given the likely age of the au pair and the fact that she is likely to be at a loss in a strange land, initially at least. But this is a question that is fraught with problems and very much depends on the degree to which the employers see themselves, or are required to be, *in loco parentis*. It is essential that the au pair be encouraged to have a life outside the employing family's and should be given her own room so that she does not have to be with the family all the time.

Whether she should be allowed to bring her boyfriend into the house overnight will depend on the employer's point of view. I heard of one au pair whose boyfriend was in hotel management. He received phone calls in the middle of the night on the employer's telephone which the employer then had to carry to the au pair's bedroom. This was surely asking rather a lot, though the boyfriend was very well-mannered about it. He made appropriate apologies and gave generous gifts, so that the parents were left speechless at what, in any other circumstances, would have been called *chutzpah*.

The best way of proceeding is probably to establish a list of rules and regulations right at the start of employment. This should be written down and cover such topics as pay, days off, hours spent on the job, and whether any light household duties are expected. Other matters well worth establishing early on with the au pair, though not written down, might well include: what name she is to call her employers by; whether the employers are willing to allow alcohol/drug/solvent abuse under their roof; the sharing of meals; contraception; theft; the extent to which children are to be allowed to watch TV.

Step-families

Divorces, re-marriages, and constantly shifting domestic arrangements between unmarried parents have reached the point that it is now almost becoming the norm for children to experience the trials (and possibly pleasures) of having step-parents, if not also having to welcome into their lives step-brothers and step-sisters. This is largely uncharted territory, as yet, and for step-parents – particularly those who do not have children from another liaison – there are no role models for them to follow.

Step-parents can be seen as intruders by their new-found children, although a real parent has invited the step-parent in, so to speak. One such step-parent says, 'You have all the responsibilities of a parent but none of the rights . . . I tried too hard to be a dad and it rebounded.' Should the step-parent attend the step-son's school prize-giving, if the real (estranged) parent wants to be there? (Probably not – this is an occasion for real parents only – even if the step-parent aspires to be thought of as such). The step-parent, in fact, frequently has to take a back seat, however difficult that may be to do.

There are signs of hope when children start referring to 'Our Wicked Step-mother' and such like. At least they are recognizing that there is a problem and that humour might be the way to solve it. It appears to be important for children to spend time alone with their step-parents to allow a relationship to develop. This is unlikely to occur if the step-parent is always talked to in the company of the real parent. Above all, the step-parent is ill-advised to try buying the respect of the surrogate children by splashing out on treats and gifts. Respect can only be earned – nor can it be gained by neglecting discipline in pursuit of a quiet life.

When a future step-parent first appears on the scene, they may first be encountered emerging from the bathroom by the children after spending a night with the real parent. Children have an unerring instinct for knowing what is going on and so the real parent should be quite frank with them about what is happening. It has been known for visiting lovers to be subjected to the third degree by children, tested and rejected on the real parent's behalf. Equally, of course, real parents may use the children for just this purpose, if too reluctant to make the move themselves. Being open about what is going on will help.

It is important to establish early on what the children are going to call the step-parent. A first name or nickname is probably preferable to claiming the special status of 'Dad' and 'Mum' – which they are not. The children should be encouraged to refer always to 'my step-dad' or 'my step-mum' rather than to cause possible misunderstanding as to the true nature of the relationship.

The step-parent or lover may also have to cope with hostility from the ex-wife or husband, particularly if involved in the ferrying round of children on visits. Much will depend on the circumstances of the divorce or separation, but an attempt to fix a meeting and establish a relationship, however difficult this is, should not be shunned.

Attempting to expunge the habits and routines of a previous partner may prove extremely difficult or impossible. It is important to proceed gradually and undramatically, gently suggesting that new routines are now called for, demonstrating how they might be preferable, and introducing them almost by stealth.

First-name terms

There is a type of progressive parent who encourages their offspring to use his or her first name. To be sure, there is something to be said for this if 'Mummy' and 'Daddy' are felt to be embarrassing. At some stage in my relationship with my own parents, it seemed to be understood that 'Mummy' and 'Daddy' were no longer to be used, and 'Pa' and 'Ma' were substituted. Sometimes, in more formal and public situations, even 'Father' and 'Mother' were used – almost in parody of 'Pater' and 'Mater'. I never could have called them by their first names, however, nor would have wanted to.

With uncles and aunts, it has become easier to call them – occasionally – by a first name as I have grown older, but I still don't forget that uncles and aunts is what they are and have not entirely given up calling them so. With 'artificial' uncles and aunts – that is to say, my parents' close friends from the same generation, though not related – it is not only easy but pleasurable to call them by their first names as we all get older. I am sure that is how they see it, too.

It is usual for married people to call their in-laws by first names, whatever the age difference, though early on they may stick rather stiffly to 'Mr' and 'Mrs' or, rather archly, call them 'Mum' and 'Dad' or whatever term the spouse uses. What boyfriends and girlfriends should call the loved one's parents is more problematical, especially if a relationship is well established. From an initially deferential 'Mr' and 'Mrs', proceed to not calling them anything at all, then *ask* them what they would feel comfortable with.

'Servants'. It is common practice to call anybody who is in an established serving position by their first name, though, a butler would be called by his surname only ('Jeeves') and a chief housekeeper or senior cook by title and surname ('Mrs Bridges'). The tendency these days in less formal employer–service-provider relationships is to assume that the employer may use a first name, though rarely is it expected in the other direction. It may well be, however, that a household cleaner, say, would prefer *not* to be called by the first name, so the person's view should be sought. Calling people whom you are trying to organize by their first names can sound terribly patronizing.

(Compare 'First-name terms' in Chapter 15 WORKING LIFE.)

Dealing with the old

Although it is almost a truism that the manners of the young are worse than they were, it is much more likely to be the case that the manners of the elderly are. This does not apply to all old people, of course, some of them have almost superhuman grace and dignity in the face of declining faculties. But there are many who appear simply to give up caring about people younger than them, when they reach a certain age. It is as if they have used up all the consideration for other people they once may have had and can no longer be bothered to extend courtesy to anyone. This is particularly the case in shop and bus queues. In conversation they crash about, often because they cannot properly hear what others are saying or have memory difficulties. On the roads, either as drivers or pedestrians, they frequently seem to believe that the simplest solution is to put their heads down, look neither to left nor right, and plough on.

Dealing with old people of this type is a thankless and daunting task, but it has to be done. And, although allowance should be made for failing faculties, for slowness and boringness, it can be done.

Pets

Other people's pets and how to survive them: the trouble with dog owners is that they tend to wait twenty minutes before saying, 'Down, Rover, I don't think Mr ——— likes you biting his ankle.' Meanwhile, the mastiff has been allowed to pong to high heaven, bark earth-shatteringly, slobber everywhere and shove their snouts in the stranger's private parts. Dog owners also pretend that it is perfectly possible to conduct an ordinary conversation with the other person while all this is going on. Only when the victim has been reduced to pulp by the dreadful smelly hound or when blood has actually been drawn (whichever is the sooner), does the dog owner ever say anything. Saying, 'Don't let him know you're frightened,' at this stage isn't much help either. About the only thing potential victims can do is to make it plain at the very beginning that they are not dog people. There is no point in pretending. With a bit of luck, the dog owner will take the hint and banish the hound.

Cat owners are usually nicer people – being one, I should know – but, like dog owners, they should reflect that not everyone is as devoted to the species as they are. Others may not enjoy being used as a climbing frame, a bed, a claw-sharpening device or a depository for cat hairs. It is quite possible, too, that other people are allergic to cats and all the pussy charm in the world is insufficient to make up for that. As for the unfortunate habit cats have of using the gardens of cat-loathing neighbours as lavatories: the only solution is for these neighbours to get a cat themselves who will see off any invaders . . .

In other words: owners of pets (of whatever kind) should always anticipate animal trouble and ask in advance whether visitors *mind* what they are more than likely to be subjected to. Animal-apprehensive visitors should not be reluctant to make their fears and dislikes known in advance and, if necessary, ask for the offensive creature to be kept from them.

Present-giving

Present-giving is a pleasant ritual when it is maintained at a relatively humble level. Gifts should never be given which embarrass the receiver by their cost or inappropriateness – in other words when they give more pleasure to the giver than to the receiver – or enable the givers to work off something in their systems.

There comes a time with most present-giving at Christmas and birthdays within the family circle when the givers begin to wonder why they are doing it. The motive has evaporated and they give simply because 'one gives'. There is a lot to be said at this stage for pondering how best the gift may be left ungiven. Or received: if having a birthday or anniversary party in middle or later life, it is quite in order to put on the invitation 'No presents, please . . .'

When ritually giving presents to young relatives – and maybe not receiving any thanks for your pains – it may be an idea to give an especially generous present at the coming of age or on some other landmark of young adulthood and announce that 'Now you're working . . .' or 'Now you've finished your studies . . . you might like to be spared having to write thank-you letters', and discontinue the present-giving. (See also 'Thank-you notes' in Chapter 16 WRITTEN COMMUNICATION.)

Occasionally, it is possible to be given the *same* present, year in, year out, by the same donor – and, what is worse, it is the wrong sort of present. In one's youth, one always receives several pocket diaries at Christmas. In later life, a non-smoker regularly receives gifts of cigars. It may be possible for an intermediary to point out these regrettable facts to the donor. Or the recipient may find an opportunity, at some suitable other time, to make plain to the donor what the position is and trust that the message will sink home. A better solution might be to ask positively for something that you want or to admire something of the present-giver's and say, 'Oh, I'd love one of those next time you wonder what to give me for my birthday.' Otherwise, you may just have to grin and bear it.

There is something rather uninspired about giving presents of money, though it is probably the most welcome of gifts (especially for the young) and is certainly the simplest for the donor to send off. Older present-givers need to err on the side of generosity. The modern equivalent of the five-shilling postal order that meant so much to them in their youth is a good deal more than a five-pound note today.'

Going to stay

This section is about what happens when you go to stay with people and try, as it were, to mesh your family life with the family life of others. Various complicated rules of thumb have been established for what you should and shouldn't do if going to stay with friends, in the country, say, for a short period. The classic observation is that 'fish and visitors smell in three days', (as in Benjamin Franklin, *Poor Richard's Almanack,* 1735, though an observation dating back to classical times), but all you can really do is to make sure you do not outstay your welcome, never mind how far you have travelled.

Try to settle how long you are going to stay at the time of accepting the invitation or before you set off. Try to arrive at a sensible time and one which bears some relation to when you said you would arrive.

'It was a delightful visit – perfect in being much too short.'

Jane Austen, *Emma* (1816)

'Don't presume on his [your host's] kindness, by attempting to stay beyond what he presses you to do, for two short visits tell better than one long one, looking as though you have been approved of. You can easily find out from the butler or the groom of the chambers, or some of the upper servants, how long you are expected to stay.'

Ask Mamma (1858)

'The first day a man is a guest, the second a
burden, the third a pest.'
  Edouard Laboulaye, *Abdallah* (1859)

'After three days give a guest a rake.'
  Swahili proverb

The inviter should make it clear whether the guests
need to bring any special clothes – for walking, swimming, tennis or riding, and right up to whether guests
will be expected to dress for dinner.

The co-ordination of getting-up times, particularly on
Sunday mornings, should be anticipated. The guest
should inquire what the usual pattern of rising is and
whether it will be all right to go down to the kitchen
and make a cup of morning tea. On the other hand,
breakfast is an easy enough meal to keep on the go over
several hours and the host will probably decline to
pronounce any set times. Still, guests should not dawdle
unreasonably long in bed – which means beyond mid-
morning and certainly not so that they miss pre-lunch
drinks.

It may be worth establishing in advance whether
churchgoing is customary on Sundays so that guests
know where they stand and can craft suitable excuses if
they do not wish to go along. 'We don't think we will
this Sunday' is a better way out than a detailed
disquisition on your beliefs or non-beliefs.

Should guests help about the house and the garden?
They should offer – maybe more than once. The host will
probably think of some small, token task which will
resolve the matter. Insisting on back-breaking tasks in
the garden is not appropriate, unless it has been well-
signalled in advance. The key point is that, in all things,
the guests should adopt the rules and customs of the
household they are visiting. For example, if they see that
the hosts always take their shoes off before entering the
house and walking on the carpets, they should do the

same. Or, rather, they should *offer* to do the same. It is just possible that hosts will loosen up on their rules when visitors come to stay.

Guests should make their own beds each day and simply throw the bedding over on the final day – rather than leave the bedding in disarray prior to its being stripped for the laundry. The question of bed-making has, however, been rendered considerably less fraught since the introduction of the duvet.

In the rare event of staying with people who have staff, guests should be prepared to find that suitcases have been unpacked for them and all their embarrassing old clothes, sexual equipment, etc. etc., have been neatly laid out on the bed for them. Tipping in such circumstances is even more of a strain than usual and it is probably best to consult with the hosts whether it is really necessary.

(See also Chapter 4 GUESTS AND HOSTS.)

Gifts for weekends away. A really good bottle of wine, especially champagne, makes an ideal gift when spending the weekend away with someone. Make it clear that you don't necessarily expect your host to consume it while you are there (unless this is part of your ploy). If he wants to, then of course he is entitled to. If you rather fancy partaking of it with him, you can surely say so. If it is a bottle of champagne – and champagne has the advantage of being drinkable at any time, with anything – then make sure you contrive to arrive with it chilled. This also helps underline the fact that you are expecting to drink it.

Boxes of chocolates somehow don't seem quite right if the weekend is being spent in the country, though no one is going to refuse them. More down to earth types of food – cheese, vegetables, meat – quite apart from seeming like coals to Newcastle, may make the hostess think you do not have great confidence in her catering abilities. Plants may be welcome (even in the country) if the hosts are keen gardeners and flowers are welcome just about anywhere.

Unmarried lovers room-sharing

This may be considered more of an ethical or moral question than a manners question and one that simply wouldn't have been allowed space in a manners book twenty years ago, perhaps not even five years ago, but it is this: you have a young couple to stay with you, under your roof (one of them might be an offspring). They are not married; but, for all you know, they may be lovers. The question is, do you arrange for them to share the same bedroom and probably the same bed?

The parental view, with one or two notable exceptions, tends to be, 'No. They can do what they like *elsewhere*, but when they are in our house, they must follow our rules.' Class can sometimes have something to do with it – with working-class 'hosts' tending to be more strict than the occasionally bendable middle. It can also be a generational matter. I know a forty-year-old man who is quite happy to let his eighteen-year-old step-son sleep with his girlfriend. But before the step-father married the boy's mother – and they had been living together for three years – *his* parents would put them in separate rooms.

Another form of the conundrum is also generation-based. What if the hosts invite a guest of their own age/ generation and he/she arrives with a young totty/toyboy. The hosts would have hearts of stone if such guests were to be kept apart. The young lover is accorded 'honorary' membership of the older generation for the duration of the visit . . .

Again, is this properly a question of *manners* or *etiquette* at all – isn't it rather one of ethics or morality? If you go back to the basic notion of manners being about courtesy and consideration for others, it is not hard to see how a social dilemma like the separate beds one, does demand respect for other people's feelings from both hosts and guests.

The hosts/parents are quite entitled to make their point of view known: it is their house and they may quite genuinely feel uncomfortable at alien behaviour, of which they may disapprove, being introduced. Making one's sexual activity obvious, flaunting it, is never much fun for other people. The lovers should not wish to embarrass the hosts by insisting on it. Lovers of the same sex need to be especially sensitive to the presumed feelings of the hosts.

Besides, it can also be the case that creeping along a corridor to unite secretly with a loved one is a rather more exciting option than having a row over being put in the same room from the word go. There is also the possibility that if hosts/parents take the initiative and go so far as to suggest that the couple might want to share a room, they might be anticipating a stage in the relationship that has not yet reached. Where hosts are unsure of the wishes of guests, it is a good thing for them to take one of the guests aside and say, 'I thought I'd put you in the blue room and —— in the pink room – is that OK, or would you prefer to share?'

Saying thank you for having me

If you go to stay with people, even if only for one night, you should write and thank them as soon as you can. Even if you don't feel they were put out by your visit – perhaps they didn't even cook you a meal, and let you share the breakfast they were having out of packets anyway – you should still do so. Even a one-night stay means that the bed will have to be changed. And, for many hosts, simply having an unfamiliar body about the house can be a little draining, even if they do not put themselves out.

As when staying the weekend (see above), the question of a present arises even after a one-night stay in town. Either on arrival or departure, the gift of a bottle of sherry, a box of chocolates, a bunch of flowers, is customary. This might seem an irritating gesture and it may be a ritual one, but it is expected.

(See also 'Thank-you notes' in Chapter 16 WRITTEN COMMUNICATION.)

Chapter 4

$\mathscr{G}$UESTS AND HOSTS

Partying is the specific type of guest and host relations that is our concern here – drinks parties, dinner parties, and informal dances. Much of what was said about formal table manners in Chapter 1 EATING IN applies here. For the other main type of guest and host occasion see also 'Going to stay' and 'Unmarried lovers room-sharing' in Chapter 3 FAMILY LIFE.

Issuing invitations

Invitations to formal and semi-formal occasions should always be issued in good time – a month in advance is about right. Any more and there may be a danger of the recipients mistaking the month in which the occasion is going to happen.

For a party or cocktail party, you will have to decide just how formal the occasion is going to be, because the invitation can be used to indicate quite subtly just what sort of party your guests should expect.

Dinner party invitations. Most usually, nowadays, invitations to dinner are given over the phone – which saves much toing and froing, if people have to juggle dates and so forth. It is a good idea, however, for whoever is giving the dinner party then to confirm the arrangement by sending a standard 'At Home' card but with the

'R.S.V.P.' crossed out and 'to remind' written in instead. This is also a useful precaution if the guests have failed to take the original message in.

With At Home and drinks party invitations, it is thought proper for invitations to come from the hostess only and, when directed at a married couple, to bear only the wife's name on the envelope (though both the invitees' names on the card.) If this procedure is followed, thank-you letters, similarly, should be addressed solely to the hostess (and probably be written by the wife of married couple.) These rules may safely be ignored if it would be completely inappropriate to stick to them. There are occasions, after all, when a hostess is not involved at all. Or, if a couple (whether married or not) is organizing an event and feels that invitations should properly be issued from both of them. Properly, the wording of any invitation has to be altered in this case. Instead of an At Home card – which can be adapted to take in almost any kind of event – one should be used that states X and Y 'request the pleasure of your company at . . . etc.' This form is also used if the host is a single person, or if two single people are hosting the occasion.

A dinner party invitation should properly give a precise time – '8 o'clock' – or '7.30 for 8 o'clock' – with the intention of getting everybody in place for the start of the meal.

Drinks party invitations. If you were to receive an At Home card like this one – a 'stiffy', 4 x 6¾ inches, with the basic information already engraved – you would know exactly what you were in for:

> *John Alexander Esq.*
>
> *Mrs Sebastian Frost*
> *at Home*
>
> *Friday, April 2nd*
>
> *R.S.V.P.*
> *106 The River Terrace*
> *London SW3*
>
> *6·30 – 8·30pm*

This is a formal drinks party. Note the precise choice of script and the capitalization of 'at Home'. You will be expected to leave before 8.30 pm, in time for your dinner elsewhere, and so will not be receiving substantial quantities of food. As black tie is not mentioned, you may safely assume that lounge suits will be worn. You are expected to answer the invitation by hand (see below). Note also that the year is not mentioned and that, if a precise time were to be given, say 7 pm, the form would be to put '7 o'clock'. Some people would move the time up the card and put the R.S.V.P. on the right.

The invitation can be made progressively less formal if a telephone number is given for the R.S.V.P. Some further indication of the occasion and its nature may be handwritten: 'Cocktails', 'Drinks', 'Buffet', 'Bridge', 'Bottle Party', 'To celebrate Donald's 40th birthday', 'For Hector Alexis', even 'Dinner'.

There is no need to have your own At Home cards printed. You can purchase pre-printed cards with lots of blanks (in fact, you may feel that you are paying a lot of money for not very much print). There are those who say that if you do buy At Home cards with blanks, they should not have any dots printed on them. If indeed this is terribly bad form, then someone ought to tell Smythson of Bond Street, the Queen's 'By Appointment' stationers, who sell them in large quantities.

You can further informalize the invitation by using phrases like 'drinks and eats' or 'Good Friday fish and nibbles', but if you do, it is probable that you won't be using a formal At Home card, or mind too much what correct form dictates. There is absolutely no need to have invitation cards engraved – or even printed – but whatever method you do choose will flag the type of party you have in mind and will make it clear what your guests may expect.

Putting a cut-off time, by which you expect people to leave, will not guarantee that they will, but again gives people an idea of what sort of occasion you are planning.

(See also invitations in Chapter 5, MARRIAGE AND DIVORCE.)

Black tie/lounge suit

'Black tie' is the coded way of indicating on invitations that men should wear dinner jackets and that women should wear evening dress. 'Lounge suit' indicates less formal apparel. It is unfortunate that women appear to be ignored in these instructions – 'Evening dress' would be just as helpful and clear an instruction.

'White tie', though rare these days, means that men should wear white tie and tails.

Replying to invitations

If you receive an utterly formal invitation, as above, you are obliged to write, by hand, an utterly formal acceptance or refusal. However awkward it may seem, this must be in the third person:

Mr John Alexander thanks Mrs Sebastian Frost for her kind invitation to an At Home on Friday April 2nd and has much pleasure in accepting.

Or:

Mr John Alexander thanks Mrs Sebastian Frost for her kind invitation to an At Home on Friday April 2nd but very much regrets that he will be unable to attend.

Note that these replies do not have to replay *every* detail on the invitation. Nor does the answerer, in giving regrets for non-attendance, have to give any reason for his inability to attend. The letter is not signed, nor does it need to be dated.

However, as the formality of the original invitation declines, so may that of the response. If a telephone number is given for reply, you do not even have to write at all, though you may prefer to. If the invitation only has your first name written top left, then this is a signal that you do not have to reply in the third person. Indeed, you can now write a short note and loosen up considerably:

Dear Mrs Frost,
Thank you very much for your invitation for Friday 2nd. I am very much looking forward to being with you.
Yours sincerely . . .

Or:

Dear Mrs Frost,
Thank you very much for your invitation for Friday 2nd. Alas, I shall be away on holiday that week, not returning till the following day, and will be unable to come.
Many regrets,
Yours sincerely . . .

The chief thing to remember is that a speedy reply to an invitation is obligatory whether accepting or declining. Whether the function be a small dinner party for eight or a dance for four hundred, the host or hostess needs to know numbers in good time for catering purposes. In addition, to delay replying might seem as if you were waiting for something better to turn up.

If you are genuinely unsure whether you will be free – and depending on the importance of the occasion – you should consider letting the inviter know what your position is. You *could* give a provisional acceptance and then absolutely not fail to confirm a little later whether you are actually going to attend or not. Whether it would be all right to decline and then seek a re-invitation, according to circumstances, I doubt.

For large drinks parties, where my actual presence or absence would hardly be noticed, I personally have sometimes found myself using the formula, '. . . am looking forward very much to being able to attend . . .' This implies some doubt as to whether I actually will or not. I suspect this is not very good form.

If a hostess does not receive a reply to a written invitation, she is entitled to assume that the person is not coming and to make other arrangements. The chances of the reply having been lost in the post are small. Should the invitee ring up at the last moment, the hostess is entitled to tell a little white lie and say the event has been cancelled and offer a barbed, 'But thank you for letting me know, anyway.'

It has to be said, though, that some inviters of the organizational rather than the private kind, hardly make it a pleasure to respond to their invitations these days. 'For security reasons' I have been told to apply for a special pass to get into a function (it did not arrive on time); for the same reason, I have almost been turned away from a function at which I was due to speak because the organizers were not on hand to advise the security men at the door; and I have received invitations to large receptions where precise time limits ('shifts' rather) were set on my participation 'because of the safety regulations'. None of this is very welcoming and, at the first hint of it, one is well advised not to get involved. As a host, if you have to submit your guests to an obstacle course, and if it is not possible to be warmly welcoming, perhaps you should think again about laying on the occasion at all.

Where an invitation has been sent to 'So-and-so and partner', it is polite of the invitee when replying to indicate who the partner is likely to be. This may head off trouble if there is to be any clash of personalities. For the host, to be forewarned is to be forearmed. If an invitation is issued to two people and only one of them is able to accept, it is polite to ask the inviter (by phone) whether the invitation still holds. The inviter will, of course, say yes, but the guest should not make that assumption.

Regrets only

These words are sometimes found in place of R.S.V.P. and reflect well-established American practice. The idea behind them might seem to be to reduce the burden of replying on busy party-goers. However, they merely serve to maintain the burden on those who are unable to attend. Too often, the formula is used on business invitations − to view a new model of car, or whatever − and in this case it has an air of inertia selling about it: as if the thinking behind the use of the formula was, if it is too much of a bother to *refuse* the invitation, because you have to write, then the chances are, you'll probably go along anyway.

This is not recommended. If an invitation is genuine, it is no trouble either to accept or refuse. Moreover, it is a politeness to do so. Nor does it require the use of a formula which implies that your would-be host believes it will be a cause for actual *regret* that you cannot attend his function.

So dilatory have some respondents been to invitations that some hosts have been driven to sending stamped-and-addressed envelopes for favour of an early reply. Others have printed an insistence that if a reply is not received by a certain date, a refusal will be assumed. These methods are quite sensible and a rather better use of the 'regrets only' technique. But the odds are that some of the dilatory, neglectful invitees will turn up anyway – without having indicated anything by way of a response – and you can't exactly turn them away at the door. It is hard work being a host or hostess.

Refusing invitations

Or, rather, refusing invitations so that people get the message . . . In Ralph Nevill's *The World of Fashion* (1923) (quoted in Chapter 5) we read that Lord Charles Beresford (1864–1919) was once summoned at the last moment to dine with the Prince of Wales (presumably the one who became Edward VII). He declined with a telegram, saying: 'Very sorry can't come. Lie follows by post.'

Great minds think alike. Marcel Proust in *Le Temps Retrouvé* (published 1927 after his death in 1922) writes of, 'One of those telegrams of which M. de Guermantes had wittily fixed the formula: "Can't come, lie follows".' And was it not Oscar Wilde who had to turn down a dinner invitation because he had a *subsequent* engagement?

These are variations on the theme of trying to indicate to would-be hosts that you do not wish to accept their hospitality or to get involved in the tedious ping-pong of being asked/asking back.

The trouble is, inviters are often insensitive to the signals that the invitee sends back. If the invitee is 'unavailable' on more than, say, two occasions this should be a sufficient hint for the inviter to stop issuing invitations. If invitees are genuinely regretful about being unavailable and would genuinely have liked to accept your invitation, they can and should undoubtedly make this clear.

Yet sensitivity on these matters is in short supply, particularly when so much store is set by what I might call 'the valueless hope' – 'Let's keep in touch!'; 'We must have lunch sometime'; 'We must have lunch some-time and I'm not just saying that . . .' How do you tell when the wish is genuine? Over to you.

'Mere general invitations mean nothing; they are only the small coin of good society. "Sorry you're going. Hope we shall soon meet again. Hope we shall have the pleasure of seeing you to dinner some day", is a very common mean-nothing form of politeness.'

Ask Mamma (1858)

It is not just a question of availability, of course. How many of us end up going to parties when we don't really want to go at all – just because we think it would be impolite or impolitic to refuse? If parties are not our thing – and most of us go through stages when we say they are not – then, for heaven's sake, we should say 'no', but nicely. It is possible to suggest that one's refusal is no reflection on the host and to suggest (more positive, this) that another sort of meeting should be arranged between you soon.

Invitations to couples

If couples of either sex are obviously living together and have sent out signals that they like to be considered as couples, then they should be treated as they wish. To send separate invitations might imply some disapproval that you do not necessarily wish to show. After all, when the day comes, it will probably not be required of the host to introduce the couple to other people *as a couple*. That they are a couple will probably be quite apparent to anyone with an ounce of intuition. If they are split at the dinner table, as is likely, then it is up to them to speak for themselves should their status not be apparent to a stranger. If a couple is homosexual, trying to alter their sexual orientation by 'getting them off with' someone is foolish behaviour on the part of the host or hostess and may only end in tears (literally).

Drinks parties

Why give a drinks party? To return hospitality or because you like making mischief, perhaps. But the only proper reason is so that a few personalities can be rubbed together, and hang the consequences. For as many guests who will look upon it as an opportunity to make friends and pick up new partners, there will be those who will feel let down because they have not done either of these things.

The chief delight of drinks parties as opposed to dinner parties is that you can take more risks, you can rub a wider selection of people together, young and old, rich and poor. And, if guests misbehave, they can be marginalized rather more effectively than at the dinner table.

Locations. There is a great deal to be said for holding a drinks party in an interesting location – in a historic house, on a boat – whatever the cost. You don't have to clear up afterwards and your home will not suffer any depredations. You can even hire people to organize parties for you, but this takes away much of the fun – particularly if they bring in guests from some arbitrary

list of people you don't know and will never expect to
see again.

Themes. Some party-givers believe in theming, presumably in order to differentiate their parties from those of
others. An invitation to a party on July 4th might bear
the instruction to bring something American (a tin of
baked beans was one person's response to such an
instruction, I recall); a party on July 14th might bring a
demand that you wear something red, white and/or blue.
Yes, this can be an imposition, but it is churlish to
refuse.

Fancy dress. Even more of an imposition, and at one
time there were rather too many such parties. It seems
a little bit of a cop-out to go and hire a complete
costume from a film or theatrical costumier. A token
gesture can be just as effective if carried out with a
little imagination. Not so long ago, just before Christmas, I was inveigled into going to a fancy dress party
at which I was instructed to come as my favourite
pantomime character. I bought a pair of Prince Charles
ears and wore them with evening dress (straightline
white handkerchief in breast pocket) and told anyone
who was interested enough to inquire that I was 'Prince
Charming'.

Food. Once upon a time, the young, the poor and
supporters of the SDP used to give wine and cheese
parties. They possibly may still, but the point about
such a combination is that guests were not simply
offered alcohol. Some sort of food should always be
supplied, from simple nibbles to elaborate buffets, to
soak up the booze. In addition, there is nothing more
annoying than to attend a drinks party – even if on your
way home or out to dinner – and have to fight off the
pangs of early evening hunger.

Taking a bottle. Whether or not to do this can cause problems where invitations are issued across generational and social divides. It is simple taking a bottle when the invitation specifically instructs you to, although you may think it an imposition for the host to ask you to bring one. He may have accepted hospitality from you in the past – possibly of a more substantial kind, too, at a dinner party – and you may feel that you should not be required to help him mount his own function.

That, of course, is how it all begins. Bring-a-bottle parties are the sort of thing the young and impecunious organize. But, as status and earning-power improve, it can seem less and less appropriate for hosts to rely on this method of party-giving. If you do decide to go along with the request, and that it would be churlish not to, it is only sensible to take fairly average wine. Bring-a-bottle parties are seldom, if ever, given by wine connoisseurs. Taking your own bottle-opener, though possibly a wise precaution, is surely taking things a bit far. The host(s) ought to do *something* after all.

Staff. To have people, hired for the occasion, to hand round drinks and food not only removes a burden from the host, it can also add a bit of fizz to the proceedings. I have encountered a special party butler who managed to get round a crammed room with the skill of a contortionist, despite having bottles, glasses, corkscrews and cigarette lighters secreted about his person. Agencies will supply all types; the children of friends will also sometimes oblige for rather less expense.

Party-hopping. Except among the young, no one expects to cram in as many different parties in one evening as can be achieved. That is about as pointless as seeing how many students can be crammed into a Mini or a telephone box. No host or hostess will feel warmly towards a guest who treats a party as a mere stopping-off point, to be left as soon as it proves too boring.

Other cultures, other manners. In America, the moveable feast approach to partying seems better established. I remember once spending New Year's Eve in Dallas and observing that it was quite in order for people to go from party to party. The saving grace was that party-hoppers took their personal bottle of hootch with them from one party to the next.

Gatecrashing. Inexcusable and never to be attempted. However, an exception *might* be made for an invited guest who brings along an uninvited guest. It really depends on the degree of formality and the scale of the occasion and whether an extra body and mouth would seriously undermine the occasion. If the pair then kept themselves to themselves and did not join in the party, that would not be a good thing. It is just possible, though, that an uninvited or surprise guest might add a little lustre and excitement to your party.

There is also the form of gatecrashing which involves extracting an invitation when it would not otherwise have been forthcoming. Say you learn that friends are having a party to which others have been invited and you haven't. Should you phone and ask your friends to dinner on the date of the party so that they can issue a late invitation? Clever calculation – but still gate-crashing.

Escaping from small parties. Difficult to engineer, this, especially if the reason for wanting to slip away is because you are bored rigid. The best thing to do is to prepare the ground from the start. Make it clear that you are only looking in, there is some other function that you have to attend to later on. Then, if the small party turns out to be enchanting, you can still linger, casually playing down the other calls on your time.

Rude hosts, rude guests. Two specific points of related behaviour are often observable especially at the more formal type of reception: the host greets you, manufactures a smile, shakes you by the hand and then almost forcibly steers you away, and onwards, so that he can greet the next guest.

Then there are guests who are forever losing eye contact with you. Why? Because they are too busy looking over your shoulder to see who has just entered the room or to find out if there is anyone more interesting to talk to. Disengage yourself as quickly as you can from such dreadful people – ideally by making it clear that you, too, have spotted someone more interesting to talk to.

At parties, guests are meant to circulate, but it can be unpleasant if you chop short an encounter too soon or too suddenly, for the wrong reason. Don't forget to take along sufficient supplies of grace with you.

Spillages. Accidents happen even in the best-regulated households. If you drop wine or a cigarette on someone else's carpet, never attempt to conceal your unfortunate action. With the minimum of fuss, inform your hosts so that they can deal with it (if they wish to), and make a fulsome but brief apology. Should you spill something over somebody else, call for assistance, make appropriate but not long-winded apologies, and make a genuine offer to pay for dry-cleaning bills. It is most unlikely that where an accident has occurred in private the victim will actually get round to asking you for the money. But the offer must be made. Consider also, according to the seriousness of the accident, whether sending a bunch of flowers or some other gesture might be appropriate next day.

The same rules apply to breakages. No attempt should be made to conceal that kind of damage. It will be discovered one day and feelings towards you may then be unspeakable.

The sensible party-giver will have damp cloths to hand ready to be brought into use as soon as they are needed.

Cleaning agents are best not experimented with at this stage. Again, the rule is that guests should not do the cleaning up themselves – the hosts may have higher or lower standards of restoration in mind.

Red wine spillages can be devastating, though as with white-wine stains, one can never be sure whether pouring loose salt over them will soak up the offending liquid. Sometimes it miraculously removes every trace, at other times it makes no difference. But, either way, it is unlikely to do harm and so is worth trying.

Surprise parties

Usually given on special birthdays, surprise parties too often end up seeming primarily to have been laid on for the benefit and enjoyment of the organizer alone. The victim is led, unsuspecting, into a darkened room, the lights pop on and there are all the 'friends' who have been in on the secret, making somewhat forced little noises rather as on a lame edition of *This Is Your Life*. For some reason, it is difficult to sustain the initial surprise in parties like these and to turn it into anything approaching enjoyment.

Arranging a birthday dinner where the subject is not aware of the identity of the invitees until they arrive is another matter and can be very gratifying.

(See also Chapter 12 SPECIAL OCCASIONS.)

Dinner parties

Something of a mystique has grown up over the throwing of successful dinner parties but it is probably the case that some people have the knack for it and others do not. Nevertheless, paying attention to certain practical matters can increase the chances of success quite significantly.

One of the burdens of providing dinner for guests in your home is that the hosts and/or cooks all too often are so busy that they get little or no opportunity to talk to the friends it has been the purpose of the occasion to entertain. So, increasingly, it is considered quite acceptable to take guests out to a restaurant, making it abundantly clear that this is your treat and that you will be paying.

It is also increasingly common for the dinner-party-giver to hire a cook and people to serve in the home, and/or to import most of the food ready-made. This is to be applauded, as it in no way detracts from the pleasure of the occasion: indeed, it may add to it, as the guests will have a host to talk to, and the cooking will probably be less at risk. Conscious of such arrangements, guests should be careful, however, how they compliment the hosts on the quality of 'their' food.

Dinner-party books. Some hostesses (and possibly, though I doubt it, hosts) keep a record of the menus and wines that they serve at dinner parties and make a note of any likes and dislikes of their guests. They also record which guests came with whom. This is all very well and conscientious; it can mean that guests don't always get served the standard dinner party repertoire. One hostess I knew, who had been sent on a *cordon bleu* course by her husband at the start of their marriage, nevertheless still only ever managed to serve one menu.

But I know one hostess who keeps a dinner-party book and who remains convinced I don't like fried onions because twenty years ago, according to her records, I left them on the side of my plate. Could it have been that the onions in question were not properly cooked? Or that my tastes have changed? The dinner-party book in question does not record. Best not to bother, say I.

'As a matter of course, young ladies do not eat cheese at dinner parties.'
Manners and Rules of Good Society (1888)

Vegetarians and special requesters. If you are a vegetarian or have some special food allergy – for example, being rendered immobile by shellfish is a quite common affliction – you really ought to tell or remind your hosts in advance, so that they can provide an alternative dish. You should never assume that people will remember your special requirements.

Napkins. Certainly these should be supplied. It is wonderful if they are proper linen ones, though they are an expensive item to launder. Some people would always rule out paper napkins, but they are effective and cheap. Either way, they should be simply folded and placed to the left of the place setting, possibly on a side plate if there is one. Folding napkins into shapes is all very well but may make your guests think you are treating the laying of your table as in a hotel or restaurant. (See also under 'Laying the table' in Chapter 1 EATING IN.)

Taking a present. This is quite a complicated question which can easily be dismissed as the kind of middle-class preoccupation that gives manners and etiquette a bad name. But it is quite *interesting* . . .

Once upon a time you automatically took a bottle of wine to a dinner party (a) because everyone had less money in those days and it helped the host if you did so, and (b) because wine seemed to cost more then and the gift of it was quite impressive. But when you grew a bit older, you began to feel that the gift was superfluous. Your host had his own cellar, was a bit choosy about his wines, and might have felt that you were imposing your tastes on him. He might also have been slightly insulted by your thinking that he needed any help.

For your part, whatever your age, you may feel that your presence at the dinner and your charming behaviour (coupled with your delightful postprandial thank-you letters) is sufficient return for the invitation, particularly when that is only in return for hospitality you have already given.

So you no longer take wine. You may also be tempted not to take wine for the reason that you are unlikely to be drinking it yourself. In which case, you might feel like taking a bottle of mineral water instead (just in case your host is neglectful in supplying any). On this last point, there is no doubt that you would be wrong just to take a bottle of mineral water. For a start, it would a bit holier-than-thou and, ten to one, your host would turn out to have cases of the stuff all ready for you, if you did. So, in this situation, you would be well advised to take a bottle of mineral water *and* a bottle of wine. After all, the gift is principally for your hosts and not to meet your needs. The same goes for taking a bottle of beer, if that is your preferred tipple. Take something for your hosts, too.

As wine has become a little less special – and as one gets older – other presents become more appropriate. A small box of special chocolates is now much more acceptable – as is a bunch of flowers.

Whatever you take, is it correct for the hosts to serve your wine or hand round your chocolates to the assembled gathering? Yes, the chocolates, certainly, and the wine, provided it is suitable for the occasion and is ready to serve (especially if it is champagne). The guest may, on the other hand, specifically state that the gifts are not to be consumed there and then but are, 'For you to enjoy . . . another time.'

If you do decide to take wine to a dinner party, bear in mind that it ought to be reasonably respectable, as it might end up being consumed before your very nose. I know of one host who virtually spat out a mouthful of red wine and expostulated that it was the worst wine he had ever tasted and that it must on no account ever be

served in his house again. The female guest who had
brought the wine as a present shrank so small that she
still hasn't recovered.

Arrival times. Promptness and lateness are discussed
under 'Punctuality' in Chapter 10 SOCIAL LIFE. When you
are invited to a reasonably formal meal – lunch or
dinner – you should make a particular effort not to be
unduly late, and never early. If an invitation is for '8
o'clock', time your arrival for about 8.10. If you anticipate being more than half an hour late, you should ring
up and state your position. The cook may be able to
delay matters, if necessary, to take account of your
lateness. One of the good things to be said about mobile
telephones is that, if you do get stuck in a traffic jam on
the way to the dinner party, or if you can't find
anywhere to park, you are in a position to do something
about it and to keep your host/hostess informed. This is
the essence of consideration.

'7.30 for 8 o'clock' means that you should be present
and ready to sit down for dinner at 8 o'clock.

Sometimes, if a guest cannot manage to accept an
invitation to eat a whole dinner, he may be invited to
drop in later for pudding and coffee. This is a pleasantly
informal way of dealing with non-availability and shows
that the host is keen to have you join in for however
short a time. But any commitment to such a procedure
should not be looked upon any more lightly than an
acceptance of a full dinner invitation. You should still
turn up, whatever transpires, and should keep your
hosts informed of any change of plan.

On a visit to Israel I found that my host had invited
people to meet me only at the conclusion of an informal
dinner that he and his wife had given me. In other
words, the guests came for pudding and coffee. This
seems to be a very agreeable custom but I have never
encountered it anywhere else, or managed to organize
such an occasion myself in Britain.

Seating plans. It is always a good idea to jot your ideas down on a piece of paper before your guests appear. Couples who arrive together should not sit together. Man/woman, man/woman is sensible if you have sufficient of each. It is the hosts' prerogative to have people sitting next to them that they really fancy talking to. On the other hand, seating people next to each other on the chance that they may get off with each other is usually doomed to failure and is best not done. At anything other than the most formal of dinner parties, it is quite in order to have uneven numbers of guests (though, understandably, most people would jib at thirteen). Nor is it important to have anything approaching equal numbers of either sex, though among young people using dinner parties as a way of meeting members of the opposite sex, any heavy imbalance may be disappointing. Generally, though, unevenness is good thing. If everyone is paired off neatly, a dinner party can be a very stodgy affair. Jagged edges, a liberal sprinkling of lone guns, can liven up the proceedings no end.

On more formal occasions there are complicated rules of precedence which I will not dwell on. Broadly speaking, the principle is that the chief guest or guest of honour (if male) sits on the hostess's right. The chief guest (if female) or the chief guest's spouse or partner (again if female) sits on the host's right.

Delayed meals. It quite often occurs that a disaster in the kitchen means that a dinner-party meal gets noticeably delayed. Hunger stalks the guests, and the host, in desperation, keeps on pouring out more drinks than are needed, to keep the conversation flowing. In such cases, it is always best to let your guests in on the tragedy. Otherwise they may wonder if the hostess is arguing with the cook – if she is not the cook herself – or is having a nervous breakdown about some other matter, or is just being wilfully negligent of her guests.

These misfortunes do happen – rather regularly – so

be open about it. Then, if the meat gets burnt to a cinder, or the fish turns out to be off, it won't come as too much of a shock if you have to send out for a take-away meal, or decamp to the nearest restaurant.

Terrible meals. If you are offered food to which you have ·an aversion, accept a little on your plate, and don't make a thing of it. If food turns out be inedible or not to your liking, leave it on the side of your plate – again, without drawing attention it. With luck, your host won't make a song and dance about it either. In any case, don't despair. Even if one course has flopped, the odds are that you won't get three in a row. You will be offered something edible eventually. Very few hostesses can make a hash of the pudding. It would take a genius to ruin the cheese.

Stack and pass. It is no doubt kindly meant when people start passing along the plates and stacking them as they go, but it smacks of the canteen and should not be done at any gathering other than the most informal – unless you are encouraged to do so by your hostess. The plates should always be passed unstacked, if they have to be passed at all. A slight reluctance to participate in clearing does not go amiss. Guests should never get up from the table to 'lend a hand' unless, again, the situation is very informal.

Guests who smoke – especially between courses. At a certain dinner party, when a young, nervous girl lit up a cigarette after the soup, the hostess said icily, 'We seem to have finished', and led the party from the room. That was the end of the dinner.

I first came across this cautionary tale in Katharine Whitehorn's *Observer* column (27 July 1980), though I have subsequently found it told about a Duke in Francis Meynell's *The Week-end Book* (1955) – though, from the way Meynell tells it, it was an old tale even them. I have also heard it adorned with the additional detail of the cook having had a tantrum over the ruination of her meal, and with the moral drawn that it is an excellent illustration of the way in which manners that are intended to put people at their ease can be used rather to humiliate an innocent or uninitiated. The girl who lit up is said to have run off in tears and had to leave the house next day.

Maybe the incident never occurred but, if nothing else, the story does point to the excessive irritation that can be caused by smokers lighting up between courses, whether in public or private. Whatever you think of smoking in general, the prospect of a smoker being unable to keep going without recourse to the weed between courses is pitiful to behold. It should not be done. If it has to be, then permission should of course be obtained from absolutely everybody.

A story is told of Paul Bocuse, the chef, eating at a table in London with a journalist who was so nervous he thought he would burst if he was not allowed to smoke between courses. Bocuse's assistant refused even to translate the request to the great man, knowing he was bound to disregard it. Finally, just as the journalist was about to self-destruct in desperation, Bocuse broke into hitherto unsuspected English, and gave him permission to smoke. 'I would rather see a man smoke,' he added, with a magnificent put down, 'than see a child cry.'

(See also 'Smoking in restaurants' in Chapter 2 EATING OUT and 'Smoking in company' in Chapter 6 NEIGHBOURLINESS.)

Wonderful meals. It used to be the convention that comment was never passed on the quality of food served at a dinner party, whether the food was good or bad. Now, rather the opposite is the case. With so many 'Foodies' about, it is considered positively unkind not to express one's pleasure. Again, be cautious, however, about asking for a recipe, as the dish may have been acquired ready-made from a supermarket or delicatessen. 'What a wonderful ——!' is consequently a much more tactful compliment than 'You're a genius with ——, how *do* you do it?'

Coffee and cigars. As it is now a minimum requirement of a dinner party that mineral waters should be available, so, too, is it a fundamental courtesy that hosts offer decaffeinated coffee (and perhaps even tea) in addition to ordinary coffee. Despite the somewhat questionable virtues of 'decaff', the thought behind it – that it won't keep the guests awake – is a kind one.

The smoking of cigars should be undertaken only with the greatest reluctance and permission-requesting – as at a public dinner or in a restaurant. Whatever the acknowledged delights of cigars, their smoke does have a way of clinging on to people's clothing. It is essential to air this clothing before the clothes are put away. Other people should be given the opportunity to avoid the necessity for such measures, just as much as they should be spared the acknowledged dangers of passive smoking.

Withdrawing. A good deal of bristling goes on these days should any hostess suggest that the 'ladies' withdraw at the end of the meal, leaving the 'gentlemen' with their port, cigars and dirty stories. Ardent feminists may well insist on remaining to smoke *their* cigars.

If guests suspect that this practice is going to be sprung upon them, and disapprove, it would be best for them not to attend the dinner. Otherwise, a quick powdering of the nose and female gossip together for a period of, say, twenty minutes or half-an-hour before the 'ladies' rejoin the 'gentlemen' for coffee and liqueurs, should be looked upon as a blessed relief and gone along with.

Passing the port. Of course, port tastes exactly the same whether it comes to you from the left or the right. Tradition, however, dictates that it should come to you from the right. Port is circulated clockwise.

The other thing about port circulation is that you should not impede it. Once upon a time, if you did, someone would ask, 'Do you know the Bishop of Norwich?' Nobody knows quite why they would have said this, but as with the term 'norwicher', the implication was clear: you were holding on to the bottle and not passing it round as you should.

Dinner-party conversation

There is a curious belief that dinner-party conversation ought to be glittering. If it ever was, then whatever happened to it? For today, unless I move in the wrong circles, one hears the occasional witty shaft – like the hostess who said, 'And while you've got your mouth open, would you ask the maid to serve dinner?' – but too often the general level of conversation is no higher than in any other situation.

It may just be a myth – something dangled before us by commentators on good food and entertaining, to go with the vision of high living they promote, which includes elegant company, fine wines, international cuisine and hand-painted place mats. In fact, these days you are, alas, much more likely to encounter utter banality of conversation at table or fellow diners being rude to each other, or otherwise ignoring the basic rules of dinner-party conversation.

Just to remind you, these rules used to be that you avoided topics of conversation which might give offence (work, religion, politics, health, money and the servant problem) (see 'Taboo subjects' in Chapter 11 SPEAKING); you talked to the person on your left during the soup, switching to the person on your right during the fish course, and so on (see 'Talking to left and right', below).

However, these days, work is invariably a topic of conversation over the dinner table (unless the host and hostess have superhuman powers of control) and, similarly, religion holds no terrors over the raspberry mousse, while the servant problem has been replaced by the standard topics of home computers, the housing market and 'our burglary'.

Talk about politics has, of course, contributed to the proliferation of that phenomenon known as the Dinner Party Bust-Up. Insurmountable breaches occur between old friends; irate guests stomp off into the night shouting, 'And for heaven's sake don't bother to apologize'; tears cascade over the dish-washer. Randolph Churchill, that scourge of the dinner party of yesteryear, had it about right when, writing to apologize to a hostess whose gathering he had ruined, he suggested, 'I should never be allowed out in private'.

The witty and memorable put-down is presumably the kind of thing that people are thinking of when they angle for glittering after-dinner conversation. The question about put-downs, however, is, 'What happens next?' When the victim has been put in his place, put down, wiped the floor with, is he supposed to say, 'Oh, ha ha, how very witty!' or 'Thank you!' – when his natural inclination must be to shrink into a very small blob in the carpet? Well, as so often in this book, I would recommend a good-humoured response. A smile may be as good as a verbal one. To react this way is not a sign of weakness. It is a sign of maturity and strength. It is also a politeness to the other guests if you do not resort to fisticuffs or a show of temperament.

The chances are, however, that you will never actually hear one of these put-downs and ripostes being uttered. Dear old Oscar Wilde may have been very good at putting such things in his plays, but I suspect he was rather less adept in real life than we have been made to think. Besides, how is that we ever came to hear of his *bons mots?* Not, surely, because overhearers scuttled away to pass them on but because Oscar himself, acting as his own public relations man, recounted them himself.

'Table Talk is so natural to man, that the mouth is the organ both of eating and speaking. The tongue is set flowing by the bottle. Dr Johnson talked best when he had dined; and Addison could not talk at all till he had drunk. Table and conversation interchange their metaphors. We *devour* wit amd argument, and *discuss* a turkey and chine. That man must be very absorbed in reflection, or stupid, or sulky, or unhappy, or a mere hog at his trough, who is not moved to say something when he dines . . .

'Table-talk, to be perfect, should be sincere without bigotry, differing without discord, sometimes grave, always agreeable, touching on deep points, dwelling most on seasonable ones, and letting everybody speak and be heard.'

Leigh Hunt (1784–1859)

Talking to left and right. The traditional way to conduct formal dinner-party conversations with those seated on either side of you was for a woman to talk to the man on her left during the first course and to the man on her right during the second, and so on – a practice known in the United States, I believe, as the 'Boston Switch'. But as for sharing conversational favours between guests on left and right, these days – well, if I am sitting next to the world's leading bore, I usually find that I make no great effort to share my favours equally between him and the guest on my other side. Yet I should. It is miserable to be stranded between two people at a dinner table while those on either side of you are both more interested in their other partners. And it is quite unreasonable to ignore anyone sitting next to you on the grounds that he might be a bore without having actually tried to make conversation. (See also 'Bores' in Chapter 10 SOCIAL LIFE.)

Talking across a fellow diner, in front or behind him, for any length of time, is also a serious discourtesy and should not be practised. It is quite in order to join in conversations being conducted on either side of you and from which you may have been excluded. Make them feel guilty.

As I understand it, when the Queen is dining formally and she turns from the person on one side of her to the person on the other, all the other diners in the hall are supposed to do likewise. As she has her husband on her right most of the time – and presumably has better things to do than chat to him during state banquets – it would be understandable if people generally on the right felt ignored in consequence.

I have also heard of an aristocratic lady, of our own day, who has been known to call out 'You may turn' to the assembled guests, presumably to make sure that everyone gets a fair blast in the ear trumpet.

A subtler, though more energetic way of ringing the changes, conversationally, is to do what I encountered when dining once at the invitation of the wife of the Headmaster of Eton. After the main course, she invited us to turn our place cards over and follow the instructions given on them. These were things like, 'Move to the Headmaster's table and sit on his left' or whatever. This ensured that one was not bound to the same fellow guests all evening and certainly brought about a more entertaining social mix. The method only works at the more formal type of private dinner party, however. A variation of this method, particularly when everyone is seated at one table, is for the women to be instructed to sit tight and for the men to move four seats clockwise, or whatever.

On the whole, though, I sympathize with the philanthropist Nubar Gulbenkian, who once proclaimed, 'The best number for a dinner party is two – myself and a damn good head waiter.' The writer and editor H.L. Mencken believed in almost the same restriction on numbers when he defined a dinner party for more than two as 'an invitation for no other purpose than boring.' No wonder I detect a move to avoid the giving of dinner parties altogether. 'Come to *supper*,' hostesses cry, in the unstated hope that people will behave themselves better – and enjoy themselves more – if the name is changed and the formalities lessened and loosened.

I heard of one British Ambassador whose dinner invitations would arrive bearing a clear idea of what the subject for discussion would be (usually something that went well with the after-dinner mints, like Strategic Arms Limitation). He was at least trying to give point and direction to his occasions – and he was, of course, answering the otherwise difficult question, 'What is a dinner party *for*?'

The novelist Somerset Maugham's response was enshrined in his observation that a dinner party was when 'one should eat wisely but not too well and talk well but not too wisely.' But for most of us the answer is fairly down-to-earth. We do it because we have to eat and realize it is good to eat in the company of others. Anyway, we remember that we *owe* a meal to those people from over the road – and have done for simply ages.

Drunks

(See 'The offer of a drink' in Chapter 6 NEIGHBOURLINESS and 'Alcohol-induced behaviour' in Chapter 10 SOCIAL LIFE.)

How to end a dinner party

I believe this is less of a problem than it once was, at least among the middle-aged. A concatenation of circumstances – the drink-driving laws, attention to duty, the need to relieve the baby-sitter – means that guests are less likely to linger in an unwelcome fashion. If you have to travel some distance before reaching home, if you have to be up early the following morning, then you should have no compunction in leaving when you want to. But try to slip out as quietly as you can and try not to precipitate a mass departure. This may be difficult, and partners should anticipate the situation, so that they can confirm with a look that one of them must begin to make the appropriate noises about breaking away.

The real problem occurs when you have guests whose body clocks are set differently to yours. Theatrical people, for example, often don't think about their hunger until about 10.30pm. They can be quite irritatingly alive at 1.30 in the morning. One hostess who often faces this problem (she is a television person, which is not quite the same thing as a theatrical) avers that, come her witching hour, her method is bravely to announce to any stragglers that, 'The bottle's in the fridge, but I've really got to leave you now.' I suspect this in itself is a sufficient hint, and that no one actually takes up the offer of the bottle in the fridge. Compare Katharine Whitehorn's tongue-in-cheek advice in *Whitehorn's Social Survival* (1968): 'Empty all the ashtrays in a pointed manner. Stay standing. One host I heard of appears to fall asleep; he then awakes with a jerk and says, "Darling, I think we should be going now".'

More pointed admonitions, such as the traditional, 'Must you stay, can't you go?' 'Come again when you can't stay so long' and 'Come, you have delighted us long enough', are unlikely to fall readily and comfortably from the lips of those in the real world outside quotation books.

Falling asleep is a common complaint at dinner parties. It is not just the effect of the food and wine, but may have to do with the associations of candlelight and, more likely, with the fact you are being kept up and on display beyond your normal bedtime. Fellow guests should be indulgent over this failing – though not to the point of putting up with snoring – as a short, actual nap can help clear the head and enable a sleepy guest to participate for a little longer. It is at the point when sleepers begin to snore or when they need to be moved, say, from table to chair, that they should be gently woken. A gentle squeeze on the arm, a softly-spoken word in the ear, ought to do the trick.

Apart from which, there are few things more amusing than a sleepy person in the middle of a social occasion. Better than a cabaret, say I.

The morning after

Thank-you letters are not strictly necessary for a dinner party, but are very much on the increase (See 'Thank-you notes' in Chapter 16 WRITTEN COMMUNICATION.) But do you thank for a birthday dinner, say, to which you have been invited and to which you bring a gift? If you have been invited to a birthday dinner, say, and have taken a gift for the birthday person, it would surely be overdoing it to send a thank-you letter to the organizer. The birthday person is the one who should do any thanking. But if it was a really splendid occasion, a guest might still feel moved to say thank-you by letter. But if not, not. On second thoughts, I would refine my credo, 'It is never possible to say thank-you too much.' It *is* possible to say thank-you unnecessarily.

Asking back. One of the more preposterous of human activities is the tit-for-tat pattern which dictates that if a person once invites you to something you are obliged to reciprocate. In fact, all you are obliged to do is to thank that person for whatever it was you were invited to. Nothing is emptier than inviting people back simply because they once invited you, or noticing when they haven't reciprocated and feeling resentful as a result. The fact is, other people don't always operate on this basis. Although it may feel natural to see social relationships in a ping-pong context – and it is obviously mutually satisfying if both sides do play the same game – it should never be assumed that this is the right thing to do.

Dances

As someone who is singularly inept at formal dancing, my only comment on this terrifying ordeal is that I am glad that I was born when I was. Somewhere in the early 1960s just when I was wrestling with the problem of my lack of interest in waltzes, foxtrots and the Gay Gordons, lo, they invented the Twist and, from then on, free-form, make-it-up-as-you-go-along dancing was introduced. Eventually, even formal dances came to be given over largely to this type of thing, and what a relief it was.

If you don't know how to dance properly, resist every blandishment to participate. Sit it out until the free-form starts. Or, if you get pushed into it, inextricably, just stand there, hope the dance floor is crowded, and don't step on your partner's toes.

The days when it was considered necessary to book your partners in advance, using the small card provided, are long gone, as has the view that to dance with one partner exclusively all night was 'simply not done'. There was a time when men were obliged to dance with the women who had sat on either side of him at dinner, and also with the daughter of the hostess, if not the hostess herself. The old idea was a good one in that favours were spread around and even the ugliest or most shrinking wallflower would probably get a go, but there we are, it has gone.

Chapter 5

$\mathcal{M}$ARRIAGE AND DIVORCE

Best Behaviour does not pretend to be a complete 'How to' guide for every conceivable occasion. This is a point worth re-emphasizing now that we have reached the point at which marriages are to be discussed. It is no purpose of this book to tell you how to organize a wedding (or a divorce, for that matter). There are plenty of publications describing in great detail how you can do this and there would be little point in reiterating their lists of things to be done and to be checked. Nor is it my purpose to provide a manual of marriage customs for Muslim, Hindu, Buddhist, Jewish and even Humanist brides and grooms. Such information, for those who need it, is easily obtainable when and where it needs to be obtained.

This chapter deals with the manners and etiquette of marriage and divorce – or, rather, those aspects of marriage and divorce over which there may hang a behavioural question mark, where there is scope for argument about what is the right thing to do, and for which advice may be sought.

Engagement

Nowadays, any formal proposal of marriage, with the man getting down on one knee, is likely to lead to the giggles, but many couples contrive to make it somehow memorable – even if, or especially when, they have been living together for some time anyway. (See also 'Leap Year proposals' in Chapter 12 SPECIAL OCCASIONS.)

Most potential bridegrooms also feel a certain obligation to mention the matter, in however light-hearted a fashion, to the bride's father. Even if asking his formal permission is a thing of the past, the bride's father may well be going to face considerable expenditure if there is to be a full dress wedding and it is a basic courtesy that he should be brought into the preparations at the earliest possible stage.

A friend of mine, in showbusiness, made a pleasant joke to his future father-in-law (who was very definitely not in showbusiness). He said, 'I know you think I come from a very unstable background and work in a very unstable world, so I was wondering if it would be all right for —— to be my *first* wife.' All too prophetic, as it turned out.

An engagement these days is an announcement of an intention to marry, usually when the actual marriage is some way off. It is in no sense a formal contract as in the days when subsequent breach of promise court actions provided journalists and novelists with some delicious situations to write about. Nowadays, particularly if the couple is to be married in a register office, there may be no formal engagement at all. The pair will simply let it be known that they going to be married and get on with it.

In this case an engagement ring will probably not be bought either. Where such a ring is bought, it is the man who pays for it.

Where a couple anticipates opposition to a marriage – on the grounds of race, religion, age difference, re-marriage, or plain 'unsuitability' – they would do well to consider how they can best win over the parents or relatives concerned. There are few things bleaker than those marriages that cause estrangement from families. If meetings are shunned, try winning over the doubters by letter, but still keep on suggesting that personal contact.

with the partner will remove all doubts. To enter into a marriage with links to one or both families severed may put intolerable pressure on one or both of the partners. Such a situation may enforce reliance on each other in the early stages of the marriage, but every effort, and repeated effort, should be made to build bridges until attempts at reconciliation are successful.

Announcement in the papers. 'Forthcoming Marriages' columns appear in national newspapers at the upper end of the market and in local and provincial papers. Whether you want to have an announcement of your engagement inserted (at some cost) is probably something you will only do if you have a large circle of acquaintance which will not hear the news anyway by word of mouth. A typical, formal announcement would be:

Mr A.B. Parker and Miss C.D. Player
The engagement is announced between Adrian Barrington Parker, son of Mr and Mrs N.C. Parker of Glebe House, Frostville, Hampshire, and Catherine Drysdale, younger daughter of Mr and Mrs J.U. Player of 25, College Avenue, London W14.

Less formal announcements would spare the couple the embarrassment of spelling out little-known first names and would not give full addresses of the parents. If the parents are divorced, then you might find, '. . . son of Mr N.C. Parker of Frostville, Hampshire, and Mrs R.E. Married of Vienna, Austria'. If one of the parents is dead, you might find, ' . . . son of Mr N.C. Parker and of the late Mrs Parker, of Frostville . . .' The putting in of full postal codes, however much it may please the Post Office, lowers the tone considerably.

Where both of the couple (or just one) have been

married before or are, perhaps, of riper years, they will probably announce their own wedding (probably not the engagement) and issue their own invitations.

Congratulations on engagements. Particularly where there has been a public announcement, it is customary for friends and relations to write to the one of the couple they know (not both jointly) and express their pleasure at the news, possibly also writing to the parents. This procedure should not have the air of angling for an invitation to the wedding, though it might help ensure that one is issued.

The bridegroom's parents will write to the bride's parents and possibly arrange a celebratory meal or, at least, a meeting, though the happy couple may well arrange this. The bridegroom's parents should already have written a letter to the bride if, by any chance, they have not yet met her. Even if they have, it is a pleasant, welcoming gesture.

Some people believe that you should not congratulate a woman on her getting engaged. To do so, it is held, is to suggest that she has, in some way, contrived to entrap him – which, of course, is quite likely the case. Why this does not apply to congratulating the male, is anyone's guess. The form is not to say 'Congratulations!' to the girl but to say 'How pleased I was to hear your news', or some such form of words.

Planning

Marriages may well be made in heaven but weddings have to be organized here on earth. Indeed, I heard one minister officiating at a wedding describe marriage as 'a paradise below', but this certainly did not extend to the planning that preceded it.

A wedding is quite likely to be the most complicated event that most people will have to organize in their

entire lives. If the significance of the occasion looms large
for them, then it is no wonder that it can all be rather a
strain. The scope for things going wrong is enormous,
there being so many fiddly little details to see to.
Someone may drop the cake, the presents may get stolen,
the best man may forget the ring, an elderly relative may
collapse, and the champagne may go flat. But, having
said that, it is almost invariably the case that, in the end,
none of this matters. People usually have a wonderful
time, they get to meet people they have never met before
or haven't seen for years, little slips are humorously
passed over, and has there ever been a wedding where
the bride didn't looked her radiant best and the bridegroom touched everybody, even despite a totally inad-
equate speech? There *is* a magic about weddings. They
are very special occasions, rich in comic human detail.
They will supply family jokes and folklore for years to
come. Indeed, the only trouble with them is that what
follows may come as the most terrible anticlimax.

Paying for the reception. Traditionally the bride's parents carry the burden of this expense, but as marriages
and re-marriages and step-relationships proliferate, it is
becoming commonplace for the other parents to contribute – say, by paying for the food or the drink, or for
some other specific element. Maturer couples will probably want to pay for their own celebrations and not
place any burden on their parents at all.

The bridegroom will pay the church or register office
costs, and for the official documentation, for any bou-
quets and buttonholes and, of course, for the honeymoon. If the bride is a working woman, however, she
may now contribute her mite. Bridesmaids traditionally
paid for their own dresses but this is less likely to be
expected of them today. This expense would now
probably be taken up by the bride's parents. The
bridegroom may well also pay all the transport costs
and for photographs. Everything is open to negotation

nowadays and provides plenty of scope for graceful generosity on all sides.

The best man. It is somehow more pleasing if the best man is a bachelor friend of the groom's, but there is nothing in principle to prevent him from being a married man himself or indeed a divorced man. It has been known for the 'best man' or 'best person' to be a woman, or for the best man to be a closer friend of the bride's – even an ex-lover – than of the groom's. But this may be playing with fire. If the marriage should subsequently flounder, the best man will probably joke ruefully that he didn't make a very good job of it.

The best man has a number of tasks (not least making a speech, see below) but his chief job is to look after the groom on his big day, calm him down (when necessary) and make sure he gets to the ceremony in plenty of time, as well as away from the reception. He is given a sum of money by the groom to cover on-the-spot expenses, tips, etc. and also has to produce the ring at the appropriate moment. Traditionally, he makes a mess of this, not being able to find it, or dropping it down a grating in the church floor, as the case may be.

A register office wedding in itself has no role for a best man – it merely calls for two witnesses – but a male witness may assume the role of the best man at any subsequent reception.

The chief bridesmaid. She is the 'best woman', if you like, and is probably an old friend of the bride's. She keeps the bride's spirits up, assists with the wedding dress, organizes the other bridesmaids, and may help the bride get ready to depart from the reception. If she is married – and there is no reason why she should not be – she is un-maided and called 'Matron of Honour'.

Is there a polite way of declining to be a bridesmaid (without offending, say, your future sister-in-law)? Not really. As with declining to be a godparent (q.v.), the waves made by a rejection are out of all proportion to the small responsibilities and inconvenience involved. Any such hostile gesture would never be forgotten.

A church wedding? Where one or both of the to-be-wed has been married before, and unless the divorced partner is dead, most churches will not allow them to have a full marriage service. In this case, a register office ceremony, attended only by the immediate relatives, best man, etc., can be followed by a Service of Blessing or a Service of Prayer and Dedication in church. Nowadays, these services can seem remarkably like the real thing – the marriage vows are made but the actual marriage does not take place.

Is a white wedding in church appropriate when the bride is obviously pregnant? There will probably rather less tut-tutting these days than would probably once have been the case. It is vital that the clergyman should be informed of the circumstances at an early stage so that he at least knows what he is being involved in and is in a position to react according to his views on the matter.

Choosing the type of service. At an early stage you should not only fix the date of the ceremony with the clergyman but also consult with him as to what the options are. If the bride does not wish to vow to 'obey' her husband, in addition to loving and honouring him, this is nowadays quite easily arranged, and is allowed for in the various revised forms of marriage service. The clergyman will also state what the fees are, especially for such extra items as organ, choir, flowers and bell-ringing. A short rehearsal in church a day or two before the wedding is also helpful.

The clergyman will almost certainly wish to meet the bride and groom before the wedding for a talk. He will give advice on the significance of a church wedding, on sex (if you're not careful), and on the meaning of life – ever poised, as Archbishop Runcie said before the 1981 Royal Wedding, between the cliché and the indiscretion.

But he will also be helpful on practical matters. If you request outlandish music for the service – 'Climb Every Mountain', for example – he may well get stroppy.

Should you wish to have a clergyman who is an old friend to conduct the ceremony in another clergyman's church, they will sort out the arrangements themselves.

The invitations. These are sent out by the bride and her mother in consultation with the bridegroom and his mother – who will have to supply names and addresses. For a big wedding the invitations should be sent out a good two months in advance as guests may well have to make travel and hotel arrangements.

It helps if you don't make mistakes on the printed invitations and, when writing in the names of the guests by hand, if you forbear to use biro or felt-tip, it will gladden the hearts of some people.

A typical invitation would read:

Mr and Mrs Average Guest

Mr and Mrs Proud Parent
request the pleasure of your company
at the marriage of their daughter
Sharon Tina
to
Mr Peter Upwardly-Mobile
at St Ethelburga's, Pinner
on Saturday, 5th May
at 3 o'clock
and afterwards at
The Marmounia Rooms, Cockfosters

42, Prospect Way
Pinner
London
PI2 3XX   RSVP

If the bride's parents are divorced, it is quite likely that 'Mr Proud Parent and Mrs Estranged Mother' would request the pleasure instead. Or, if both parents are dead, somebody else might be doing the inviting, or, if people are only being invited to the reception, the invitation would read, ' . . . at a reception after the marriage of their daughter . . .' Another form is '. . . request the pleasure of your company at a Service of Blessing following their marriage, and afterwards at . . .'

Who to invite to the wedding? Don't forget 'artificial' uncles and aunts − your parents' friends who have acquired this status and who may well mean more to you than actual uncles and aunts. An actual written invitation should also be sent to the bridegroom's parents, even though they know all about the occasion anyway.

What not to wear at weddings. Women should not wear dark clothes. If verging on the black, they may be mistaken for funeral garb and give people the wrong idea of your intentions towards the happy couple. Green is also frowned on by some people, for some reason.

What should women do if they find they are wearing the same dress as, say, the bride's mother? Laugh it off, dear, laugh it off. There is nothing that can be done, except to make a thing of it and congratulate each other on their excellent taste.

If formal morning dress is worn by guests, in addition to the bridegroom and best man doing so, I think it is a very good thing if top hats are left at home (or wherever they were hired from). They should certainly not be worn for the photographer, except by budding Fred Astaires and show-offs.

Spouse and children from an earlier marriage. To have the debris of a previous liaison present at the sealing of a new one can, however unlikely it may seem, aid the process of coming to terms with what has happened. In fact, it is a very good sign if the parties involved can agree to this sort of forgive and forget move. Former spouses should endeavour, however, not to take anything approaching a prominent role in the re-marriage celebrations. It has been known and it has not been well received.

The present list. Yes, it is unromantic, positively industrial, to have a list of presents that you would like to receive, but it is a quite normal way of doing things and may help to avoid excessive duplication of presents. Few marriages would be any the better for starting off with five identical toasters. The form is for guests, when they have received their invitations, to ask which store has your list and then for them to consult it in person or by phone. The list should have items at a wide range of prices, so no one will feel pressured into paying more than they want. Guests can also more easily share the cost of items this way. It makes very good sense that people should know exactly what you need and your specific tastes in terms of colour, manufacturer, line, and so on.

'As soon as our engagement appeared in *The Times*, wedding presents poured in . . . the majority were frightful, and they came in cohorts – fifteen lamps of the same design, forty trays, a hundred and more huge glass vases. They were assembled at Grosvenor Place . . . When the presents were all arranged, Lady Evelyn looked at them all reflectively.

'"The glass will be the easiest," she said. "It only needs a good kick." She said silver was more of a problem. "Walter and I had such luck, *all* ours was stolen while we were on honeymoon".'

Diana Mosley, *A Life of Contrasts* **(1977)**

If you do not wish to have a list, you should at least have some suggestions to give people when they ask you about presents. Couples who have been married before or who have already set up substantial establishments together or individually may well try to discourage present-giving altogether, though an insistence on 'nothing practical, please' may result in some rather interesting, if token, gifts. Gifts of money should not be solicited, but may prove the most welcome gift of all. It is, however, agreeable if the money can be said to be being put towards a specific use – and this can be mentioned in the thank-you letter.

On the other hand, people who give specific gifts as wedding presents do buy a kind of immortality. The chances are that, if the marriage survives, in years to come it will never be forgotten that, 'That was the clock Aunty Dot gave us as a wedding present', or, 'Oh, look, here are the fish-knives from Mrs Snodgrass that we've never used . . .'

How much should guests spend on wedding presents? It all depends, but it should certainly not be less than the estimated cost per head being paid by the father of the bride per head to entertain people at the reception.

A present should be given if an invitation has been received. If invitees are unable to accept, then they are not bound to give a present though some sort of gesture is appropriate – an invitation to the couple to come and have dinner at a later date, perhaps.

Present giving may also take place between bride and groom, though they may well feel this is taking things too far. The groom may also wish to thank the best man and bridesmaids for their part in the ceremony. In my time, I have received a silver port label and simply one of the wedding photographs for my performing this role. Both were good to have, but a personal note from the groom (and even a separate one from the bride) would have been quite sufficient as far as I was concerned. The bridesmaids may be given a small piece of jewellery and may be allowed to keep their costumes (if these are in

the gift of the groom). I think that the mothers of the
bride and of the groom also tend to be given presents.
Did I hear that a cactus plant was thought appropriate
in one case?

Thank-you letters. It is only sensible to make sure that
you know very clearly what present has come from
whom. Keep labels attached. Write down the details.
Then when it is time to write thank-you letters, you
can make them appropriate. To avoid the situation
where you would have to spend the early, post-
honeymoon, weeks of your marriage writing thank-you
letters, it is quite in order for you to start on this task
before the wedding day. In other words, you can thank
people for the presents before you are married. It
makes sense for the couple to share the thank-you
letters, according to who knows the sender best. This
might be a very good moment to tell people what style
the bride will wish to adopt following the marriage –
'Mrs Andrew Newly-Wed', 'Jennifer Single', 'Jennifer
Single Newly-Wed', or whatever. That could save a lot
of bother late on.

In the event of the wedding being called off, the
presents will have to be returned (see 'When it's all off'
below).

The wedding ring. This is chosen by the couple jointly,
the bridegroom pays for it and the bride wears it. If the
groom wishes to wear a wedding ring, it is given to him
by the bride and the blessing of the rings becomes part
of the marriage ceremony. This is common practice on
the Continent, especially in Roman Catholic marriage
services; in Britain, much less so. The officiating clergyman may have to adapt the standard wedding ceremony
in order to accommodate it.

Hen parties/stag parties. These are best not held the night
before the wedding. As much as a week before is not

unusual – anything rather than have a hungover groom (or even bride) feeling less than good on the big day.

The wedding ceremony

As for seating in church or in a register office, ushers (formal or informal) traditionally seat relatives and guests according to whether they know the bride or the groom. In a church, the bride's side is on the left facing the altar, the groom's on the right. If strictly adhered to, however, this can mean that one side would quite likely be fuller than the other, so it is a good idea if guests other than the immediate families simply go where there is more room. In a register office, it is more of a free for all, though the immediate family should be allowed to sit in the front rows.

Children at weddings. Children should only be taken if specifically invited – but usually they are welcome. A sprinkling of noisy brats is a harbinger of things to come. Babes in arms would be rather too much of a harbinger and should probably be left at home.

Bringing presents to the ceremony. It is understandable that some people should wish to bring their presents with them rather than send them in advance, which might require laborious wrapping up and expense. But it would obviously be pretty poor show to bring them into the church, and even taking them to the reception only means that someone other than the happy pair will have to deal with them. Much better if they can be delivered to a mutually agreed place beforehand – usually to the bride's home, or to the groom's, if the bride is not known to the guests.

The bride's privilege to be late. Not in our church, it ain't. In the film *Sailor Beware*, because of the bride's lateness, the church organist has to keep on playing 'Jesu Joy of Man's Desiring' or 'Sheep May Safely Graze' *ad nauseam*. This is no fun for anybody. The bride should not be late, unless she wishes to get her marriage off to a very bad start indeed.

Photographs/videos. It is all too easy for the photographic element in weddings to become the be-all and end-all of the occasion. This should be resisted, however much your desire is to have the best possible record of the event. Think very hard about whether you want to have a photographer clambering over you, especially during a church marriage service. Do you really *need* to have pictures of yourself taking your vows?

(See also 'The intrusiveness of photography and video' in Chapter 7 PUBLIC BEHAVIOUR.)

Cause or just impediment. In the Anglican marriage service – as in the ritual reading of the banns of marriage during Sunday services in the period preceding the wedding day - there is an opportunity for anyone present who knows 'cause or just impediment' why the marriage should not take place 'to declare it'. A slight frisson goes through the congregation on the speaking of these words, lest anyone should suddenly stand up and say, 'Yes, I have.' This is no more than ritual. If anyone knows just cause (perhaps knowing that one of the bridal pair is about to commit bigamy), they can take the appropriate steps before the wedding day, and discreetly.

It is not done for whoever is giving away the bride to say 'I do' when the the clergyman asks, 'Who giveth this Woman to be married to this Man?' The person should merely step silently forward and pass over her hand. There is no reason why a woman should not give the bride away – the original Anglican service speaks of the bride's 'father' or 'friend'. Possibly, however, the clergyman may have a strong view on the matter.

Worries about forgetting words. Some clergymen make the repetition of the marriage vows especially difficult by not presenting them to you in bite-sized phrases for you to repeat. It has been known for people to make a hash of this. The Prince and Princess of Wales both made a slight hash of it at their wedding in 1981. It is not the end of the world if you do, though it might be a better world if clergymen offered you shorter, easier-to-remember phrases to repeat.

Difficult guests. Weddings have a way of healing old wounds rather than reopening them. It has been known for old family squabbles to be patched up 'for the sake of the children'. But, having said that, I seem to have been to a fair number of weddings where already-married couples have not been on speaking terms and where a parent who has remarried has had to come face to face with the spouse that was ditched. When two such people are still not talking, a quaint little ceremony like witnessing the signing of the register can become richly comic, with each side studiously avoiding the other. They can only be left to get on with it and it would be unwise to try to build bridges.

The reception

After the marriage ceremony, and after photographs have been taken from every angle outside the church door or porch, the bride and groom will be the first to leave for the reception. This means that they will be first to arrive and are able to stand inside the door and receive their guests, usually accompanied by both sets of parents. Brides have been known to get quite worn out as every guest exercises the right to kiss her. Her cheeks may get reddened by too much male stubble brushing by. At this point, both bride and groom should work quite hard introducing people to their parents and explaining to each other who long unseen relatives are.

Sending telegrams. If you have been invited to a wedding but are unable to attend, you are not under any obligation to send a present. However, some sort of gesture is appropriate and to send a telegram is the most obvious. Even though telegrams have lost most of their distinctiveness now that they are 'telemessages', they are usually well received. It is good if they can be worded to suit the couple but it is best to eschew in-jokes that are unfathomable to anyone else. Rather watery formulae that tend to get trotted out include the rhyme: 'With —— as the Captain/And —— as the Mate/ We'll be looking for the crew/At a later date.' My favourite telegram contained the Biblical quotation, 'Go not empty to thy mother-in-law' (*Ruth 3:17*), which could have meant anything or nothing.

The speech proposing the bride and groom's health. This task may be undertaken by the bride's father, though it may best be consigned to an uncle or senior friend of the bride's family. All he has to do is to propose a toast to the bride and groom, but usually he will make some humorous but positive comments on the bride's early years (if he can remember them). It is all too easy to be patronizing towards the groom ('don't really know 'im, but seems a nice enough chap'), and this sort of thing is best avoided.

The bridegroom's speech. All the groom has to do is to respond to the foregoing toast on his own and his new wife's behalf, and then to propose a toast to the bridesmaids, if there are any. He traditionally thanks his wife's parents for bringing her into the world and, where appropriate, for laying on the reception. Should any of his or his new wife's parents be dead, this is certainly the moment to remember them and to say how much they are missed on this day of all days.

The groom should also thank the guests for their presence and their presents. A special word of thanks should be given to any individual who has provided or arranged the flowers. He should not say any more than this, and should certainly not give a clearly premeditated speech. The more self-effacing and shy he is, the better. 'It is the bride's day really,' people will say inaccurately, but at this point, let it so be. I once heard a bridegroom declare in his speech just how much he loved his wife and, regrettable though it may be, it did sound a little arch of him to say it at that stage.

On no account should notes be used for this speech. If he forgets anything, his wife can usefully prompt him, thus demonstrating from the word go how useful a partner she is going to be.

The best man's speech. Traditionally, the best man responds on behalf of the bridesmaids. He may bulk out the beginning of his speech by reading out a selection of the better telegrams received, if he has not already done this earlier in the proceedings. As most of them will be repetitive, and signed by relatives and friends not known to most people present, it is quite in order for him to edit these very heavily. Just a few funny ones (if necessary made up) and perhaps those from abroad will be quite sufficient.

He should then attempt to be charming and to make everyone think what a much better catch he would have made for the bride than the groom. If he is still a bachelor himself, this is obviously an excellent occasion on which to showcase his charms. Weddings do tend to lead to weddings (rather on a par with 'One funeral makes many . . . '). The likelihood is, however, that the best man will attempt to embarrass the bridegroom (and everyone else) with some far-fetched stories of the bridegroom's pre-marital days. A little light innuendo does not go amiss, but telling jokes, smutty or otherwise, just for the sake of it, can be embarrassing for everyone.

As with speeches by Royalty, the warmth of reaction to speeches made by anyone at a wedding is out of all proportion to their intrinsic wit or worth.

Cutting the wedding cake. This is the last event in the proceedings and does not have to be fitted in with whatever other food is being served, though there is often pressure to bring it forward so that the caterers can get to work on cutting it up and putting it on plates. Nor does it have to be connected with any speeches. In fact, it is chiefly what is now termed a 'photo opportunity' – it is a symbolic cutting. With this out of the way, the cake can be taken away and readied for serving at the appropriate moment later on.

Small portions of cake at one time used to be posted off in special silver boxes to those who had been unable to attend the wedding – and some was even retained by the bride as a keepsake, perhaps to be consumed on the first wedding anniversary or even at much later ones or at christenings.

Going away. The bride and groom change into their 'going away clothes' and everybody assembles to wave them off. Their 'departure' is largely symbolic: it is quite possible that they will still be around to look in at any post-wedding party later in the day. This is not sacrilegious. Pretending to 'go away' is not the only acting the couple have to do on their wedding day. 'Going away' also gives guests the opportunity to leave without appearing to be rude.

Throwing confetti is now illegal where it is done in a public place as it contravenes the litter laws. Consequently, some churches and reception places make a fuss about this. Biodegradable confetti is, however, available and disappears after a good shower of rain, if it is not nibbled away by birds first.

Displaying the presents. This is only practicable if the reception is being held in a private house and, besides, is a rather odd convention, chiefly pandering to the nosey. Presents should be displayed with their gift tags. A sheet listing the names of those who have given cheques should be given some prominence, though it should not, of course, state what the amounts are.

Practical jokes. I know from a film of my own parents' wedding that they departed for their honeymoon with the inevitable tin cans tied to the back of the car – where there was also a large card stating 'AISLE ALTAR HYMN'. The jokers who enjoy this sort of thing have grown more adventurous over the intervening years. Honeymoon-bound couples are now quite likely to find their get-away cars covered in crazy foam and thus they are instantly recognizable as newly-weds to everyone on the roads and at their first-night destination.

The answer is to arrange for a going-away car – perhaps a chauffeur-driven one – to which this sort of japery may be applied. This car will then take you to your own vehicle which has been hidden away and which contains your honeymoon luggage. This also lessens the chance of people filling your cases with confetti, so that the slow dribble of confetti from your clothing keeps on reminding everyone at your honeymoon destination why you are there. I have also heard of one couple who had several clocks placed in their luggage with alarms primed to go off every half-hour during their wedding night.

Newspaper announcements. These may be arranged in advance so that they appear at the first opportunity after the wedding and while the happy pair are tucked up on their honeymoon. A typical announcement in the Marriages column would read:

CHRISTIE:DRAGON – 24th April, 199–, at
St Mildred's Church, Hampstead, RICHARD
DAVID CHRISTIE, eldest son of Mr and Mrs
T.N. CHRISTIE of Welwyn Garden City, to
SUSAN BERNADETTE, younger daughter of
Mr and Mrs P.T.M. DRAGON of Church
Row, Hampstead, London NW3.

If the marriage took place in a register office, the vague
phrases 'took place in (London)' or 'quietly in (London)'
may be inserted instead. The full address of the bride's
parents may be given to facilitate contact.

The honeymoon

The honeymoon destination is traditionally kept a secret,
for no very good reason except that it may lessen the
chance of colleagues from work wishing to try to contact
either of the couple about some crisis. It may also put
off any practical jokers from the family who may wish to
make merry. It is part of my family's lore that my
grandmother had to be dissuaded from ringing up her
son, my uncle, on his honeymoon, 'just to see that he
was getting on all right'.

When it's all off

If a newspaper announcement of the impending marriage
was inserted at the time of the engagement, then a brief
cancellation notice should be inserted when matters
come unstuck:

The marriage arranged [or 'previously announced'] between
Mr U.R. Difficult and Miss I.M. Also will not [now] take
place.

The newspaper will probably require signatures of both parties.

Any engagement ring should be returned to the ex-fiancé and any presents already bestowed by friends and relations should be returned to them, accompanied by a note of thanks and regret from one of the sad pair. If invitations to the wedding have been sent out by this stage, guests will have to be written to and informed, preferably in individual notes and probably from the bride's mother or whoever was in charge of the original invitation list.

Wedding presents do not have to be returned to sender in the case of a divorce, though probably any family heirloom that was bestowed on the pair should be retained by the one from the family in question.

Divorce

As far as I know, putting an announcement of impending divorce in a newspaper is not something that has caught on. Usually one partner – the one who feels less guilty? – will phone round friends saying, 'I think you ought to know that – — and I have split'. The word will no doubt get passed on from there.

Dealing with other people's divorces. The chances are, though not necessarily, that if you are friends with a married couple you will have come to know them through either the man or the woman, rarely both. So when divorce looms, it will be difficult not to take the part of the person you originally knew. This is understandable and it can prove impossible to resist siding with that partner. On the other hand, you may have come to know the other partner very well while the marriage lasted or may be justifiably aghast at the way your old friend has behaved.

To avoid taking sides during divorce proceedings may

be difficult, but taking sides can only serve to make a horrendous situation worse. If you can't avoid doing so, at least try not to stir things up. A discreetly low-key approach will probably ensure that when the dust has settled you will still be friends with the party you really prefer anyway.

Transitional affairs. It is not a good idea to assume that, after a period of (possibly) enforced good behaviour while the divorce dragged its slow length along, either partner is just dying for it and needs to be kitted out with a new sleeping partner. Worst of all is if you kit them out with another divorced person of your acquaintance. Curiously enough, it is possible for people to survive without a lover and to attempt to supply presumed needs just after the emotional drubbing most people suffer in a divorce, is not only meddling but unfeeling.

Propositioning divorcees. To add to the burden of a divorce – and, in some cases, to widowhood – must be added the assumption on many men's part that a woman in such a position is bound to want their attentions. Quite the opposite is likely to be the truth and the idea is especially unwelcome if accompanied by the spoken (or unspoken) belief that the woman must be 'desperate for it' under these circumstances.

Chapter 6

$\mathscr{N}$EIGHBOURLINESS

There is more to being neighbourly than just living next door to someone. Neighbourliness is the behaviour that might be expected wherever one human being is next to or near to another and thus embraces such matters as noise and smoking as well as the charitableness of the good neighbour.

Uninvited callers

It was once commonplace for house doors and gates to have on them a small notice saying 'NO HAWKERS OR CIRCULARS'. For some reason this practice appears to have fallen into disuse – perhaps because few of the people the notices were designed to deter could read or because they failed to recognize themselves in the guise of 'hawkers' (itinerant salesmen) or 'circulars' (printed advertisements).

The menace has not diminished, however; it has rather been augmented by the arrival of inanimate, though no more welcome, masses of junk mail. So what can be done to discourage market researchers, Jehovah's Witnesses and other religionists, insurance and other salesmen, from knocking at your door, uninvited?

Putting up a notice is still likely to have little effect, for the reasons given above. You can try simply not answering the door, if you have means of identifying the caller. Otherwise, all you can really do is to answer the door and attempt to deal as briskly and finally with whoever is there before the salesman gets his foot in the door or the religionist gets too far into a set *spiel* along the lines of, 'We was wantin' to share our thoughts on God with you . . .'

It has been suggested that a rapidly delivered statement that you are a God-fearing, churchgoing person will soon see the latter off. This does not seem to be borne out in practice, though. Not all of us are fitted to do what a certain white-bearded old gent is reported to have said to two startled Jehovah's Witnesses – 'Good, I'm Jehovah – how are we doing?'

For those with a little time and mischief on their hands, there is something to be said for inviting such visitors in. They rapidly run out of things to say when the expected opposition to their sales pitch is removed. There is nothing quite like the disappointment on an insurance salesman's face when, having guided you through his sales procedure and handed you the pen and the bottom line of an agreement, he hears you decline to sign. But this method is only recommended to those whose sales resistance is impregnable.

The best approach is never to buy anything or agree to anything that is brought to you by an uninvited caller. As with beggars and tramps of old, word soon gets round if a householder is a soft touch. The same probably applies to charity collectors (but see below) and certainly to representatives of political parties. You are in no way obliged to admit your political allegiance to anyone who comes knocking on your door. That is why we have secret ballots in elections. Being listed as a 'don't know' is discreet, even if it doesn't sound very distinguished.

If you have time on your hands, answering questions put by market researchers and opinion pollsters can make you feel wanted – though my experience is that these activities take up more time than you usually want to give them and the questions are often phrased in ways that are unrewarding to answer.

Needless to say, inviting people over the threshold of your home should only be done if they carry convincing documentation and if you feel you are in a strong enough position to deal with them if they turn out to be other than what they say.

Unannounced callers

Neighbours and friends dropping in on you unannounced can be both a pleasure and a burden. I suppose it must seem appalling if I say that, living as I do in central London, even my next-door neighbours almost always phone up first before calling round. I expect this rather formal behaviour decreases proportionately to the distance one travels from Marble Arch, but I wouldn't change it for anything less formal, not even if I was living in a croft in the Orkneys.

Borrowing and lending

There are fewer greater strains on neighbourliness than requests to borrow – even if the traditional request of a 'cup of sugar' can hardly be described as borrowing. It is hard to say no. 'Neither a borrower nor a lender be' is not a maxim that is easy to follow in real life. So, if you are landed with a borrowsome neighbour, about all you can do is, firstly, make sure you do some reciprocal borrowing (even if you don't really need to) just to keep your end in and, secondly, tell the occasional little white lie: 'No, I've just lent it to somebody else', or whatever. Gradually, the borrowsome one may get the message, though some people are such compulsive borrowers that they will not change their spots. And they're probably borrowed spots anyway.

Should you be a borrower yourself, repay in kind as soon as you are able. Borrowed money should be repaid in absolutely no time at all. If declining to lend money, it is a pleasant little joke to say that you don't ever carry money with you – 'like the Queen'. This can be a useful and tactful way out of some borrowing embarrassments.

Handing over cash may be a trifle embarrassing, even when it is warranted. There is much to be said for putting money in an envelope before handing it over. It is more discreet and good security.

'Lady Dorothy Nevill, so Sir Edmund Gosse tells, preserved her library by pasting in each volume the legend: "This book has been stolen from Lady Dorothy Nevill".'

quoted in *The Week-End Book* (1955)

Charity and charities

There are two things to be said about charities. The first is that they appear to be a necessary way for society to give help to the needy and suffering. How much better they probably are at doing this job than any conceivable state-run schemes. The second thing to be said is that people do not often give to charities unless they are asked. It is at this point that fund-raisers and charity workers can become a pain. It is obviously a nice point – the one at which gentle persistence in the pursuit of donations turns into behaviour that is a nuisance and an imposition.

I prefer to choose which charities I am going to support and to keep that choice to myself, just as much as I keep my vote to myself in the secret ballot. The trouble with some charity workers is that, one suspects, their activities have become an end in themselves. The act of rattling the tin gives them some sort of buzz, even if the net result is not of much use to the charity. At a more elevated level, this is where one begins to wonder about uncomfortable questions – like how much of the benefit, both moral and financial, is going to the charity and how much to the fund-raiser?

'Charity vaunteth not itself, is not puffed up.'
1 Corinthians 13:4

'Above all things have fervent charity among yourselves: for charity shall cover the multitude of sins.'
1 Peter 4:8

Charity workers have a tendency to *expect* cooperation – in particular from celebrities (who, in show business, at least, are often extremely generous with their time and efforts). I have heard of quite extraordinarily insidious remarks being made about celebrities who have declined – often with good reason – to go along with some fund-raising scheme.

There is an old saying (dating back beyond the 17th century) that 'charity is cold' – referring to the unfeeling nature of much charitable giving. I do not think charities these days can be said to be cold, but they can be unnecessarily calculating. Arm-twisting cannot be justified, even if it is for a charitable end.

Begging

The well-mannered person is never to be found begging, except for asking other people's forgiveness or pardon (though before using the words 'pardon' or 'beg pardon', have a look at 'U and Non-U language' in Chapter 11 SPEAKING). But, leaving aside the higher forms of surrogate begging (see the foregoing 'Charity and charities'), the well-mannered person is quite likely, in this day and age, to be accosted by street beggars of one sort or another.

The cities of Britain since the late 1980s have witnessed a rise in the number of beggars or, at least, in their public visibility. There are the buskers in the London Underground, who at least aspire to give something in return for alms; then there are the pathetic wrecks who stretch out their palms – usually from within cardboard fortresses in which they appear to sleep and on which are written slogans about their plight – often phrasing a request in terms of, 'Have you any change, mister?'; and then there are the walking beggars who accost you, often with some attempt at apology in advance for having the temerity to trouble you. I do not know whether to include a fourth category – what appear to be mothers, accompanied by muddy-faced children, pulling out all the organ-stops to loosen your purse strings.

This last is the deeply suspect face of beggardom, indeed just the sort of thing to give beggaring a bad name. One can't help but feel being got at by such people. Even if newspaper articles had not aroused one's suspicions, it might occur to one that mud had been applied to the children's faces in order to enhance the appeal. Any hint of calculation or organization in soliciting is liable to have the opposite effect to that sought. Lurid tabloid tales of beggars who make a substantial living and then spend the night in the lap of relative luxury, or even drive off in cars, should be discounted, or at least only held to be true of a tiny number.

Now, it must be said at once that there is no certain way you should respond to a request for money in circumstances like these. Your response will depend on any number of factors and, whatever form it takes, will not be easy or make you feel any better about life once you have done it.

The simplest response is to make none. You can comfort yourself with the thought that the welfare state should mean that there is no call for anyone to seek money in this way. There are hostels for vagrants. No one should need to beg.

In which case, however, why is it that begging has without question increased in recent years, if not to a medieval pitch, then at least almost to sub-Continental levels? Here, your answer may be political. In Britain, more people are unemployed than ever before. A tough government cut away many of the benefits of a caring welfare state. The contrast between the haves and have-nots widened visibly. In which case, you may feel that the unfortunates who resort to begging need some sort of supplement, to compensate for whatever a particular government has failed to do for them.

So you give. There is the view which I have heard voiced by a clergyman – and clergymen, of course, are particularly prone to being asked for alms – that it is better to risk being conned by ninety-nine than to deny help to one genuinely needy person. By giving, however, you may wonder whether you are providing any useful kind of relief. If you give a pound or a fiver, you may just be contributing to the beggar's alcohol fund. By proffering any amount of money, you may be lessening the likelihood that he or she will ever pull out of the mud, get a proper job, smarten up, and do all the sort of things the haves always think the have-nots ought to do.

It is an impossible conundrum and, clearly, not one you are liable to solve at the very moment when confronted with the human manifestation of it. You should make a small donation – and feel a fool for the rest of the day for having fallen for it. Or you should say 'not today, thank you', or make no response at all, and walk on – and feel bad for all of the next three minutes.

There really is no correct way of behaving towards beggars, and well-mannered persons allow themselves to feel uneasy about the whole problem. It will be interesting to see if the system experimented with in Berkeley, California, makes any difference. There, people may buy coupons to hand to beggars, and these coupons are then redeemable against food, services and non-alcoholic items from cooperating stores and organizations. The system has the merit of sorting out the inveterate winos from the genuinely needy, and of focusing charitable giving. It deserves to be more widely experimented with.

'A true Englishman is a kind man at heart, but has an unconquerable dislike to poverty and beggary. Beggars have heretofore been so strange to an American that he is apt to become their prey, being recognized through his national peculiarities, and beset by them in the streets. The English smile at him, and say that there are ample public arrangements for every pauper's possible need, that street-charity promotes idleness and vice, and that yonder personification of misery on the pavement will lay up a good day's profit, besides supping more luxuriously than the dupe who gives him a shilling. By-and-by the stranger adopts their theory and begins to practise upon it, much to his own temporary freedom from annoyance, but not entirely without moral detriment or sometimes a too late contrition. Years afterwards, it may be, his memory is still haunted by some vindictive wretch whose cheeks were pale and hunger-pinched, whose rags fluttered in the east-wind, whose right arm was paralyzed and his left leg shrivelled into a mere nerveless stick, but whom he passed by remorselessly because an Englishman chose to say that the fellow's misery looked too perfect, was too artistically got up, to be genuine. Even allowing this to be true, (as, a hundred chances to one, it was) it would still have been a clear case of economy to buy him off with a little loose silver, so that his lamentable figure should not limp at the heels of your conscience all over the world.'

Nathaniel Hawthorne, *Our Old Home* **(1863)**

Smoking in company

The world is seldom more sharply divided than into the ranks of those who smoke and those who don't. People do, of course, pass between the two ranks, but if they have given up smoking after long indulgence (and with difficulty) then they acquire, more often than not, all the passionate conviction of the religious convert. Over the past thirty years, the accumulation of government health warnings on the one side and pro-tobacco lobbyings on the other, means that more than any other subject outside the Middle East conflict, smoking raises passions and provokes irrational responses.

I have never been a cigarette card-carrying person myself. True, in my student days, I can remember returning from abroad with two hundred duty-frees and smoking them almost without a break. But I was so *mean*, I never felt an overwhelming urge to go out and buy a fresh packet. Having consciously or unconsciously avoided women who smoked, I then – of course – had to marry a forty-a-day-er. She, subsequently, in heroic fashion, gave it all up, seemingly just by handing whatever she had left in a packet, and her lighter, for me to dispose of.

I occasionally have a cigar after dinner, so I am probably as guilty as more full-time smokers on occasions – guilty of being unfeeling towards others. The simple fact is that it is well-nigh impossible to smoke without in some way offending other people. Even if you smoke in a hotel room all on your own, you will be leaving traces of air-pollution likely to cling to the furniture until the next guest checks in.

So, having a foot in both camps, I can see perfectly well that it is next to useless trying to impress on smokers that they should be reasonable to non-smokers. Too much depends upon the activity. It is a pleasure (and most pleasure is selfish); it is a symbol of all sorts of things (not least of defiance, nowadays); it is a right to be fought over. And it is simply not compatible, as I've just indicated, with being thoughtful to other people.

So what should non-smokers do in the light of the provocation? Although they are in a majority in Britain, they may notice a curious fact: that when they go out for a meal in a restaurant, they are often outnumbered by smokers. It is as though smokers congregate in restaurants with the particular aim of harassing the opposition.

There is nothing more dispiriting than to see new-arrivals sitting down and parking on the table their car-keys, filofaxes, cigarette packs and lighters. You know what you are in for. Then they light up – just as you are about to start eating, and a wisp of smoke drifts up your nostrils and into your mouth, just to off-set the subtle flavours of food and wine. Probably the smoker will then rest one elbow on the table, and hold the cigarette aloft while the air-conditioning draws it over your food.

What is to be done? Well, the first thing the non-smoker has to do is to attempt a reasonable response. If non-smokers are in a restaurant which does not have smoking and non-smoking zones, and very few do, in a sense they know what they are in for. The trouble is, many non-smokers take a wholly unrealistic view of the way the rest of the world should treat them.

I am thinking of a well-known anti-smoker. He is quite likely to refuse to enter a room where people are smoking and remain ostentatiously outside. He would certainly refuse to sit at any meal-table where a smoker had lit up, or threatened to. He is quite likely to become involved in fisticuffs with smokers who do not bend to his will in theatres and other low places of entertainment. But he rarely explains *why* he takes such a line. (It is because he has an allergy.) He also, quite clearly, expects too much. If he rings for a cab and it arrives having previously been occupied by a smoker, he sends it away. If he had really wanted a smoke-free cab he could quite easily have specified this. His irrationality is every bit as contemptible as the selfishness of the smokers he condemns.

Non-smokers can, of course, put up with smoking, and probably make themselves even more miserable. Making martyrs, however, is not what this book is about. Is there anything that can be done or said? Well, you can fan away the smoke in a rather obvious way but the smoker does not usually take the hint. Or you can take the course recommended in the cartoon which showed a non-smoker saying to a smoker, in a restaurant, 'Thank you for not smoking: I hope my food isn't interfering with your cigar', but you would have to be a true health Nazi and have a lot of courage actually to utter that line.

Other remarks you could use include, 'Oh, not one of the minority, are you?' 'Oh, I'm so sorry, I thought for a funny moment that somebody was smoking in here, but then I thought, surely, no one could be so foolish . . .' 'Don't you find it makes your clothes smell?' In response to 'Do you mind if I smoke?' reply: 'I don't care if you burst into flames'. But ridicule provokes smokers rather than provides a remedy.

I sometimes think that what's needed is some sort of retaliatory device – a portable spray which I could whip out of my pocket and squirt in the direction of the offender, but one which didn't ruin my food or make the place smell like a tart's boudoir. It would give the smoker a taste of his own medicine. But I doubt if I will ever find such a thing.

The only useful tip I have on the subject comes from a non-smoking inspector on one of the food guides (and who, presumably, in the course of her working life had to suffer a lot of provocation on this score). She told me that she found it very effective to say to smokers, 'I wonder if you'd mind holding your cigarette in the other hand' (i.e. away from the food). This, she said, tended to have such a devastating unsettling effect on the smokers that they put out the offending objects immediately.

'"You won't object if I smoke?" – "Certainly not – if you don't object if I'm sick".'
Sir Thomas Beecham, replying to a woman in a non-smoking railway compartment

'For a man to go into the street with a lady on his arm and a cigar in his mouth is a shocking sight, which no gentleman will ever be guilty of exhibiting; for he inevitably subjects the woman to the very worst of suspicions.'
Arthur Martine, *Hand-book of Etiquette and Guide to True Politeness* (New York, 1866)

People often say that manners are the lubricant that oils social machinery. And yet I wonder, what is the best method by which to achieve a normal social compromise when it comes to smoking? There is irrational behaviour on both sides. Non-smokers should not assume that only they are on the side of the angels. It will do their cause no good if they are as objectionable about smoking as smokers can be by doing it. Non-smokers probably need a code of conduct just as much as smokers do. Such a code would emphasize that mediation and compromise are much more likely to be achieved by cool, considered argument than by confrontation. Tone of voice may achieve more than specific words.

(See also 'Smoking in restaurants' in Chapter 2 EATING OUT, under 'Dinner parties' in Chapter 4 GUESTS AND HOSTS, and 'Smoking' in Chapter 10 SOCIAL LIFE.)

Sharing illnesses

In Samuel Butler's novel *Erewhon* (1872), people who are ill get sent to prison. I have always thought this an excellent idea, not least because when I am ill all I want to do is hide and keep out of the way of other people until I am better. Unfortunately, most people have other ideas. But, surely, if you are suffering from an infectious illness – a cold or influenza – it is the height of ill-consideration to go out to dinner with, or even just to meet, other people?

It could be that the other people are prepared to take the risk in meeting you and it is probably the case that even if you warned them of your condition, they would not withdraw their invitation. But it is surely the minimum of politeness to warn them in advance and give them the option of breaking the engagement.

The offer of a drink

There are still hosts who will automatically press a glass of something alcoholic into your hand as soon as you arrive. They are only doing this to be sociable. They do it unthinkingly because they have been conditioned to do it.

In which case, take the drink and don't drink it. Rather than enter an argy-bargy situation, it is much better to accept a drink and not drink it than to risk seeming unfriendly by making a fuss. By not drinking, you will also make it impossible for your host to top up your glass. At this stage, he may become aware that you would prefer something else. Or, you can ask him for something else *in addition* to what you already have, and get what you want in that way.

The same applies to wine served at the dinner table. If it is accepted and then left undrunk, the message will get across. If you have started drinking and do not wish your glass replenished, it is quite in order to put your hand over it as a gesture to prevent this. Besides, these days, mineral water is so generally available and aware-ness of the penalties of drink-driving so widespread, that someone on the entertaining side will most likely take pity on you.

Surreptitious refilling of glasses is, indeed, a problem.

It can be difficult to keep track of how many you have had, if people do this. But the rule still holds. If you genuinely don't want to drink, accept the first glass and then don't touch it. In any case, hosts are unlikely to want to waste wine on guests who do not appreciate or enjoy what they are given.

The pre-dinner drinks tray should nowadays have red and white wine and mineral water on it and not simply spirits and cocktail mixers, as was once the form. This enables people to control their own drinking, if they so desire, as well as reflecting the move towards wine and mineral water drinking that has been a feature of recent years.

'If there is a gentleman at the table who is known to be a total-abstinence man, you will not urge him to drink. He will suffer his glass to be filled at the first passage of the wine, and raising it to his lips, will bow his respects with the rest of the guests, and after that his glass will be allowed to remain untouched. As little notice as possible should be taken of his total-abstinence peculiarity. And, if he is a gentleman, he will carefully avoid drawing attention to it himself.'

Arthur Martine, *Hand-book of Etiquette and Guide to True Politeness* **(New York, 1866)**

Although alcohol consumption remains static in Britain, it is probably the case that being drunk is much less acceptable than it ever was. Heavy social drinking would seem to be much less in evidence than was once the case. Possibly those who drink for drinking's sake (and have rather more than the maiden-aunt-like 'just a little drop to be social') go about their pleasure more in private than they used to. It is just possible, I suppose, that drinking will go the way of smoking in this respect.

Whatever the case, it is still unforgivable to make

people drink if they do not wish to, or to drink more than they would wish to, or to get drunk when it could be lethal to do so.

(See also 'Alcohol-induced behaviour' in Chapter 10 SOCIAL LIFE.)

Neighbourly noise

I am the living proof that it is possible to survive neighbourly noise. In my flat-dwelling days, I have experienced Jim Reeves records coming up through the floor at two in the morning and what sounded like Polish clog-dancing coming down through the ceiling all night. So when I bought my first house, I made sure that it was detached, and vowed never to live under or over anybody again. (I now live in a terrace house where interesting sounds enter sideways.)

Neighbourly noise is one of the greatest aggravations that anyone can experience. A survey carried out by the Building Research Establishment in 1988 found that one family in five was seriously worried by noise at home. And the short answer is that it is very difficult to do anything about it. An Englishman's home is his castle, even if it now has less than fortress-thick walls, and your average Englishman feels that it is a basic citizen's right for him to be able to play his favourite music at the threshold of pain, particularly towards three o'clock in the morning.

The patient neighbour can request gently that the noise level be reduced. A response is unlikely if a party is in full swing but, on occasions, the 'reduced' does end in complete cessation. A complaint to the police seldom produces any result as the boys in blue are as reluctant to get involved with this sort of matter as they are with marital disputes. Besides, they can only act if a criminal offence is committed.

The neighbour can make an official complaint through

a magistrate's court under the Control of Pollution Act, 1974, Section 59. Most local authorities now have Environmental Health Officers and they can deal with 'unreasonable' noise in the same way. A noise abatement notice is issued and then any infringement can result in a fine. The legal powers of the EHO's are limited, though, and their powers of persuasion may be no more than the ordinary citizen's, and it all takes time. Mediation by specially-formed local groups is on the increase and can provide an alternative solution in relatively petty disputes where confrontation might only be aggravated by recourse to the authorities.

It is almost impossible to lessen through-wall or through-floor noise without major structural rebuilding. Acoustic tiles, floating ceilings, floor infill and other devices are only fractionally effective. Taking a shotgun to your neighbour, as not infrequently happens, is not recommended. In some cases, about all that can be done is to move – and hope that when people come to view the property, the noise isn't coming through the wall . . .

If the problem is deaf old people with the TV on full blast, then it may be possible to encourage them to listen on headphones, particularly if these are sent to them as a gift. You may get somewhere if you pitch your appeal along the lines that the noise is ruining your life, causing you sleepless nights, etc. But this may be a forlorn hope.

A related problem is the sort of noise you get over the garden wall in summer when otherwise civilized people are quite likely to dead-head the roses while listening to the afternoon play on Radio 4. Very irritating. (I once stormed out into my garden to remonstrate over the wall, to find that my neighbour was listening to a programme I was on...)

In the end, it all depends on the way in which the request to reduce the noise is pitched. Don't expect it to change anyone's habits for more than a day or two. And, though it certainly ain't manners, you could always resort to retaliation. Match your neighbour's loud music with yours. Or, in the words of one anonymous advice-giver, 'Don't get annoyed if your neighbour plays his hi-fi at two o'clock in the morning. Call him at four and tell him how much you enjoyed it.' He may not get the message, but it won't half make you feel better about things . . .

But the main thing is to attempt to do something about the problem. Many people are genuinely unaware that their noise is disturbing others or are completely oblivious to the fact that it may not be something others wish to share.

A noise from above

Of all life's lessons, the one I learned most painfully was, 'Never live in a basement flat beneath a transcendental meditationist'. I was living in a basement flat in Notting Hill with my newly acquired wife when, one morning about eight o'clock, there occurred what can only be described as an *earthquake* over our heads. Then complete and utter silence.

Next morning about the same time, *another* shattering crash. On the third morning, I could take no more of it and rushed upstairs to berate the occupier of the flat above – or at least to discover what had occasioned these appalling noises.

He opened the door wearing pyjamas and looking rather sheepish.

'What the hell is going on?' I asked politely.

'Er . . . have you ever heard of TM?' the youth responded.

'Yes.'

'Well, I've been flying . . . '

Which was how I discovered all about transcen-dental aviation, and how yogic pilots sit in the lotus position and bottom-jump into the air . . . and land with a shattering thud if they fall out of bed in the flat above you.

I'm pleased to say my remonstration had the desired effect and we never had to put up with it again.

If you are living in shared accommodation or next door to people who you think may be troubled by it, when giving a party, let them know in advance. They may not wish to accept your invitation to pop in for a drink, but at least they can brace themselves for the onslaught. The annoyance caused will be considerably reduced if they can put a face to the people who are the cause of it. They may even make arrangements to keep out of the way.

Personal stereos

When people first wore headphones and started walking around listening to their Sony Walkman machines, I thought it would only be a matter of time before one of them was flattened by a bus. I almost wrote 'fortunately flattened by a bus' because there is something rather irritating about people who are visibly enjoying a private pleasure which others are unable to share. All that the others can share is the odd, rhythmic scratching noise that spills out of the headphones and which is curiously annoying if you have to share a bus or train with them.

The point is, surely, that locked in a private world and less likely to respond to warning noises, the users of these otherwise excellent devices may be putting themselves in danger. About the only thing you can do is to hold up a written notice in front of their faces, asking, 'Are you all right?'

Mobile telephones

I think the dilemma, if that's what it is, over the use of mobile telephones was first brought home to me – not sitting in a restaurant or driving along a motorway, as you might expect, but in, of all places, the Royal Albert Hall. During the interval of a Promenade Concert, I became aware that a man sitting behind me was using the august setting and that moment to phone a restaurant and book himself a table for dinner after the concert. Yet I have to say that any feelings I may have had about the inappropriateness of his behaviour in a concert hall were mingled with the thought that the man behind me was in possession of a rather useful little gadget. Very shortly afterwards I went and bought one for myself.

But I still twitch when I hear other people using mobile phones in restaurants or see people using them as they drive along the road (which may be illegal, anyway, see below). To receive incoming calls on mobile phones in public places and to subject other people to the annoyance of hearing them ringing, as well as to the ensuing conversations, is bad manners. There is much to be said for only using mobile phones to make outgoing calls, and not even doing that in a public place, if people have to hear you doing it.

A Chancellor of the Exchequer called mobile telephones, 'One of the greatest scourges of modern life', but they are not. They are an extremely useful communications tool, not some frivolous, unnecessary perk, and all users should not be punished just because some people operate them in a way contrary to the common good. Mobile phones are an example of a new arrival on the scene for which etiquette has to be established. This is not a matter of life and death, but the people who use mobile phones must be aware of their irritation factor.

(See also *Car phones* in 'Motoring offences', below.)

Alarms and excursions

There is obviously something wrong if a device meant to prevent crime in all probability doesn't, and causes indescribable misery and aggravation in innocent people. For some reason, burglar alarms appear to be very unreliable devices. They frequently go wrong and, when they do, there is next to nothing that can be done to stop them making a noise. Having a burglar alarm visible may deter burglars from thinking of entering a property; whether an alarm once set off stops them from proceeding with a robbery is debatable. Meanwhile, people who live near business properties which have alarms that sound continuously all over a weekend, for example, are made to feel suicidal. Even house alarms that stop and re-set themselves after twenty minutes can be deeply unsettling. Clearly, insurance companies should think twice about liability linked to an insistence that alarms are fitted and used. The police must be given a reliable contact number for when emergencies occur, as otherwise they are obviously unable to take measures to stop alarms ringing.

Car alarms are an even worse problem. Although car-theft crime is of almost epidemic proportions, particularly in city centres, it is extremely debatable whether car alarms act as any sort of a deterrent. The dawn chorus – if not all-night chorus – of malfunctioning car alarms is a price hardly worth paying, given the disruption and sleeplessness it can cause in innocent hearers. Car-owners whose vehicles are fitted with these devices should make sure that they are properly fitted and, indeed, should ponder whether they fulfil any genuine security function.

Covetting thy neighbour's skip

I don't know what happened before skips were introduced (for household use, that is to say, in about 1970).

Presumably, builders' rubbish sat in a mound until it was taken away by lorry instead of being kept in a large metal container parked at the kerbside, as is now the norm. Useful though they are, skips also constitute a temptation. Neighbours may feel like dumping their larger, more difficult to dispose of rubbish, in someone else's skip.

Clearly, it is not right to creep out in the dark to do this. The well-mannered thing would be to *ask* your neighbours if there was any objection to making use of their skip. Promise a *quid pro quo* in due course. It is quite possible that what you add to your neighbours' skip will be stolen out of it by somebody else long before it is driven away, in any case . . .

Motoring offences

Motoring manners are rather special because people who may be politeness itself when they are pedestrians can be turned into monsters of depravity once they are safely, as they might think, placed inside a suit of armour or, in this case, a four-wheeled tin box. I have been given a statistic from the General Accident insurance company which suggests that 47% of road accidents can be traced back to some form of bad manners on the road.

Unfortunately, people rarely see bad driving as bad manners. People who would never poke you in the back and tell you to get a move on if they were standing behind you, think nothing of blasting at you with their horns if they are in a car. Selfishness rises to new heights when people take to the roads where they think there is some divine right of unhindered passage.

Key moments of bad manners on the road occur when, for example, at a road junction or traffic lights, drivers wishing to turn right do not indicate that they are going to do so until it is time to move off. You, meanwhile, have positioned your car behind theirs and can't get round them. Not parking your car in alignment with the kerb can make it difficult for other people to park – or can mean that they are denied the opportunity of parking at all. On the motorway, cruising at your own speed down the centre or outside lane, forcing others to overtake dangerously, is provocative – especially if it is done in an attempt to stop other drivers going at a fast speed of which you disapprove.

And so on. I suppose the point to make about good motoring manners is that, unlike some other types of manners, there really is no scope for disagreeing with them, or for arguing whether they are necessary or not.

What should you do if you find yourself being driven by a drunk – or simply by an over-fast, dangerously combative driver who makes you fearful for your safety? In the case of drunkenness, though this will undoubtedly be a difficult matter, you should make every effort to prevent the driver from breaking the law by driving, and attempt to make the journey in another way. The penalties for not doing so hardly need explaining.

In the case of a bad but sober driver, don't be shy of making your lack of comfort apparent. Many drivers work off their aggression when they are behind the wheel of a car, but try to show them how unhappy this makes you. Don't grin and bear it. It is more than your life – and certainly your equanimity – is worth to sit and cringe.

Transferring to a back seat may lessen some of your apprehension, but then you might transform yourself into as bad a peril – a passenger who distracts and irritates the driver. Back-seat drivers should have their condition pointed out to them, politely and firmly. It is only possible for one person to drive a car at a time, and it is better for that person to make the odd mistake in following a route, say, than for an attempt to be made at driving by committee.

'My daughter, aged four, was patiently sitting in the back of the car while I drove and my husband map-read our way through a complicated German city. He did not appreciate it when I turned *left* and he had instructed me to turn *right*, but my daughter offered us a practical solution: "Daddy, why don't *you* drive and let Mummy shout at you?"'

quoted in *Eavesdropping* (1983)

A frequently encountered problem on the roads is the other driver who simply wants to pick a quarrel. It seems that as soon as they get behind their steering wheels, they see it as their duty to alert other motorists to any shortcomings they may have. There is the flashing of lights, the tooting, the car window being wound down for an earful, after the most innocent of manoeuvres has been accomplished.

If you feel up to lowering your window, too, and letting fly with a stream of matching four-letters words, you are welcome to. But, bear in mind, you never know precisely what sort of beast you are dealing with. He might leap out of his car and aim a kick at yours – or worse. Do you really want to have stand-up fisticuffs with him? Or you may decide to ignore the pest – not always the best policy, though, as this could enrage him further. Probably it is best to acknowledge him with a weak smile and sheepish grin. All this says is that, in the old Scottish sense, you 'hear' him – meaning, you take in his message but aren't necessarily going to do anything about it.

Crash etiquette. It has been drummed into motorists so effectively that they should on no account admit liability after a car crash or motoring incident that the resulting atmosphere between the parties can seem churlish to say the least. On two occasions in my life (to date, at any rate), I have shunted other cars at road junctions.

Drivers at the rear in such incidents are always deemed culpable – they should not have been so close. I knew this and, on the second occasion, I made a point of expressing my regret at the inconvenience we had both been caused by the incident (which is not the same as admitting liability). I can't recall what I said on the first occasion but it obviously had the required soothing effect. When the shunted party's costs had been sorted out, he wrote to me and said he looked forward to bumping into me again in happier circumstances.

Car noises. Horatio Hornblower should generally be discouraged. A gentle toot may remove some minor obstacle, but driving 'on the horn' is an aural pollutant and is just the sort of thing to get the backs up other drivers. Sitting in your car with the engine running for long periods can be extremely irritating for people living nearby (especially at night), as is sitting inside a car with the radio or tape-player on at full blast, for the same reason.

Car phones. Everywhere I look these days I see car telephones in use – and being used while the caller is driving. People who have these devices fitted seem to use them all the time – perhaps to show the world what dynamic and in-touch lives they lead. It would be interesting to know how many accidents have been caused by people driving into things when using their car phones. Clearly, if they have to be held in the hand, they cannot be good for your driving. Even if they are fitted to the car, the process of dialling or even conversing is not good for the concentration.

As far as I can discover, it is not actually illegal to drive along while using a car phone, but it would count against you if you were to be involved in accident.

It also imposes on the person you call from a car to have to bear with you while reception comes and goes and frequently breaks down all together – particularly when the motive for your call is only that you are bored with a motorway and want something to do, or because you simply want to show off that you have such a handy little gadget.

Personalized number plates. There is, I suppose, something to be said for the Spanish Ambassador to the Court of St James being driven about London in a car with 'SPA 1N' on the number plate, though one might assume that certain diplomats from the Middle East would prefer not to disclose their identity in this way, for security reasons.

Again, if you are the sort of person who needs to drive around in a big car with a small number plate stating 'PEN 1S', that is your problem. Trumpeting your ownership and flashing your wealth may only result in your car being vandalized before the next, plainer one.

The buying and selling of customized number plates has become big business. Note, however, that the Queen who might well feel entitled, and could afford, to show off in this way, is the soul of discretion: she has no number plates at all on her official cars.

'Whatever the other monkey wants to do, let him do it. Give him a smile and wave him on. It won't cure him, but it *will* cure you . . . Relax. Be grateful. Be humble. Be kind. Be human. Mind your manners. Enjoy this wonderful machine and help others to do the same.'
Paul Gallico (1897–1976), 'Easy Gallico Method for Deflating the Pumpkin and Restoring the Humanities to Driving', in *Esquire*

Handicapped people

The principal failing people have in dealing with the handicapped is brilliantly encapsulated in the title of the

BBC Radio 4 series *Does He Take Sugar?* This phrase, pinpointed originally by social workers, represents the unthinking attitude that leads people to talk to the companions or relatives of the physically handicapped rather than directly to the people themselves.

Much the same goes for the tendency to shout at the blind, as if their hearing was deficient as well (rather the opposite is, of course, the case). A normally spoken offer – 'Do you want any help?' – when about to cross a busy road or standing at the bus-stop – is usually much-appreciated.

Far from embarrassing a handicapped person, a direct question about how they came to lose a limb or what they find most difficult doing is often a perfect way to break the ice and establish friendly relations.

Stutterers. It is a fact of life that stutterers do not take the easy way out. Instead of saying, 'No', they say, 'I don't really think so', and, with all the repetitions involved, you may feel that they are taking up whole decades of your life. Never mind. The rule is, never hustle stutterers – and *never* supply or finish off the words they are trying to get out. Let them take their time. Only in that way may they sometimes be cured.

Chapter 7

PUBLIC BEHAVIOUR

The whole concept of manners depends upon people being social and having to interact with other human beings. You could be exquisitely well-mannered on your own, in private, but that would not be manners, because there would be no one to be considerate or courteous to.

Similarly, you could be well-dressed in private, but although that might be functional, in that it might keep you warm, it would not achieve what has become the prime reason for wearing clothes – that they enable you to mix with other people and become a social being. So it is with clothes that we begin to look at public behaviour, deportment in public.

Clothing

This book is not a guide to taste – which may well be something you either have or don't have, anyway. But some things about what you wear are just 'not done' and contribute to your overall image, if not your overalls image. An unobtrusive, effortless, style of clothing is what men, in particular, should aim for, though getting British men out of the various 'uniforms' they seem to hanker after has been a long process and, to date, not entirely successful.

It would be presumptuous of me to give much guidance to women on this front. Although there are specific occasions when women are expected to conform to rules (not entering the Enclosures at Henley and Ascot, for example, wearing trousers or too-short skirts), the only real rule is not to go over the top. It is much better to be under- rather than over-dressed. If your basic attire is modest, you can always pep it up with the addition of jewellery from your handbag when you discover that everyone else has put on the glitz. If everyone else is in jeans, you can easily go into reverse mode. Generally, though, if you are in doubt about what to wear at a public or private function, ask the organizer or the hostess what would be appropriate.

I would merely observe that it is one of Nature's laws that many women who have not been favoured in physical shape are equally unlikely to have been favoured with an ability to disguise the fact. They draw attention to their bad points unerringly.

Black tie. Evening dress for men – the traditional 'penguin suit' – makes women seethe because it does not require men to spend any time asking, 'What shall I wear?' About the only problem it presents is in tying the bow-tie – and this should, naturally, always be hand-tied rather than ready-tied. Coloured bow-ties may suit larger-than-life characters but are best avoided with evening dress. It is no longer necessary for men to wear shiny black patent leather shoes with evening dress: discreet black shoes of almost any type will suit just as well. A white pocket handkerchief *may* be worn in the breast pocket, but is not necessary and is frowned on by some.

Buttons. The buttons on a jacket or waistcoat should never all be done up. The bottom button is usually left undone on a waistcoat; only the middle button of the three on a single-breasted jacket, or just the top and middle ones. On a double-breasted jacket, both the operable buttons should be done up when standing, but the lower one may be undone when seated.

Handbags – for men. For whatever reason, these have just not caught on in Britain the way they have in continental Europe. The British male is apparently wedded to his wallet. There was a period when handbags did flourish but most men seem to have discovered what the Queen knew all along, that handbags have to be carried all the time or parked somewhere (so that you can worry about them). In working life, the executive briefcase continues to hold sway with the personal organizer and the portable phone as all-too-apparent handbag substitutes. Men will not, apparently, put their masculinity at risk, however practical something like the handbag may be. (I seem to recall someone trying to launch 'Hamlets' – tights for men – in the early 1960s. Men did not take to them either.)

Hats. 'If you want to get ahead, get a hat' was the slogan used by the Hat Council in Britain back – oh, it must have been in the 1930s and 1940s. Although hats haven't died out, the wearing of them has sharply diminished. If I go to speak at a Literary Luncheon or to a Ladies' Luncheon Club nowadays, I often comment on the fact that whereas once I would have been confronted with a sea of hats, now I am lucky to see one or two. They can't even award a prize for the best hat. Even at the annual Conservative Women's Conference and the Tory Party Conference, hat-wearing is not what it was.

Men, for their part, have largely – except for the odd eccentric – stopped wearing hats as part of their professional uniform. Bowler hats and rolled umbrellas in the Civil Service or in the City are now few and far between. Homburgs and Anthony Edens are *nowhere* to be seen in the media. When was the last time you saw a television news reporter wearing a hat, except to make some fanciful point or other? The race course is the last refuge of the chap's hat.

At the same time, male wearing of hats solely for fashion purposes – to enable the wearer to look like

something out of a gangster movie or a cigar commercial
– has probably increased. Alas, the raising of the hat to
women, or the alternative light touching of the brim, as
a gesture of greeting and respect, rarely comes as part of
the package.

This is to be regretted. Of all the outmoded, irrelevant
gestures that go to make up traditional 'good manners',
touching the hat had genuine charm. They say it
originated in the raising of the vizor when suits of
armour were worn, but possibly it seemed a little like
forelock touching?

'That touching of the hat is a very rare piece of
courtesy from working men in Australia. The con-
victs are forced to do it, and so the free men make it
a point of honour not to do so.'
    **Henry Kingsley (1830–76), *The Recollections of Geoffry
    Hamlyn***

Should hats ever be worn *indoors* by men? Once hats
were *never* worn indoors, but now there has been a
slight change. Singer George Melly never stops wearing
one, for example, though he is an entertainer and, for
that reason, can get away with it. If the hat is a fashion
hat, there can hardly be any objection to it being worn
indoors, though perhaps in recognition of its changing
status, it should be raised and lowered as frequently as
possible.

It is probably only among fashion-hat wearers that
you will find men who can bear to remain 'covered'
when under someone else's roof. If they can, there may
also be the suspicion that they have some dreadful
problem with their scalps which needs to be concealed.
But, in essence, there is nothing wrong with it and if
only entertainers did it, that would be a pity.

When should women de-hat indoors? They might feel
the urge when they get to the reception after a wedding
– in which case they might take their cue from the

bride's mother or simply do whatever makes them feel comfortable. Men would probably prefer them to stay covered, if only because finding somewhere to park a wedding hat can cause problems.

Pocket handkerchiefs. As a rule, these should never be bought in a matching set with a tie, though if the design is pleasing there is no particular reason why the rule shouldn't be broken occasionally. The handkerchief should never be placed in the breast pocket with a straight line at the top parallel with the top of the pocket. (This also applies to a white silk handkerchief worn with evening dress – though, as stated above, this is not an essential item anyway.) The handkerchief should simply be stuffed in the pocket casually, with no edges visible. The amount showing or hanging out will depend on the effusiveness of the wearer's personality.

There is an exception to this, and that is the Prince of Wales, who frequently sports a pocket handkerchief with a straight line across the top, for reasons best known to himself. On the other hand, he is in a position to do what he likes.

There are those who think that nothing should ever disfigure the breast pocket of a town suit. A country suit, sports jacket or blazer might well look very naked without a handkerchief, however.

Pockets. On the whole, only inside pockets should be used for carrying things, and then never anything bulky. Breast pockets should never have a comb, pens or pencils stored in them, unless the wearer wishes to be mistaken for a train-spotter – hence the damning code initials 'CITP' for 'Comb In Top Pocket'.

Standing with hands in pockets is to proclaim that one is in casual mode. From boyhood to the grave, men are exhorted to extract them, with little apparent success. It is utterly bad form to shake hands with the other hand still in a pocket. It is unspeakably bad form to perform any sort of function publicly in this mode.

Shoes. Black shoes will go with most, dark, formal suits and must be largely unnoticeable. Some form of colour coordination with the rest of the clothing is otherwise allowable, though, for some reason, grey shoes – especially light grey – and beige shoes, not least with buckles and other decorations, are suspect. Tassels have the imprimatur of the Prince of Wales and are now widely worn.

Socks. Dazzling socks intended to contrast with the rest of your clothes should only be worn by the foolhardy or by entertainers. Darkish socks, without any pattern, are the safest choice. Americans have a way of cutting their trousers too short and this only emphasizes any poor choice of sock. On no account should a band of skin be visible between sock and trouser (whether the wearer is seated or standing).

Ties. Once almost compulsory except on holiday, ties are now frequently omitted. Choice of tie is best restricted to the discreet, but many men find it difficult to observe this rule. Whatever the case, ties should not be looked upon as long-term investments, as they are bound to get marked the first time they are worn and they lose most of their lustre once they have been cleaned.

Tying a Windsor knot (a somewhat fuller though better-balanced knot than the basic, and named after the Duke of Windsor who popularized it) was an activity once held in low esteem, though no longer. Any scheme of tying which puts the bottom tip of the tie with any amount of shirt showing below it, is wrong. The bottom tip of the tie should fall slightly below the waist or belt.

Club or organizational ties, although providing useful conversation-fodder on first acquaintance with the wearer, are often sartorially restrictive and are best avoided, if only on aesthetic grounds. The same goes for tie-pins (which are best avoided whatever they look like) and cuff-links (which should be as plain as possible).

(See also 'Sexual dressing', next, and 'Dress' in Chapter 2 EATING OUT.)

Sexual dressing

As with flaunting one's bedroom activities in other people's faces, it is never the done thing to advertise one's sexual wares through one's clothes. That is to say, dressing sexually beyond a certain degree is offensive. People who are uninvolved with you, and never likely to be, just aren't interested in your breasts or the hairiness of your chest and shouldn't be forced to look in that direction.

Sexual display in public

If there is one form of sexual display calculated to make you not know which way to look, it is when couples indulge in behaviour of an intimate nature – from snogging through to heavy petting – in the street or, indeed, anywhere in public. Onlookers' attitudes vary: some people just laugh, others get quite worked up about it. And yet, one does not have to be a retired colonel from Eastbourne to say that the public expression of what ought to be a private matter between two people is unacceptable. Far from being rather sweet and touching – 'They're so carried with each other, they don't realize anyone else is near' – it is unacceptable behaviour, and all the more so for being quite impossible for a third party to interrupt.

On a very minor point: for women publicly to adjust their make-up with a mirror or literally to powder their noses, is to indulge in a form of sexual display – or, rather, to engineer a form of sexual display which may in its final form be acceptable but which should only be prepared privately.

Breastfeeding in public

Fat, as the book title had it, is a feminist issue. Breast-feeding in public has gone the same way and evokes both passionate support and opposition. Although in the PAS survey just over half the sample interviewed (men and women) said that, to them, breastfeeding in public was perfectly acceptable, this does nothing to lessen the quandary many mothers still find themselves in on this issue.

Subtlety and discretion may well be employed – it doesn't have to be done as a campaigning gesture – but breastfeeding in public, which means anywhere other than mother and baby locked alone in a room, still has the power to unsettle onlookers. At the very least, mothers should ask the immediate company whether anybody minds and should try to gauge what reaction would be in the wider context of, say, a restaurant. It has been well put that, 'Breastfeeding only takes place between intimates.'

Public nudity

Topless sunbathing has taken an age to reach British shores and, given the weather, this is not entirely surprising. It is best only done in the privacy of one's own backgarden or by the side of hotel swimming pools where it is obvious that it is acceptable. In public parks or on a crowded beach, it can be done discreetly, but not everyone wishes to look at pasty, raw and uncooked flesh and their feelings should be respected. Fortunately, though, the British are gradually beginning to get quite grown up about this.

But if you argue that it's not in order for women to breastfeed in public – and that it is not in order for men to urinate in public either – and if what we might call 'sexual display' is involved in both these activities, couldn't you also say that it is no worse for a woman to adjust her clothes for breastfeeding purposes than for a man to go around without his top on? A double standard operates here, needless to say. If the man (or woman) doing the showing off is genuinely attractive, objections tend to evaporate pretty quickly. This is, of course, grossly unfair on unattractive people who may wish to let it all hang out, too.

If men or women wish to flaunt their nakedness, should they hesitate before doing so in front of the older generation? Should a woman ask if anyone would mind her taking her top off – thereby drawing attention to it – or should she not simply go ahead and do it discreetly? Ask the older people quietly whether they have any objection. If you do ask, it is most unlikely that they will say no.

Jacuzzis and saunas. In public jacuzzis and saunas, the rules about the degree of nudity allowed and whether the sexes can mingle will probably be spelt out in a clear fashion. Owners of domestic versions who invite guests to partake should have warned them in advance of the possibility and should say what the house customs are.

Lavatory terms

This is a curiously neglected area of concern, except for the matter of what name or euphemistic phrase you should give to the place. Frankly, you go to the lavatory – even if the Latin root of that word has to do with washing, which is not the prime purpose of your visit. The most popular American euphemism – 'going to the bathroom/restroom/washroom' must, however, be discounted for the same reason.

'Martha, will you show her where we keep the . . . er, euphemism?'
Edward Albee, *Who's Afraid of Virginia Woolf?* (1962)

'Toilet' is marginally less descriptive (from the French for cloth or wrapper). What is more it sounds niminy-piminy and has been fatally degraded by use in most public places, on motorway signs, etc. – perhaps for no other reason that it takes up less space on signs than 'lavatory'. 'Loo', which has the saving grace of extreme brevity, is still slightly precious. It may (though this can be argued about) have a pleasant origin as part of a pun (Water-loo) and has long escaped its original upper-middle-class usage and become generally accepted (though not in the US).

No, 'lavatory' it has to be – though in a public place, the inquiry, 'Where is the Gents'/Ladies'?' can't really be faulted, unless you are seriously concerned that the world should be divided into Gentlemen and Ladies, rather than Men and Women.

Euphemisms of the 'I'm just going to the little boys' room' or 'I'm going to send a telegram to Hitler' type are best reserved for the type of company where everyone else says the sort of thing. (See also 'U and Non-U language' in Chapter 11 SPEAKING.)

As for what one finds inside a lavatory, it is, of course, the height of bad manners to comment subsequently on the material used for the seat cover or the design of the brush holder. These reflect your host or hostess's taste and it is terribly bad form to dwell on such matters (except, later, in the comfort of your own home, where no one can hear you and you can laugh to your heart's content.)

Little research, fortunately, has been carried out as to what happens in multi-occupancy public lavatories. Conversations should not be conducted between people at or in adjacent urinals or cubicles. Introductions should not be made at all in these places. Gossip or business should on no account be conducted (except after rigorous checking whether enemy ears are listening from other cubicles). Ostentatious handwashing and drying afterwards is the mark of the well-mannered and hygienic person. For the most part, an eyes down, notice no one, mumbling demeanour should be adopted by all.

Queuing

It is really rather unfair the amount of stick we British have had to take because of our addiction to queueing. It is, after all, quite the most civilized way of achieving order and fairness in obtaining goods and services.

'An Englishman, even if he is alone, forms an orderly queue of one.'
George Mikes, *How To Be An Alien* **(1946)**

The problem is when people who are not born queuers – by which one means foreigners, especially undisciplined, pushy Middle-European and Mediterranean types – come over here and blithely ignore the rules. Patiently pointing out that there is a queue and which way it is headed is usually sufficient to bring the poor things to heel. Other mutterings might range from the polite, 'I believe I was next' to the educational, 'There are such things as queues, you know . . . '

But there are queue terrorists, some of them British and particularly the elderly, and by and large it is best to let them be. Fortunately, as banks and post offices have now, at last, organized themselves with regard to queuing, one is no longer subjected to having to play queue roulette – trying to work out which line is moving fastest and then choosing the wrong one.

Swearing

Is swearing still socially unacceptable? Of those habits that you might feel entitled to indulge in under your own roof, whatever you may do in public, swearing is still the most contentious. The thing about swearing is that even those who might be expected to swear a lot are quite likely to say they disapprove of it. In the PAS survey, a very high 84% of the sample found the use of four-letter words *in public* to be unacceptable. And this went beyond 90% in what one might think of as tough-talking areas like Yorkshire and the North-East. The poll confirmed that women are more likely to disapprove the use of four-letter words in public than men.

In private, one supposes that few people would disapprove of a four-letter word unleashed at the moment when hammer has just landed upon thumb or in other situations of comparable, minor misery. Never mind that the f-word is now a commonplace in films and on TV, there is still much disapproval reserved for people who swear in real life, and particularly in front of children, and for men who swear in the company of women. Curiously, it would seem that those who complain about blasphemous and obscene language in the media are much more concerned about the words used than they are at the visual depiction of sexual or sacrilegious behaviour. This may have something to say about the power of words but it underlines the fact that swearing, though it can be entertaining in some cases, should not be treated lightly.

How refreshing it was in 1983 when Prince Charles addressed 13,500 schoolchildren at an open air rally in Western Australia and the blustery wind whipped away the top sheet of his speech. 'Oh God, my bloody bit of paper,' he exclaimed, before going on to quote from an 1897 homily, including the advice, 'Swearing is contempt-ible and foolish,' and, 'Vulgarity excludes one from good society.'

In the audience

It is not just other people chattering that can make being part of a theatre, concert or cinema audience such an ordeal. In a lifetime of suffering, I have seen almost everything. A performance of *Così fan tutte* by the English National Opera was ruined in the last five minutes as a man in the most expensive seats started taking flash photographs. Admittedly, the prohibition of such activity was tucked away in small print in the programme, but nobody sitting near him in the audience did anything about it, and the theatre management fluttered ineffectually on the sidelines.

Most bizarre of all was the audience performance during the run of the stage-play *A Walk in the Woods*, starring Sir Alec Guinness. Even before the curtain went up, my wife pointed to a woman a few rows in front of us and said, 'She's got a baby with her'. After the initial reaction that, no it couldn't be, it must be a doll, had moved on to, well, perhaps the baby sitter failed to show, it was time for the curtain to go up. And, lo, ten minutes into the play, the baby started yowling and, after a while, the mother had to take it out.

After the interval, we were in for more entertainment from the audience. A couple of theatre-goers had been drinking well and were now sat (wearing evening dress, let it be said) with a bottle of champagne between them. After a while, every time Sir Alec uttered one of the play's modestly distinguished lines, a voice would say out loud, 'Oh, wow, such poetry!' and sentiments of that type. The curious thing about this performance was that it was almost entertaining. The rest of the audience was stunned into wonderment at what would be said next. Either way, I don't expect Sir Alec regarded us as one of his best audiences.

So why are audiences often so badly behaved? In a sense, it is the fault of managements. Like today's clergy, they are so glad to have you in the building they never dream of pulling you up. They never enforce the photography rules, or rarely bring them to people's attention in an effective way. They continue to sell confectionery in packaging that makes a confounded rustling noise when opened.

But, I suppose, the main culprit is television. People are so used now to being able to watch performances in the comfort of their own homes, where they can make remarks in loud voices about what is going on, that they naturally feel there is nothing wrong doing the same in a public auditorium.

And it is not just chatter. Years ago, I was in a provincial theatre as Sir John Gielgud was going through one of his great Shakespearean death scenes. Suddenly, some person at the rear of the 'Gods' decided not just to have a sweet, but to drop a whole box of Maltesers, so that they cascaded all the way down to the front row. Sir John died a little quicker than usual that night, I am sure.

So what should you do? Turn round and glare; politely request people to shut up. It is not a fun task, but if you don't do it, people will just carry on regardless. If you suspect that you are an offender, please note that overtures are not there to be talked through; tall people or people wearing large hats and hairdos should do what they can to keep their heads down; above all, try to regard a visit to the theatre or concert hall as an occasion, and not as a live TV show.

Corporate sponsorship of plays and concerts has introduced another hazard – less-than-acceptable behaviour by invitees of the sponsors. This may consist of talking loudly during performances which they otherwise would not have attended (and are not accustomed to attending), taking their seats late after accepting hospitality before the performance or during the interval, and generally behaving as if they owned the place. Patrons who have actually paid for the tickets and have not been on the receiving end of corporate hospitality may have good cause to feel resentful.

Having to climb over people who are already in their seats is difficult enough even when you are not late-comers. The form seems to be that you should move along the row, almost with your back to those who are half-standing or still seated, all the while beaming thanks and apologies, however phoney these may be. People should stand to let you go by if there is the slightest difficulty in your getting through.

Silent moments. It is not only in plays and concerts that silence is golden. There are moments even at rowdy sporting events when it is polite to shut up – at rugby matches, for example, when a kick at goal is being taken. It is bad form to shout at Wimbledon, particularly during a service, though Centre Court umpires seem recently to have been fighting a losing battle on this score. In any sport, spectators should remain silent when a player is concentrating.

Applause. There is no doubt about it, applause is a very odd thing – banging your palms together like that. There is probably too much applause these days – largely the fault of radio and television performers who engineer applause, not as a token of appreciation but as a kind of aural glue to hold proceedings together and also to provide punctuation for the work in progress.

Applause at concerts is in its own league. Accompanied by soloists trooping on and off the platform and conductors waving up individual soloists from the orchestra for a bow, it can often go on for a very long time and be quite exhausting. One can't help feeling sometimes that the audience is applauding in order to show that it has got its money's worth rather than solely out of appreciation for an exceptional performance. Eagerness to applaud can also spoil the magic of a poignant last note and the moving pause that can follow it. People who are unable to tell when a piece of music has come to an end shouldn't try to lead the applause. Either they should wait for others to start, or they should observe whether the conductor has put his baton down on his desk – the sure signal.

Opera audiences are also, of course, a separate species. They like to applaud individual arias and shout 'Bravo', and if they really want to do these things, they should not be stopped. Booing, however, is quite another matter. It is a bad form of criticism because no one is to know why precisely you are doing it. What is the root of your complaint? How do you boo scenery in a way that makes your point? There are other ways of showing that you feel your ticket money has been poorly spent. But it is part of the opera tradition to boo, however unlikeable a trait it is, and it is unlikely ever to be stamped out.

Applause in church. Quite frequently, concerts are given in churches and chapels and members of the audience are understandably reticent to applaud, as though the giving of thanks and appreciation in God's house was something new. However, unless a request has been clearly been given that applause would not be appreciated, applaud by all means. The performers still need it and, in any case, applause helps make an occasion out of an event.

The free expression of laughter in church is also to be encouraged though, to be sure, rather less likely to be obtained after so much conditioning.

Standing ovations. It is now quite impossible for a political or trade union leader to make a conference speech without being accorded the ritual staggering to the feet of rank and file. The same vertical expression of applause is also encountered with unavoidable regularity these days in theatres, concert halls and television studios. I was once invited along to one of London Weekend Television's *An Audience With . . .* shows and, despite a less than remarkable peformance from the star, we were all somehow provoked into giving him a standing ovation (it is even available on video – and there I am doing it). I swear there were little pins in the seats which stuck up at the right moment to make us comply.

I suppose it is a very Continental thing to do and makes good pictures for the TV cameras. Alas, if you sit out a standing ovation, not only is your view blocked, but it looks as if you are making a rather more sour protest than you may intend. All I am saying is that this common occurrence *devalues* the compliment it is intended to bestow. The standing ovation should be reserved for the most special of occasions. I recall going to hear José Carreras give his first recital at Covent Garden after he had conquered his leukaemia. He was accorded a standing ovation as soon as he stepped on to the stage and before he had sung a note. And quite right, too. But people don't come back from the dead every day so we should reserve a special way of showing our appreciation when they do.

Noises off. In vain each year at the Promenade Concerts at the Royal Albert Hall, a notice is inserted in the programme pointing out (not least because the concerts are also being broadcast) that the amount of noise generated by audience coughing is louder than that of some of the orchestral instruments.

Well, there is not too much that can be done about a bad cough – though equipping yourself with cough sweets is sensible and considerate – but what about the new curse of civilized listening, watches that go beep on the hour? It is hard to imagine what possible benefit to mankind anyone could have thought would flow from this invention. Who needs to be told when the hour is upon us? Chiming clocks, of course, have done it for centuries – but no one carries such time pieces around with them when other people are trying to make beautiful music.

The merry beeping of the hour – each one going off, of course, at a slightly different moment – is a curse of modern life almost on the same level as car and house burglar alarms. The solution is simple. They should be switched off, and never turned on again. If people want to use their watches as alarms, they can use them for that purpose – but obviously they would have no need to do this in a public auditorium during an entertainment.

Noises on. Foot-tapping among a concert audience is one thing. Another is the occasionally objectionable extraneous noises made by performers . . . There is one famous conductor I can think of who crashes audibly about his rostrum. There are pianists (and not just jazz-pianists) who grunt and groan *above* their breath. And there was a Swiss cellist I once heard perform, whose heavy breathing was so much louder than his playing that any thought he may have had of a career making CDs was out of the question . . .

Audience participation. Of the more formal kind, that is. This is not to be encouraged where it is not expected. A theatre-goer does not pay to sit in the most expensive stalls in order to be mocked by some comedian who can't raise his laughs any other way or to be included in the production, as it were, by some director who has barmy theories about audience 'involvement'. Although this sort of thing can be funny – mostly for other members of the audience – it is embarrassing and fundamentally bad manners from the performers. An audience member who is drawn out of the anonymity of a darkened auditorium is not being treated considerately and that, as needs often to be said, is the basis of manners.

Dressing up to be entertained. It is a compliment to the artists if audiences at plays, operas and concerts look upon attending the performance as something special – not just like stopping at home to watch television. Dressing up to do this is the most obvious manifestation of this attitude and, though putting on full fig for the opera may seem curiously inappropriate for a minimalist production of Berg's *Wozzeck*, for example, it is at least better than expecting to grace a Mozart opera in T-shirt and jeans. If you wore the latter at Glyndebourne, I suspect you would probably get stones thrown at you. At the Royal Opera House, Covent Garden, it is increasingly common to see jeans-clad persons next to tiara-wearers. Of course, it can be argued that music sounds the same whatever you are wearing, but I am not so sure that it does. The point is, though, that if the audience does not perceive the occasion as something special, then it probably won't be.

Objectionable smells

Frankly, I like catching a brief, tantalizing whiff of someone else's scent – even another man's aftershave reassures you that he is at least trying. But it should be a *brief* whiff. Otherwise, a heavy session with the scent bottle can pollute the atmosphere around a person just as effectively as puffing a cigarette. And just because you think the smell is irresistible (perhaps that is why you chose it), and just because you think it is sweet-smelling, that doesn't mean to say that someone sitting next to you in an audience, or at an adjacent table in a restaurant, will take kindly to having their olfactory nerves 'deafened' by your interesting scent or your butch aftershave.

The trouble with scent is, of course, that the wearer rapidly loses awareness of it. The other problem is that even the most expensive concoctions can end up smelling like a tart's boudoir or an athlete's locker if allowed to get out of hand. The day of the neutralizing spray may not be very far off.

Revolving doors

One gesture more complicated than the simple act of holding open a door for another person, is what to do when confronted with a revolving door. Never mind what kids might want to demonstrate to you, only one person should go in each 'compartment' of a revolving door at a time, and no one should attempt to make the door revolve at anything more than medium walking pace. Revolving doors can be frightening – particularly if you are carrying luggage – and should be treated with the utmost caution.

Electrically-driven revolving doors are quite common now but should also be kept at arm's length, so to speak. It is probably overdoing it to go in first before a woman, push the door all the way round, before emerging *after* her – as a letter-writer to *The Times* once suggested was correct form.

I have always imagined that it was a revolving door that gave rise to the alleged (and much-denied) exchange between Dorothy Parker and Clare Boothe Luce. Luce is supposed to have waved Parker through first with, 'Age before beauty . . . ' Parker is supposed to have responded with, 'Pearls before swine'. Most of us have still not progressed beyond the 'After you, Claud' – 'No, after you, Cecil' routine that was celebrated in the 1940s comedy show, *ITMA*.

The intrusiveness of photography and video

About twenty-five years ago, I went to see the Grand National at Aintree race course. It occurred to me even then that what I was attending was not some great national occasion with its own distinctive atmosphere but an event that was being staged almost solely for the benefit of television viewers at home.

The race course was like some huge 'set', everything seemed to be geared to the cameras, and the actual atmosphere of the course was no more heady than it is backstage at a film studio. Except, they don't re-run the race if there's a technical breakdown, or resort to re-takes.

Little did I imagine the extent to which television would, in the intervening years, take over almost every event you could think of − so much so, that participants in everything from great national occasions to events supposed to have a degree of local character and charm about them get turned into actors, or people playing at participation.

Little did I imagine, either, that the same effect would become apparent at what was then a private, amateur level, through the invention and widespread adoption of the domestic video camera. It is too easy nowadays for weddings to become events staged for the person wielding the camcorder and, however pleasing it may be to have the resulting photographs to chortle over in the years to come, something is lost in the process.

Much the same goes for still photography. I suppose there is a reason for the incessant flashing, clattering, scratching and whirring of press cameras at all public events nowadays. But does it extend to Uncle Joe's Instamatic with the flash at his nephew's christening? You don't have to go along with the belief of certain primitive peoples that cameras are capable of stealing your soul. But they do detract from the atmosphere of many occasions.

It also doesn't say much for the souls of guests at weddings or of holidaymakers on tour, if their experience of occasions and places is only enjoyed through a view-finder at the time. Indeed, it seems their enjoyment is only to be expected at a later date. Recollection in tranquillity was a phrase used about poetry, not involvement in events. The act of photography should not be a substitute for life.

Nowadays, there is too much television coverage, too much videoing, too much photography for anyone's good. This is not to say it should be banned, just limited. Obviously the results can be very enjoyable, but intrusiveness is a high price to pay for this. Photographers of all kinds should think before they get to work – and, where appropriate, certainly ask permission before they do so.

(See also under 'The wedding ceremony' in Chapter 5 MARRIAGE AND DIVORCE.)

Correcting mistakes

Elsewhere (see 'Eavesdropping' in Chapter 2 EATING OUT), it is made plain that you should never correct mistakes in other people's conversations (overheard in restaurants, say). It is also unfeeling to correct people's facts or grammar in a pedantic way during conversations or discussions in which you are taking a direct part. Let their mistakes go unnoticed – except by others who have noticed them for themselves.

However, if an error concerns you – someone repeatedly gets your name wrong, for example – it is only sensible to put the matter right at the earliest opportunity, while making a little joke about it.

Incidentally, other people should never be told that they are 'wrong' in what they think or say, though they may well be told they are 'mistaken'.

Responding to rudeness

How should you respond when you observe someone being rude to another person or just generally behaving rudely? Do you intervene? Do you make your own discomfort known? Do you join in? Do you dissociate yourself from the rude person? Do you try and conciliate?

This is a difficult one. On the whole, it is probably best not to upbraid the person who is giving the offence at the time. If, say, he is behaving badly towards a waiter in a restaurant, it should be possible for you to indicate to the waiter by your tone of voice and demeanour that you are not in agreement with the behaviour he is being subjected to. A moderately demonstrative show of kindness and fairness on your part may also rub off on the rude person and make him aware that he has gone too far.

Dealing with muggers

It does not take any great adherence to victim theory – in which it is believed that victims bring attacks (of any kind) upon themselves – to appreciate that, to some extent, those who are attacked may deserve it. Nor is this to enter that controversial and dubious legal area of 'culpable negligence' – in which, for example, a woman seems to become a rape victim merely because she is a woman and because she has the temerity to want to walk out at night.

What one is saying is this: it is possible to head off trouble by anticipating it and by ignoring it. If you identify a difficult, drunk or threatening person some way ahead of you and take suitable avoiding action, you may be able to lessen the possibility of an unpleasant encounter. Avoiding eye contact with a potentially difficult person *may* also help you avoid getting into a situation which could lead to your being robbed, assaulted or worse.

Easy to say, I know, and not much help in certain dire circumstances, but worth thinking about and contriving to bring about.

Eating in the street

This is probably not the offence it was once considered to be. There are some people who still disapprove of the sight of others snacking as they walk along in a public place, but with the proliferation of so-called fast-food outlets, the only problem is not so much how the food is consumed but how the packaging is disposed of. Even if the eating is not offensive, creating litter is.

Litter

The well-mannered person does not create litter nor leave it lying about, under any circumstances. If you cannot find a rubbish bin, take your litter home. If you witness someone else leaving litter, should you go up to them and politely say, 'Excuse me, I think this is yours' or 'I think you left this by mistake'? Irony is lost on most people and especially on litter louts. You could be brave – or you could bin the offending litter yourself and live to fight another day.

Chapter 8

$\mathcal{R}$ELATIONSHIPS AND SEX

Manners between the sexes is the subject of this chapter. The view that 'All's fair in love and war' might seem to rule out manners in relationships and sex, but surely they are as necessary there as in other little courtesies between men and women. Little courtesies that can mean so much – like a man carrying a woman's bags, helping her on with her coat, walking on the outside of the pavement – and which may well add to the allure of a member of the opposite sex – but not just the special etiquette that can be, or even should be, demanded when things get physical.

The little courtesies sometimes involve the physical, too, of course.

Men opening doors for women

If there is a key aspect of behaviour which is supposed to speak volumes about the way men treat women and what women expect of men, it is the question of whether a man should hold open the door for a woman to go through first. It has to be said that division of opinion over whether such masculine gestures are necessary is not restricted to men. Women may feel inclined to suspect the attitude behind the held-open door. But faced with the reality of this simple old-world courtesy, many women – perhaps most – react differently, and accept the gesture.

167

In the PAS survey, it was found that a clear majority of men and women – 81% – agreed that men *should* open doors for women. There was almost no difference between the male and female view on this point – though whether, of course, men actually do it every time, in practice, is another matter.

It was interesting that the opinion poll found that even 62% of people between the ages of fifteen and seventeen were in favour of men opening doors for women.

'Marriage indeed may qualify the fury of his passion, but it very rarely mends a man's manners.'
William Congreve, *Love for Love* (1695)

'When a lady whom you accompany wishes to enter a store, you should hold the door open and allow her to enter first, if practicable; for you must never pass before a lady anywhere, if you can avoid it, or without an apology.'
Arthur Martine, *Hand-book of Etiquette and Guide to True Politeness* (New York, 1866)

But if in polite society there is still no question as to whether men opening doors for women, to allow them through first, is the correct thing to do, there is an interesting exception. Most Saturday lunchtimes I go with my wife to a particular Italian restaurant of which we are inordinately fond and where we have been going for more than a dozen years. Having previously booked our table by telephone, we arrive at the restaurant and have to pass down a very narrow corridor before we get to the head waiter who will give my wife a kiss and then show us to our table.

Now then, the question is – even in rather less familiar surroundings – who should have gone through the restaurant door first – me or my wife? Ask a group of business people in the City who would go first if they were in that position – the man or the woman? – and they would tend to reply, 'The woman *always* go first', but the occasional brave soul will reply, 'The booker of the restaurant table always goes first, irrespective of sex'. And quite right, too, in my opinion.

So, is there a point to be made here? Even if it is normally considered bad manners for a man to go through a door first, there is a good practical reason for him to do so in this situation. Such a pragmatic approach to manners can surely not be called into question. It makes life easier and more comfortable and therefore must be a good thing.

Opening car doors. It is a pleasant thing to hold open a car door for a woman (or an older person of either sex) but here the point at issue is clearer. Car doors are often stiff and unwieldy and it is much easier for another person to operate them than the person who is going through the door. Opening the door from the inside and pushing it outward is a rough way of doing things, though as a gesture it is not entirely negligible.

More than twenty years ago, I had occasion to give a lift to that splendid old bat, Lady Violet Bonham Carter (or Baroness Asquith as she probably was by then). To this day, I still cringe at the memory of opening the door for her from inside my car. I should have been on the outside, holding it open for her, aged eighty something, frail and not a little grand. Terrible and enduring are the punishments for getting these things wrong.

Men giving up their seats for women

The second key aspect of what one has to call 'gender-related manners' is what happens when a man offers his seat to a woman on a bus or train, and these days doesn't know whether the offer is going to be spurned.

Giving up one's seat may be written in the traditional code of conduct, but I think without doubt that any such automatic gestures have been much less in evidence over the past, say, twenty years. I must admit to having altered my own behaviour on this point. An element of calculation has entered in to the gesture, for me and for many other men. I ask myself, is she old, is she pregnant, is she going to throw the offer back in my face?

But whereas holding open a door for a woman is no more than a nice thing to do, giving up one's seat may involve other, more practical considerations, as any woman might tell you. A man is not to know, when he is weighing up the probabilities of being snubbed, whether the woman is pregnant or having a period. There is also the argument that if men like seeing women wearing high-heeled shoes, they ought to let women take the weight off their feet at every opportunity.

Men standing up for women entering a room

The third gender-related act to be mentioned is a kind of blend of the first two, as it's just a nice gesture but also has to do with standing up: the business of men standing up when a woman enters a room. These days, I observe a kind of reluctant levitation at such moments. A sort of grudging stance which looks very funny, with men in general only halfway stirring, and like the Grand Old Duke of York's men, neither up nor down.

It is a very pleasant gesture and should be encouraged – and not just when a woman, especially an older woman, comes into a room. It should be done when an older or senior man comes in, too. Hardly any trouble is involved and the gesture can be as natural as a handshake.

(See also 'Assumptions about women' in Chapter 15 WORKING LIFE.)

A walk on the outside

Various reasons have been advanced for the traditional positioning of the man nearest to the edge of the pavement when he is walking along a street with a woman. In olden days he might have protected her from mudsplashes – and might still – or have taken the full force of chamber-pots being emptied from upper storeys, or been able to pull out his sword without cutting her up.

Nowadays, it could be argued that the woman is more vulnerable to beggars and others lurking in shop doorways, if she is on the inside, but the rule holds. It is an agreeable expression of fairly meaningless courtesy. Besides, it has been suggested (by a woman) that women can use the positioning to check how they look reflected in shop windows, should they so wish.

The custom maintains only a tenuous hold on behaviour, however. One wonders if it will go the way of other male protectiveness measures regarding women. It once used to be thought that a man should precede a woman down stairs, so that, if she fell, he could break her fall.

The effects of feminism

There is the story of the staunch feminist who rebuked a courteous male with the words, 'You don't have to hold the door open for me because I'm a lady', to which the man replied, 'I didn't. I held the door open for you because I'm a gentleman.' Then again there is the story of the irrascible broadcasting personality, Gilbert Harding, who, if a woman failed to acknowledge his having opened a door for her, would say, pointedly, 'Thank you madam for allowing me the pleasure of opening the door for you.' But that was in the 1950s, before the rise of modern feminism.

I can't say that I have experienced the feminist

backlash myself in these kinds of situation, though every other man I know seems to have been treated to some woman's rough tongue of late. One man in his fifties told me of an encounter he had at a bus-stop when he stepped aside to let an elderly woman get on first, with a cheery, 'After you, madam'. She launched into a 'suffragette tirade' about equality of the sexes, 'etc.', he recounts.

Nigel Dempster, the gossip columnist, has an excellent put-down which was delivered to him in, of all places, Harrods. Rushing into the store to pick up something before catching a plane, he failed to hold open the door for an elderly woman who proceeded to berate him for his misdemeanour. 'I am not a doorman,' he expostulated. 'No,' she replied, 'but I hoped you were a gentleman.'

So, to what extent can women, should women, expect to be treated in a special way at these possibly trivial moments, if they also want to be treated as the equals of men in more substantial matters?

It is time to grasp the nettle. I say I am sure that my own attitude to giving up my seat to a woman has changed over the past twenty years and it is no coincidence that the women's movement has been active during this time. So, can militant feminism be blamed for any diminution of men's good manners on these points? Some men think it has had a disastrous effect and other men adopt a rather wistful tone when recalling how the old courtesies have waned.

I must say I have always expected to encounter more robust feminine dismissal of these traditional male courtesies. But in most cases, where I have expected to find a hard line being taken, I have been surprised to find almost coy acquiescence. Yet could it be that a decrease in male gallantry represents a reaction on men's part to accepting women as their equal? One could say these polite male gestures date from the days when women had no choice whether men cocooned them with solicitousness. So would it not be natural for the gestures to disappear when women can stand on their own two feet?

Nevertheless, if men are not exactly recoiling from kind gestures being thrown back in their faces, there is, shall we say, a good deal of confusion on their part as to what rules currently should apply in manners between the sexes. But, then again, perhaps men have no real need to worry, because most women are inclined to recognize their dilemma.

Dating

Who pays? Can sex reasonably be expected as a *quid pro quo*? In the PAS survey, a series of questions on manners between the sexes was asked on the subject of dating, and especially about the first date. 72% of all people interviewed agreed that the man *should* pay for the meal on a first date, but were less certain that he should pay for meals on subsequent dates. The figure was 21% for those who would not expect the man to pay.

To the question of whether the man might reasonably expect sex on the first date in return for paying for the meal, a massive 90% of both sexes firmly disagreed with that expectation – though almost 10% of the men in the eighteen to twenty-four age group did appear to think it reasonable.

Some brave souls among the women apparently thought it might be a good idea to insist on paying their share to reduce any sense of obligation. Nevertheless, as one put it, although she didn't expect the man to pay these days, she rather hoped he would . . .

Women paying

There is still an underlying assumption that where a man and a woman are together and a bill has to be paid

– in a restaurant, or anywhere else – the man should do the paying, or should at least organize and oversee the process. What has happened is that it has now become an easy and natural process for any such assumption to be torpedoed by mutual agreement. Of course, a woman can pay for a meal or a taxi if she wants to, the only difficulty occurs in persuading waiters and others to go along with her intention. Such people are still programmed to do things the old way.

(See also 'Sins of waiters' in Chapter 2 EATING OUT.)

Lonely-hearts columns

Finding one's intended has not become any easier with the general loosening up of sexual morality over the past few decades, not least because it has little to do with sexual morality. People still have to overcome shyness, still have to have opportunities to meet suitable partners, still have to deal with the embarrassment of making proposals and being rejected.

Hence the growth in dating agencies and the popularity of lonely-hearts advertisements. It is hard to say how successful dating agencies are – but they seem to stay in business and undoubtedly produce some results, and they should not be rejected for any snobbish reasons.

Lonely-hearts advertisements are popular (at least among people who read them for entertainment), even though the number of male respondents to advertisements from females far outweighs the other kinds. There are obvious risks in all this and the advertiser should take care to retain anonymity, even name, address and telephone number, until he/she finds how things are going. Any trial dates should be on neutral territory. There will be many disappointments in this kind of rather contrived mating, but there will, too, be undoubted successes.

Match-making

Attempts by the already-married to dupe others into their condition should not be encouraged. To try to get others hitched is an unfortunate pastime of a certain type of (usually) woman. There is nothing wrong with lighting a blue touchpaper and retiring to a discreet distance to see the firework ignite (or fizzle out), but match-making of any less subtle kind is not good manners and is almost bound to fail, anyway. People will not be mated; they like to mate themselves.

On the other hand, a third party can play an important role in the igniting of a flame. In a way reminiscent of a certain type of diplomacy, if A tells B that C is interested in B (even if this is not the case), and if A then tells C that B is interested in C, there is a terrible inevitability about the fact that B and C will suddenly discover a mutual passion. (See also 'Unmarried lovers room-sharing' in Chapter 3 FAMILY LIFE.)

Terms for lovers

When a couple are not married, there is sometimes a certain amount of thrashing about for a name to describe the two people concerned. 'My partner' seems to be emerging as a sort of winner in these stakes, closely followed by 'the person I live with'. Other less likeable suggestions include 'cohabitee', 'committed partner', 'life partner', 'constant companion', 'householdmate', 'live-in boyfriend/girlfriend', and the old 'common-law wife', but most these terms sound too much like sociological categorizations.

Jokey nonce terms – like 'virtual spouse', 'bosom companion', 'LASER' (for 'Loving And StablE Relationship' and 'POSSLQ' (for 'Person of the Opposite Sex Sharing Living Quarters') – are best left where they came from. Loud trumpetings of 'my lover' won't go down well with everyone and smack of wearing it on your sleeve.

In more formal circles, the question can cause a certain amount of heart-searching because these days it is simply not on to slap 'Mr and Mrs' on people when they aren't. There is a delightful story told of Frank Giles, a former editor of the *Sunday Times,* whose wife, being the daughter of an Earl, should correctly have been addressed as Lady Katharine Giles. When an invitation arrived from the British Ambassador in Rome addressed to 'Mr and Mrs Frank Giles', the journalist pointed out, deferentially, that, 'Well, actually, I'm afraid she's not strictly speaking "Mrs Giles" . . .'

'Oh, never mind,' he was told by an Embassy official, 'nobody bothers about that sort of thing these days. Bring her along anyway.'

I think the point should be that it is quite in order to indicate that there is something more than acquaintance-ship between a man and a woman, or indeed between two members of the same sex. But anything which begins to identify precisely what they get up to in the bedroom – 'My lover', 'My bed-mate' – is being forward to an unwelcome degree.

Curiously, as early as the 1930s a pleasing solution was apparently to hand in, I think, the Roosevelt White House. If someone was being invited to stay or to attend some social occasion, the partner was referred to as 'the person you travel with'.

Walkers

I suppose they have always existed but it was when people started referring to them as 'walkers' that they become a recognizable species – and, indeed, welcomed as a laudable institution. Walkers are (usually) men who act as companions at social events to women who are divorced, widowed, single, or who may, for some reason, be unaccompanied by their husbands.

The walker tends to be a safe, middle-aged figure – though it is unkind to assume that he is homosexual. It is quite wrong for hostesses to start tinkering with this purely social relationship and to hint that it might develop in another way – or, indeed, to start engineering such a development. Such attempts are doomed to failure. Walkers are walkers because they are safe, reliable, convenient, and no threat whatsoever.

Making passes

I am assuming here that passes (sexual advances) can be made male-female, female-male, and between members of the same sex. If you welcome the pass, then there's nothing more to be said. But on the whole, the issue is raised when people object to proposition making.

Depending on the nature of the pass, the most humiliating response is to ignore it. Simply not noticing will almost certainly lead to a second attempt. If you can show that you are *consciously* ignoring the pass, then so much the better.

If the pass is gross and unmissable, you can try and say something like, 'I hope you didn't *mean* that, did you?' But even that might give the person who is pressing unwanted attentions, the opportunity to insert a foot in the door, so to speak. You want to avoid the possibility of anyone invading your space. Once people are in the space, it may be impossible to get rid of them.

Flirting

This has acquired a bad name, but is good fun and perfectly agreeable if it is seen by both parties as a substitute for actual sexual behaviour and not to be acted upon literally. The matter is put into excellent context by the Rev. Sydney Smith who wondered, 'How

can a bishop marry? How can he flirt? The most he can
say is: "I will see you in the vestry after the service".'
For the most part, flirting is like shadow-boxing, and
about as harmless. This is not to confuse it with sexual
harassment.

(See Chapter 15 WORKING LIFE.)

Sexual manners

Since the arrival of AIDS, casual sex is just not what it
was and yet one hears people claiming that it has not
made any difference to the way they carry on. 'Good
manners' is the mildest way of describing precautionary
measures that might mean the difference between life
and death. AIDS can be an enforcer of morality by
default, if you like, just as, even if by default, through
the use of condoms, it can lead to the avoidance of
unwanted pregnancies.

Yet whenever I have raised the question of sexual
manners with people, I have been greeted with inevitable
giggles. This surprises me, because there has been a
significant change in the openness with which sexual
matters can be discussed – with the important qualifica-
tion that this change is by no means universal.

Coming as I do from a generation which suffered all
the hideous embarrassment about buying contraceptives
over the counter from obstructive chemists, I can still
only marvel at the way people now talk quite merrily
about condoms and related matters on every occasion.

There is generally very little willingness to concede
that manners are important in the bedroom or to grasp
that raising the subject of sexual diseases is a fundamental courtesy to a potential partner. But surely they
do, and it does, on every front, from personal hygiene to
being sensitive to the sexual feelings of one's partner, to
even more fundamental matters.

Raising the question of sexual diseases with a new

partner and what to do in the precautionary line may be considered a great turn-off. But it has to be addressed somehow. It may be considered good manners in a heterosexual partnership for the man to take care of the mackintoshes, overcoats, johnnies or whatever people like to call them. For the woman to be dishing them out and saying things like, 'Oh, I have to say this to all my lovers . . .' may not have quite the reassuring effect intended.

Indeed, one wonders just how capable people are these days of dealing with such tricky matters. If, as we are told, men are in a state of terminal dither on basically frivolous matters like whether to open doors or to stand up for women, one wonders whether they are really going to be capable of mustering the wherewithal to cope sensitively with what has become a matter of life and death.

Coming out with it. A person's sexual orientation is his or her own business, unless the person wishes to make it known. Therefore, to ask someone straight out, 'Are you gay?' is not good manners. In such cases, one is tempted to revamp a celebrated reply by Gore Vidal, and say, 'I don't know. I've always been too polite to ask.'

Clothing. (See 'Sexual dressing' and 'Sexual display in public' in Chapter 7 PUBLIC BEHAVIOUR.)

Manners in bed. This book is not a sex manual, so let it just be said that manners do apply in sex. For example, it would be ill-mannered to expect partners to indulge in any sexual practice they did not wish to indulge in or to adopt any position you are not willing to adopt yourself. This is not to minimize the difficulty of understanding when a 'no' is supposed to mean 'yes', but most people are quite capable of reaching the right conclusion, even in the heat of the moment.

It is obviously unfortunate if one of the partners lets

slip that he or she is thinking of someone else, though preventing this from happening, if it is going to, is probably impossible.

Afterwards, even among the most intimate, it is simply not done to reveal and discuss the sexual proclivities and performance of previous partners. To reveal such matters in a derogatory or even a complimentary way to a third party is to destroy the essence of intimacy.

One-night stands and thank-yous. It is probably true to say that the participants *know* when they have taken part in a one-night stand, even if one or both of them would like to leave the option open about seeing the other again. There once was a sort of rule that the man would contact the woman the following day, by phone or with flowers, to say thank-you or just to acknowledge that something had taken place. It may lessen any let-down if intimacy is followed by some touch of kindness, though I suspect in today's climate that a one-night stand rarely extends to such graciousness.

If the relationship is going to take a step further forward, then some such gesture would seem to be mandatory after a 'first time'.

Friends of lovers. Friends are good to have if you are having an affair. They provide a sounding board or reference point for your feelings, but they should never be misused. They should not be asked to tell lies on your behalf, to cover up your relationship and keep it from people at your place of work, for example. Friendship does not have to extend to that. Friends may choose not to give things away, but nothing more should be expected of them.

Rejection. The rejection of a suitor or the ending of an affair is one of the most difficult manoeuvres to accomplish without hurting the other person's feelings. It can scar people for life and, whatever they may have done to disappoint you, that is not a condition you should inflict upon anybody. A good-humoured suggestion that, 'I do not think that we are right for each other' is many times better than a curt dismissal or brush-off. A 'Dear John' letter may be a less awkward method for the sender than a face-to-face rejection, but even one of those should be followed by a phone call, however final the sender may have want to make the letter, and however reluctant the sender may be to allow the matter to end in mutual recriminations. The manners of rejection amount to not causing pain, though causing sorrow is unavoidable.

Chapter 9

$\mathcal{S}$ERVICE AND THE CUSTOMER

The interface, as some would call it, though battlefield might be a better word, where customers meet what are known as service providers and especially shop assistants, is one of the most fraught areas of modern manners – possibly only exceeded in aggravation by what happens when ordinary people come up against officialdom.

The shop assistant who is more interested in finishing a conversation with a colleague than in serving you and the bank clerk who continues talking with a colleague even while serving you, or who visibly messes about while the queue of people waiting for attention grows ever longer, are prime examples of the kind of behaviour that makes customers boil.

Can customers get their own back in situations like this? Regarding the problem of shop assistants who stand chatting while the customer waits to be served, a correspondent has what she calls 'a very satisfying solution . . . I see how many items I can pick up from the shelves and *replace in the wrong position* before the staff realize what I am doing. Then they are very quick to ask what I want . . .'

There are occasions when this kind of consumer terrorism seems justified.

Not before time, shop assistants and other front-line troops as they are often called (note the continuing battlefield imagery) are now, in many cases, being put through training courses with the express purpose of having their manners brushed up. It usually shows, initially at least. The customer can usually tell from the surprisingly warm 'Hello', the eye contact and even the gentle touch of the flesh, that someone has been put through the sheep dip of 'customer care'.

Large firms and organizations are bringing in what are called 'customer care consultants' or 'courtesy consultants' because – or so they say – they realize there is a quantifiable benefit in treating customers properly. If all other things are equal in terms of price and quality of product, noticeably better service can possibly gain them the edge over their competitors.

Usually the training takes place on two-day courses during which an attempt is made to show the employees who deal direct with the public how they might improve their manners and their communications skills. But as many customers as are impressed are turned off by it when they are subjected to the 'have a nice day' experience.

The other side of the coin is the behaviour of customers towards the very same shop assistants and service providers. How to deal with an irate complainant takes as much skill and as many training courses as an employer can provide. As yet no one has instituted manners training for customers and complainers.

(See also Chapter 14 TRAVEL AND TIPPING and Chapter 15 WORKING LIFE.)

The rise of consumerism

The current emphasis on customer care is an inevitable response to the demands of consumerism that have been steadily with us now in Britain since the 1960s. My view is that the consumer backlash we have witnesssed is not quite the shining crusade that its proponents would like to think it is. There is a good deal of red tape that has been introduced in the name of the consumer which we could well do without, and there is a good deal of whingeing, unjustified complaint-making, and rather too much trying-it-on by customers. Just because mechanisms and procedures for complaint have been established, consumers they think they ought to use them. This has resulted in manufacturers and service providers adopting defensive postures that do not always become them.

Equally, the committed consumer is not always placed in a better position because of the safeguards and procedures that have been instituted as as a result of the consumer uprising. It now often requires even more energy and persistence to make a point when a manufacturer or service provider has installed stonewalling procedures, especially if it has all been done in the guise of 'customer care'.

Is 'customer care' training necessary?

Actual persuasion hardly comes into selling these days. Shop assistants in supermarkets, for example, largely only facilitate a customer's transaction. And, surely, if you are selling something, it is commonsense to be pleasant to the person you're selling to. But apparently a lot of shop assistants have never grasped this fundamental point. What a strange thing it is, in consequence, that they have to be taught to behave like human beings.

Yet, does the solution to the problem have to take the form of a freeze-dried ritual, from which all spontaneity and genuine personal warmth has been removed? Some trainers would argue that a 'script' of precise words to say is necessary in order to prevent things going wrong and because most people have difficulty stringing two words together anyway. Some managments fear that if their sales staff are given free rein to be warm and friendly, they could lose control over them.

Why is 'customer care' training not enough?

The horrific nature of the 'charm schools' run by 'customer care consultants' comes partly from their blatant efforts to stick a smile on anything that moves. After all, it is only a short slip of the tongue from 'junk civility' to what can often seem like 'junk servility'. Training sessions for the tip of the retail iceberg that shows are not enough if their influence does not extend back through the organization and is not reflected in all the organization's activities, at all levels. Sprinkling 'Disney dust' on the front-line troops, as one expert puts it, is valueless if it means that it only cultivates a civility that is less than skin deep, a mere surface politeness.

But one should spare a thought for the poor shop assistants, the check-out persons and service providers, upon whom the 'Disney dust' is sprinkled. They may or may not like, and may or may not carry off with aplomb, the strange rituals they are given to perform. And one can't help thinking that they would find it much easier to be better mannered towards customers if they weren't rushed off their feet, the victims of low staffing levels, and if they did not have to endure all the other pressures that afflict anyone in business when times are hard.

'A haven of quiet quality where the staff's desire to please is both genuine and absolute, and not the product of a two-day course at a corporate charm school.'

Leeds hotel brochure (1992)

Complaints

As you may imagine, there is also training available for those unfortunate people who have to earn their living by dealing with customer complaints over the phone. There is quite an art in reassuring an irate customer without resorting to bad manners. The worst thing is for the person whose job it is to field complaints to lose control. The person should use all the techniques available to reassure the complainant, speaking firmly but kindly to convince the caller (however difficult) that the complaint will be pursued, the matter will be taken up with the right person, and a response will be forthcoming just as soon as possible.

As for the complainers: it will clearly be counter-productive if they lose their cool and start blaming the employee personally for all the ills they have experienced. They should not be personal, if they can avoid it.

It is the case, unfortunately, that certain large companies and organizations have 'customer relations' departments whose chief aim is to fob off complaints. Worse, they do this by pretending to be 'caring', even to the extent of naming the person to whom complaints should be addressed. It then transpires that the named person does not exist and never has done.

If you are complaining, it is important to be level-headed and calm, as well as tenacious. Whoever fields your call will be putting out feelers to ascertain whether you have a genuine complaint and how much determination you really have to get something done about it. A display of reluctance and disbelief on their part may be part of a calculated plan to screen your complaint, if not to try to dispose of it. Depending on the complainer's skills and determination in combatting this defensive posture (or, indeed, the lack of any posture at all, which can be just as disabling), you may fight your way through to a more senior person, even up to the manager or chairman, if you are adept enough at persuading your way past their secretaries.

However successful you are – and you may need considerable reserves of will-power to make any progress at all – you should make sure you keep a note of the progress of your complaint. Write down dates and times of phone calls, keep copies of correspondence and, especially when dealing with faceless minions over the phone, always try to find out their names (if they will divulge them) and acquire a reference number for your complaint (if they operate such a system.) This might just save you having to relate the details of your complaint over and over again to a different person every time you call to chase it up.

Apologizing

Oddly enough, in the light of the foregoing, I believe there is too much of it. Elsewhere in this book (in Chapter 16 WRITTEN COMMUNICATION), I advance the view that it is impossible to say 'thank you' too much. Here, I would just like to say that this does not apply to apologizing. Of course, I do not mean that a heart-felt, genuine apology is ever out of place, though the effectiveness of such an act of contrition is lessened if you go on about it too long. Nowhere is this more the case than in customer relations.

What I really mean is that these days there is too much *synthetic* apologizing. Everybody apologizes for everything and, even if they mean it, it is not the right way to make amends. The past masters of this are public transport bodies, and especially British Rail. Presumably, somewhere in that organization, there is a Head of Apologies, with a huge staff of Deputy Apologizers and Assistant Apologizers (Acting) under him. It has to be said, though, that sometimes BR's apologies are touched with a surrealist genius, especially when they are dressed up as something else – a benefit, for example, as in this perfectly genuine apology from an Inter-City steward: 'For the benefit (*sic*) of passengers, only cold meat and salad will be on the menu for dinner tonight. This is due to the buffet car being the wrong way round.' Normally, however, the standard apology goes something like: 'British Rail apologizes for the late running of this train and for any inconvenience that may have been caused' – never mind the pain of having to listen to that kind of wordage being routinely trotted out.

Incidentally, when giving apologies it seems important never to be too explicit as to the cause of whatever has gone wrong. If trains arrive late it is 'because of late departure' (but no apology for that); at airports, planes are late taking off 'because of the late arrival of the incoming plane'. Or, in other words, things happen – or, rather, don't happen – 'for operational reasons'.

The thing about all apologies is that they should not be necessary in the first place. Therefore, the best form of apology is to correct the basic failure and to make sure it does not happen again. What one wants from British Rail is not copious apologies; simply, what one wants, is for the trains to run on time.

Making amends

An apology is, however, the minimum anyone should expect after being given poor service or having being inconvenienced by a service provider. But even if an apology is forthcoming, it will have no effect if it is grudgingly given, if it has to be extracted, and if customers are so furious at what they have been put through that the memory of it cannot be erased.

This raises the question of whether any other kind of soothing balm can be applied. If aircraft are unduly delayed, it is fairly standard procedure for free drinks to be announced (even if they would have been forthcoming anyway.) Apart from any legal obligation there might be to compensate for inconveniences of this kind, making such a provision counts as a worthwhile gesture. And a gesture is often all that is needed.

A voucher or a small gift, even a simple letter (however pro forma it may be) can do wonders towards assuaging anger and frustration. It is, again, the gesture that counts – even if the complainant may turn round and say, 'I don't want a bloody widget, I want my bloody holiday back!'

Any failure to apologize or make a gesture can produce a reaction that may well be out of all proportion to the actual offence. Twenty years ago I stayed in a hotel in Amsterdam that was part of a well-known international chain. Having accepted my luggage for safe-keeping during my final day there, the porters managed to lose it among the many bags of a Japanese tour party. When it was eventually found – by which time I was chewing the carpet and about to catch my plane home, luggage-less – there was no hint of apology forthcoming. No offer (as I fondly imagined) of a free night's stay somewhere else in the chain, not even a spot of ritual grovelling. Could it have been because to apologize would have been to admit some liability? I don't know – but I have avoided those hotels ever since. I expect my gesture has gone unnoticed, but it is the only one I could have made.

Other sins of sales people

There is not a great deal to be done about sales people who hover over you and won't let you browse in peace. You could end up buying something just to get them off your back, and that is probably what they are banking on. 'Just browsing' will help you buy a little more time to yourself. Otherwise, you will probably find yourself having to go elsewhere.

There is an increasing forwardness among sales people, just as there is among waiters. One even notices it among people as staid as guides at National Trust properties. They feel they have to buttonhole you and engage your interest. They should politely but firmly be put in their place.

Telephone selling

There are two types of telephone selling, both of them on the increase. One is where you are phoned, probably at home, and an attempt is made to sell you some product or service because the vendor has identified you from a mailing list or other source, or because you have previously bought the product or service and need reminding of its availability and excellence.

The other type, known as 'cold calling' is when the seller simply works through a list of telephone numbers, hoping to sell you something simply on the basis that (a) you own a telephone and (b) you answer it when it rings.

This kind of selling must be a miserable way to earn a living, but unfortunately it appears to work, or it would not be persisted with, and so it will continue. Most sales people have been put through a training programme and/or work closely to a script. It is very insidious. As with uninvited door-to-door callers (see Chapter 6 NEIGHBOURLINESS), it is often difficult at first to disentangle from the blah of words precisely what you are being offered. But, unless you are desperate for companionship and actually want to chat to telephone sales persons, the best thing is to cut off the chat in its tracks, just as soon as you twig what it going on. Say, 'No, I have all the life insurance, pensions advice, gardening products I need – and please do not ring me again.'

Alternatively, try to persuade the caller to put his pitch in writing. Junk mail, however annoying, is easier to deal with and dispose of than a phone call.

If you are faced with a persistent business caller, it will become easier to identify what is happening. In which case, it may be worth asking the caller to make a

note on his call sheet that you should not be called
again. It might just sink in. Apart from this, there is no
way to get yourself taken off telephone sales lists as
there is from mailing lists.

A comparable annoyance to members of the public is
what market researchers and opinion pollsters refer to
as *sugging*. You are walking down the street when you
are approached by someone carrying a clipboard or,
alternatively, such a person knocks on your door. They
ask whether you would mind answering a few questions
and it is only when they are getting towards the end of
their list that you realize they are in fact trying to *sell*
you something and couldn't give a damn for your
opinions. This is selling under the guise of research
(hence, sugging) and is extremely annoying. The only
way to avoid it is to ask the 'pollster' right away, 'Are
you trying to sell me something?' If they have not begun
by showing you some sort of identity card, the chances
are the answer will be yes.

Debts

How do you get money out of people who owe it to you,
or ensure that a payment or repayment is made promptly? Short of sending round the heavy mob, there are
only one or two ways of bringing this about that can
justifiably be included in a book on manners. I am not
sure that this is one of them: I was once owed some
money for some articles I had written for a new
magazine and had reasonable fears that the publication
might fold before I had received my due. Calls to the
editor – when they were not fielded by another member
of his staff – failed to produce any result. Unfortunately
for him, he had, at a more euphoric moment in our
relationship, given me his home telephone number. So I
took to ringing him up at mealtimes, rather late in the
evening (though not in the middle of the night), and at

weekends, and made my interest in payment known in a civilized and patient manner. And, lo, quite soon into this process, one morning the editor arrived in person at my front door, bearing the much sought-after cheque.

Of course, that kind of sustained campaign takes a lot of energy and application, but it is curiously rewarding. It is the modern equivalent of hunting, I suppose – there is almost as much pleasure in the chase as in the final resolution of the problem.

The important thing to remember when pursuing moneys due is to establish at a fairly early stage in the game a specific person, whose name you know, at whom you can aim the drip, drip, drip of your attack. You are unlikely to get anywhere simply dealing with an anonymous voice in 'Accounts'.

The trouble is, though, that in time the chase can come to be *more* important to you than the payment of the debt. This is probably the point at which to adduce the only useful piece of advice I have ever been given by a multi-millionaire. He told me, 'Know when to cut your losses'. Pursuing a debt may be important to you for all the wrong reasons; money in itself doesn't matter; try to sense the moment when it is sensible to give up, to forget, and to move on to the next thing.

The basic principles, though, of firmness and persistence can be applied on the broader front to businesses or officialdom from which a reply to a request of any kind is not forthcoming. Proceed coolly, politely, firmly and regularly. Send copies of earlier letters and invoices each time you write – this, if nothing else, will demonstrate to your target that you are organized and unlikely to abandon your pursuit easily.

Dealing with the police

An awkward question of dealing with officialdom arises with the police. There is no denying that the police have an immensely difficult and obviously very risky job, which no one envies. However, it also has to be said that, as people to deal with, the police are unpredictable. They can be immensely helpful and supportive if you are the victim of a crime, or if they need your cooperation. But they can be most unhelpful and positively bloody-minded if they don't want your help.

Of course, there are still bobbies of the old school to be found. Some others also have charm and capability of an admirable kind. However, many of the police go around calling everybody (and not just criminals) 'chummy' and saying things like, "Ere, mate, you're nicked!' (I have been present when both these have been uttered). Again, treading cautiously, I have to report that there is something about many policemen that is suspicious, patronizing, overbearing, supercilious and really rather unpleasant to have to deal with.

But how *do* you deal with this? The first thing is not to attract their attention in the first place, of course. The next thing is to realize that you can never get the upper hand with them and should not even try. The best thing is to bite your tongue, take whatever they throw at you lying down, and don't exacerbate the situation. Anecdotal evidence suggests that any attempt to be clever at their expense, to point out their failings (or your rights), to prevent them from being their natural patronizing, overbearing, etc. etc., selves will only end in tears (your tears).

So let them go through their little routines without saying anything. Rub them up the wrong way and you'll regret it. However hard it grates, just keep quiet. But when they do ask you to speak, answer them politely. Irony is lost on them, or rather it grates on them.

If you have read books on body language, office politics, and the like, you might feel inclined to do things such as getting out of your car, when stopped by the police, so that you are not in an inferior position with regard to them. To stand up and attempt to achieve equality of height with someone who may be about to ask you questions is understandable but it may easily be misinterpreted. Even though it is only in places like the United States where a sudden movement could make a policeman think you were about to pull a gun on him, and make him take drastic action to disable you, there is the same readiness to be suspicious here and the same tendency to overreact. So, be docile in your movements as well as in your manners.

Having written this, I realize that it is very close to the advice given to people likely to fall victim to aircraft hijacks: don't risk any heroics, keep a low profile, maintain a polite rapport, never respond to verbal abuse. Well, you know it makes sense.

At the hairdresser

If one was to devise one of those informal laws of everyday life, one would be, 'The second time you go to a new hairdresser, it won't make you so happy'. Don't ask me why, but the shock of the new is often gratifying and seldom repeatable. It is then up to you to campaign vigorously and continuously to make sure your hair is cut the way you want it rather than the way the hairdresser does.

And the second law of hairdressing is that hairdressers always cut off more than you want. It is strange that hairdressers fail to realize that the less they cut off, the more often you will have to go to them, but this simple lesson of economics does not appear to have occurred to them.

Inanimate bank clerks

It says a lot about a lot of things, especially about the level of personal service in banks, that many people prefer to queue up to get their cash from an impersonal 'hole in the wall' dispensing machine than get it from a human cashier with (possibly) less queuing involved.

But there it is. When using cash dispensers, it is a relief if the person operating the machine does not have the next in line breathing down his or her neck. Otherwise the user will feel vulnerable, and may suspect that the person behind is taking in personal information. Even inanimate service involves manners.

Chapter 10

$\mathcal{S}$OCIAL LIFE

According to the dictionary, 'to socialize' means 'to act in a sociable manner'. Sociable manners are what this chapter is about.

(See also 'Embarrassments' in Chapter 3 FAMILY LIFE.)

Shaking hands

Everybody knows that men used to shake hands using their right hands to demonstrate that they were unarmed and, in particular, not carrying a sword. Now shaking hands has become the universal gesture of greeting, far more popular than kissing, bowing, or rubbing noses like the Eskimos or Maoris.

And a good thing, too. I love shaking hands with everyone, even when it is completely uncalled for and even when not even the semblance of a deal is being struck (the handshake being, of course, the traditional way of sealing an agreement).

I suppose there are some who might say there is too much of it. And there are some people who seem to like to use the handshake as their way of demonstrating to you what bone-crushing strength of character they have. Some men seem to view the handshake as an extension of their virility, which is unfortunate. It is sensible, anyway, not to bone-crush a woman's hand – decorated rings will cause pain to both donor and recipient. Apart from which, let the handshake continue. Gloves should usually be removed first.

'Have you noticed how people shake your hand?
There is the *high-official* – the body erect, and a
rapid, short shake, near the chin. There is the
mortmain – the flat hand introduced into your palm,
and hardly conscious of its contiguity. The *digital* –
one finger held out, much used by the high clergy.
There is the *shakus rusticus*, where your hand is
seized in an iron grasp, betokening rude health,
warm heart, and distance from the Metropolis; but
producing a strong sense of relief on your part
when you find your hand released and your finger
unbroken. The next to this is the *retentive shake* –
one which, beginning with vigour, pauses as it were
to take breath, but without relinquishing its prey,
and before you are aware begins again, till you feel
anxious as to the result, and have no shake left in
you. Worst, there is the *pisces* – the damp palm like
a dead fish, equally silent, equally clammy, and
leaving its odour in your hand.'

The Rev. Sydney Smith, in 1820

'You need not stop to pull off your glove to shake
hands with a lady or gentleman. If it is warm
weather it is more agreeable to both parties that the
glove should be on – especially if it is a lady with
whom you shake hands, as the perspiration of your
bare hand would be very likely to soil her glove.'
   **Arthur Martine, *Hand-book of Etiquette and Guide to True
   Politeness* (New York, 1866)**

Sometimes you find yourself extending a right hand to
someone who is unable to shake it. Maybe this is
because they are holding something in that hand, or the
right arm is in a sling, or they have some disability. The
thing to remember is that it is only a gesture – so just a
touch is as meaningful as a grasp. Also, a light grasp of
the left hand, if appropriate, is just as pleasant – and

even rather refreshing. In any case, you don't have to believe in Masonry and secret societies to shake hands using the left hand.

Endearments

It is unfortunately the case that endearments have fallen foul of the law as far as the Sexism Police are concerned. What in essence are mere sentence-fillers like 'love', 'dear' and 'darling' are amiable little terms capable of being used by either sex about the other. Alas, too often, 'dear' in particular has been used by men with a patronizing tone of voice and 'darling' by both sexes in the context of a reprimand whose hard edge it is sought to soften. No one would seriously suggest that such endearments ought to be banned but neither should they be overused automatically and unthinkingly.

Meaningless courtesies

As has been said, 'How are you?' is as much a meaningless gesture as is – often – the statement, 'We must have lunch some time.' The English have a peculiar penchant for these little sayings that are merely supposed to oil the wheels of social intercourse and not to be taken literally. 'How lovely to see you!' is another expression which, if taken literally, could leave the addressee into all sorts of difficulties.

The meaningless courtesy can be seen as insincere. Or it can be seen as a coded form of speaking, designed to exclude (if not just hoodwink) the outsider. Why do the English often say the opposite of what they mean – and expect their hearers to grasp what they are up to? Well, it might also have something to do with wanting to be kind, to maintain the smooth tenor of existence.

Compliments

It is a failing of the English, especially, that they are not good at receiving compliments. They are embarrassed by them, blush and look away. But this should not prevent anyone from making compliments. The simplest way of accepting a compliment is to say, 'Thank you', and smile.

Sometimes people are reluctant to pay compliments to famous people they recognize in the street. Americans, on the other hand, have a curious way of dealing with celebrity. Either they make little whooping noises of recognition (like a chat-show audience) or they *applaud*, rather as the British usually do with Royalty. A reluctance to pester famous people is to be encouraged but I remember how someone once told me how she had encountered a well-known actor on the London Underground. It took a bit of doing, but she said to him, 'I've always admired your work – thank you for all the pleasure you have given me,' and did not linger, which I think was splendid.

'I don't mean to be rude, Miss Woodhouse, but you are looking very pretty this evening.'
Jane Austen, *Emma* **(1816)**

'*Lord Darlington:* Ah, nowadays we are all of us so hard up, that the only pleasant things to pay *are* compliments. They're the only things we can pay. *Lady Windermere:* I don't like compliments, and I don't see why a man should think he is pleasing a woman enormously when he says to her a whole heap of things that he doesn't mean.'
Oscar Wilde, *Lady Windermere's Fan* **(1892)**

Different cultures make compliments about different things and in different ways. The humorist Frank Muir once wrote to *The Times* about an incident that had occurred to him in Piccadilly, London. A small woman of

South-east Asian appearance had told him admiringly that he was wearing the most beautiful trousers she had ever seen – and then proceeded to pinch him on the left buttock. 'In my country,' she explained to the sceptical Mr Muir, 'we always give a pinch when we give praise.'

It used to be thought incorrect to compliment a woman on getting engaged to be married (see Chapter 5 MARRIAGE AND DIVORCE). It was thought that this might be construed as congratulating her on having ensnared her man. Similarly, do you compliment a woman on getting pregnant – or could this be construed in some dark way? I do not think there should be hesitation in either case these days.

Compliments that go over the top should also be accepted without demur – 'The most beautiful woman in the world' 'Oh, that is my favourite girl's name'. It may be gross flattery, it may be slippery and opaque. Accept it, however. As with presents that you don't like, it is the thought that counts. And if it cheers you up momentarily, why not enjoy it?

Engineered compliments. For years I have been intrigued by those little puffs you find on the covers of novels, especially American ones, in which a Well-Known Person writes something flattering about the contents – 'This is the book that I would like to have written' – Jeffrey Archer; 'Another little gem' – Graham Greene.

These are not extracts from reviews but are endorsements solicited by the publishers through the method of sending an advance copy to the Well-Known Person who, so they hope, will look upon the work favourably. If he or she does not, then presumably whatever he or she comes up with will not find its way on to the book's dust jacket or into advertisements. But it is an pernicious process and, surely, of questionable value in attracting purchasers. I suspect that most book-buyers on seeing Frederick Forsyth endorsing Jilly

Cooper, or whatever the combination is, will merely assume that they are all part of the network and pay no attention.

So what do Well-Known Persons do – particularly if the author is known personally to them? They could try writing something equivocal along the lines of Disraeli's 'I shall lose no time in reading it'. They won't be able to get away with Groucho Marx's blurb for an S.J. Perelman book: 'From the moment I picked up your book until I laid it down, I was convulsed with laughter. Some day I intend reading it.' They could say, 'Now this is what I call a book!' or 'I have never read a book like this before!' or 'I shall always treasure this book'. Or come up with something unusable: 'Reminds me of Hieronymous Bosch at his peak . . .' But it would be best, on balance, if they politely declined the invitation and said they have always made it a rule not to.

Clearly this is not a dilemma that many people will face, but it raises the question of the solicited compliment which you are more likely to encounter when asked to give references (See 'Giving references' in Chapter 15 WORKING LIFE.)

After the show

If you meet a performer after the show, it is quite all right to come out with a cliché like, 'Darling, you were marvellous!' – even if darling wasn't. So much has been made of this potential embarrassment that it is now virtually impossible to say anything backstage after a show without actors wondering if you are having them on. But there is sense in not committing yourself *too* deeply in praise of a performance you have just witnessed.

Among the equivocal remarks that have been devised to get over the difficulty are:

'You old rogue!'
'You've done it again!'
'Well, how about *you* then?'
'Beautifully *placed* performance, laddie, *beautifully* placed!'
'Well *found*, old boy! Well found . . . '
'What a performance!'
'It was so *you!*'
and – 'What can I say . . . ?'

More barbed, and thus to be avoided, are these from people within the profession: Ernest Thesiger's '*You* couldn't have been better!' and Richard Maney's 'Well, nobody got hurt'; Max Beerbohm's or W.S. Gilbert's 'My dear girl, *good* is not the word!' and Beatrice Lillie's, 'Darling, I don't care what *anybody* says – I thought you were marvellous!'

I myself was treated to a cleverly ambiguous compliment once when I had been showing the TV programme I had made with one producer to another such. As the final credits rolled, I turned to him and said: 'What do you think?' He replied simply, 'Amazing!'

Name-dropping

A colleague once remonstrated with William Clark, a journalist and later Downing Street press secretary, on the grounds that he was an incorrigible name-dropper. 'Funny you should say that, old boy,' he replied, 'the Queen Mother was saying the same thing only last week.'

It *is* a dreadful habit and difficult to discourage, unless you are capable of showing the name-dropper either that you have absolutely no idea who the dropped names are or that you are completely indifferent to the fact that the name-dropper knows them.

False modesty

Or, rather, unnecessary modesty. Let me take myself as an example. I sometimes find myself, in company, saying 'when I was at college' or 'when I was at university' – this is when I am not trying to deny that I had any further education at all. What I am aiming at, though, is to lessen the repercussions of admitting to 'When I was at Oxford . . .' – simply on the grounds that I expect the company to be overwhelmed by such a revelation. Readers may be able to think of similar reticences in their own life.

Although I am not, obviously, very good at it myself, I think the best thing is not to be embarrassed by any achievement that one may have. It is better to come straight out with whatever it is, because it is bound to emerge in due course, and, by having tried to hold back the information, one is likely to have only made matters worse.

Drug-induced behaviour

It has long been one of my tenets that if there is no obvious explanation for something then it probably has to do with drugs. This is especially so in the case of behaviour. Unlike alcohol, drugs tend not to be the obvious cause of a person's erratic actions and moods. Only the more sophisticated observer will be aware of the tell-tale signs that would confirm this. The use of drugs (for purposes of entertainment, in the widest sense) is intolerable and no one expects even a well-mannered person to pretend otherwise.

How to behave towards people on drugs? Very difficult to say, and advice simply to avoid them may not be helpful. As with drunks (see below), it is pointless to express disapproval, but even more important not to show hostility. Patient, tolerant and kindly behaviour (however difficult to produce) is about all that I can suggest.

Alcohol-induced behaviour

How do you deal with a drunk? Of course, it rather depends where they stand, or stagger, on the scale from the amusingly tipsy to the roaringly embarrassing. A reasonably familiar type is the person who, slightly oiled, comes along and makes spiky, difficult conversation at a drinks party. It may be difficult for you to work out what they are driving at, except that you will sense a general air of hostility. Here, a firm injunction to 'go away' has been known to do the trick. The shock often renders a drunk speechless. Or you can effectively freeze drunks out by excluding them from your conversation with other people and, perhaps, by so angling your body that they get the message.

Indeed, ignoring is usually the best way of dealing with most kinds of drunks, as any attempt to sober them up – with offers of mineral water or whatever – is likely to be perceived, even by drunks, as patronizing, spoil-sport behaviour. Gentle, humorous, even affectionate, guidance towards the exit can be tried, though in some cases this will be resented, too. An offer to arrange transport home may be appreciated. If the drunk resides in your own home, then steering them towards a bedroom (or bathroom) is all that can be advised – with help offered in the removal of clothes, spectacles, and other breakable items about the person. Possibly the worst thing to say to a drunk is that he is drunk. Suggest, rather, that they are 'not feeling very well'.

Above all, as I say, a tone of amused and kindly patience is more likely to get results than a condemnatory or patronizing one.

(See also 'The offer of a drink' in Chapter 6 NEIGHBOURLINESS.)

Irritating behaviour

For whatever reason buried deep in their psyches, some people exhibit irritating mannerisms. When repeated frequently these can be infuriating. The question is, should you and how can you get them to stop? If a person cracks his knuckles or jingles coins nervously in his pocket or clears his throat every few seconds, there really isn't a lot that can be done. To bark, 'Don't do that!' would be to reduce the fellow to the status of a child and could well result in a child-like response. All I can suggest regarding a compulsive coin jingler is to encourage him to spend some of it.

To make a physical gesture against irritating behaviour may also be resented. I once found myself in a theatre watching a very tense murder mystery play only to be distracted by a woman stranger sitting next to me who systematically and manically was *shredding her programme*. Unable to bear it any longer, I gently laid my hand upon hers in a restraining gesture. She almost died with embarrassment, presumably at having exposed her innermost state in this way.

No, other people just shouldn't do these mad things, but all the rest of us can do is to glare and hope that someone may get the message across to them some time.

Smoking

A curious habit of cigarette smokers in social situations is to refrain from offering the packet to others. This is very odd. Could it be that smokers are so ashamed of their habit that they do not wish to draw attention to it? Or is it that they do not wish to encourage others to join them in their terrible affliction?

Whatever the case, people are still going to notice when a person is smoking. It is only polite, even in such a controversial area, for the smoker to offer cigarettes to any companions – cigarettes which may then be politely declined. The smoker ought to be asking permission to light up, anyway – so not to offer the cigarettes is doubly bad-mannered.

(See also 'Smoking in company' in Chapter 6 NEIGHBOURLINESS.)

Television snobbery

It is to be hoped that the disdain for television that was once *de rigueur* no longer exists. 'Oh, we don't have one of *those*', 'We've no time to watch it, anyway', 'Yes, we have one - for the servants' – those were the kinds of things people used to say. The quality of the pro-grammes on offer may or may not have improved, but the chief objection to television – that it is disruptive of home and social life – no longer obtains. The happy proliferation of home video-recorders has meant, for the past decade and more, that no one ever has cause to insist on watching a favourite programme at the time of transmission. It has transformed social life in a way that was once inconceivable. But it is still not right to inflict a TV programme – or, for that matter, a video – on visitors to your home or to other people in it.

However, there are one or two aspects of television of which it is still reasonable to disapprove. The intrusive-ness of the medium as a whole is discussed in Chapter 7 PUBLIC BEHAVIOUR. At a more personal level, there is an expectation by programme-makers that people should kow-tow to their wishes and needs and always co-operate with the medium. But it is a perfectly proper and understandable thing for people to want to protect their privacy. Not everyone thinks that an invitation to appear on television is like a gift from God, or that an intrusion into their privacy is what they have always been waiting for.

Should you ever be in the position where a TV, film or

commercials company wishes to operate in your own home, you should be warned that you are likely to end up saying, 'Never again'. Any amount of money that may be offered will hardly recompense you for the bother involved. If you think the proceedings will somehow bestow glamour upon you, they won't.

As for appearing on television, even if you are a professional, you may well emerge from the experience wondering what has hit you or, at least, feeling slightly scruffy. Few people have big enough personalities (or egos) to exert complete control over the way they are depicted on television or, indeed, in the media generally. It is only something to be entered into with your eyes as wide open as you can get them. Always question why you are really doing it.

Appearing on television manners are, alas, often to be found washing over into the lives of mere viewers. The conversationalist who sells himself as blatantly as any book-plugger on a chat show, the egoist who basks in the spotlight of attention just like any anchorman, the pompous person, the bore – these are all TV types who should, on no account, be taken as role models by anybody seeking to be considered a human being, at least in ordinary life.

Television-watching manners include not insisting on having the set switched on, with or without the sound up, when you have visitors. Turning the sound down when you are talking over the telephone is a basic courtesy, too. The best televisions are those which can be hidden away and which don't dominate the room. Even a blank television screen can be a threat, almost demanding to be switched on.

Punctuality

'The politeness of princes' is what they call it – and one can't help muttering that it is a politeness that must come more easily if you have a prince's equerry, chauffeur and a police escort smoothing the way for you . . .

But when does lack of punctuality and, indeed, over-punctuality become a problem?

'I owe all my success in life to having been always a quarter of an hour before my time.'
Horatio Nelson (quoted in Samuel Smiles, *Self-Help*)

There are certain occasions when lateness is unforgivable. If you fail to arrive at the correct time for a dinner party, it can obviously cause grief to the cook. If a bride arrives late for her wedding – whatever the tradition involved – she can thereby establish a terrible precedent for the rest of her married life. I know of one bride who was *forty-five minutes* late arriving for a church wedding. This merely served to confirm what was a congenital condition. The marriage only survived after a fashion and she went on through life driving her friends suicidal with her lateness and, possibly worse, being the cause of lateness in others.

There is only one thing to be done about unpunctuality: don't set yourself impossible targets. Allow ample time to make journeys, especially in cities and on motorways. You never know what disaster may crop up unexpectedly.

Above all, don't be afraid of arriving early. There is no particular shame in that; just park yourself out of the way and *wait*. Never show up early. It is most unlikely that your host (of whatever type) will be glad to see you ahead of time. Additionally, if you are a punctu-holic and congenitally early, you will drive people to distraction every bit as much as if you are always terribly late.

Passing on the stairs

I can recall what I took to be the first genuine example of someone passing a test of manners with flying colours. In the mid-1950s, on a visit to London, my family was staying at a little place round the back of Harrods. One day the owner clucked that a member of the Royal Family had just departed. Indeed, she had been visiting a portrait painter who had his studio there. 'And,' the owner said to my mother, 'your boy stood to one side as she came down the stairs.' This was my brother, not me. Thank God, he did.

Somewhere along the way, I have heard that people coming downstairs ought to take the bannister side as, should they stumble forward, they need to have something to hold on to. Whereas people mounting the stairs would stumble upward, so to speak, and would have less need to grab at a handrail, if there was only one available. This is probably poppycock, but it does give one a basis on which to assert one's authority if it ever came to a debate on the matter . . .

Slang

'The new slang – you do it ever so well!' is a compliment paid to Eliza Doolittle in George Bernard Shaw's *Pygmalion*. Indeed, slang is a good deal more entertaining than standard speech and, one day, may well transmute into standard speech. But slang does not travel well between social classes (though 'Roller' for Rolls-Royce and the adjective 'brill' seem to crop up almost anywhere) and should be avoided where it can stereotype you or be misunderstood.

Americanisms are rejected by the purist, but I say, if the Americans have a better word for it, then use it. These days I even find myself saying 'movies' instead of 'the pictures' or 'film' or 'cinema'. To insist otherwise is like sticking quaintly to 'wireless' instead of 'radio'.

Stiletto heels

These are another modern dilemma. How do you convey to some fashion plate that she shouldn't carve up your floorboards, shred your carpets, and pit your tiles with her stiletto heels? These high, narrow heels, which have a fearsome pressure per square inch, have been a problem since the 1950s. People should really have no qualms about asking wearers to remove them or to put on a rubber tip. The most entertaining solution, as is to be found in some old Italian villas open to the public, is an overshoe which allows you to skate over polished floors. Entertaining and protective, too. Wearers should be accommodating.

Social kissing

When did social kissing get out of control? I don't mean sexual kissing, but being kissed by mere acquaintances, often on more than one cheek. So rampant is this kind of social kissing, it has almost replaced the handshake as the standard form of introductory gesture. It may be thought to be getting out of hand, especially when people are quite unable to anticipate whether they are being proffered a 'one-cheek jobby', a 'two-cheek jobby' or even a 'three-cheek' one.

Though social kissing is widespread in some circles, it appears not to be so among, shall we say, less sophisticated circles, where kissing someone you barely know, even on one cheek only, is almost unknown. So one has to remember that kissing manners vary from place to place.

I'm all for lots of social kissing, but there's no escaping the fact that it is a ritual that can have about as much style as dodgem-car driving. It *is* possible to indicate to the kissee what sort of buss you are about to implant. Shaking the person by the hand as you go into the clinch enables you to steer yourself first to one cheek and then to another (and even back again) without too much room for confusion. Left, right, and left again seems to be the preferred aiming order.

There are two types of kisser who should not be encouraged, however, even among enthusiasts: social kissers who aim for the lips and women kissers who leave lipstick all over men as a result. If you wish to avoid any sort of kiss that you don't like, the clever thing to do is to put your hands to the sides of the kisser's head and guide the mouth to more appropriate territory – from the lips to the cheek or forehead, for example. This is a delightfully disarming gesture and will never be taken amiss.

There is also the question of the noise some people make when executing that type of social kiss where the lips and cheeks barely touch, if at all. As a substitute for contact, they emit a sort of 'mmmmmwwwuhhhh'. This is entertaining and adds to the gaiety of nations, but is not favoured by all.

'He [President Carter] is the only man since my dear husband died to have had the effrontery to kiss me on the lips.'
Queen Elizabeth the Queen Mother, quoted in 1983

Some enthusiastic kissers also couple their activity with fondling the backbone of the kissee. This is presumptuous of them, more sexual than social, and may lead to reactions that they wot not of.

Kissagrams

As compared to the spread of social kissing, these are probably the worst imports of the 1970s. Kissagrams, gorillagrams, strippagrams, even plain old singing tele-grams, and all embarrassing eruptions into birthday parties and other events are only justifiable to the extent that they keep otherwise unemployable people off the streets. And that is not saying much. As with surprise parties (see Chapter 4 GUESTS AND HOSTS), the only people who seem to enjoy them are the people who arrange them. The 'victims' may be genuinely embarrassed by any sexual by-play.

On one occasion at which I was unfortunately present, the victim was so surprised by the arrival of a bellydancer-gram that he slipped, hurt his back and had to be taken to hospital. And this was supposed to help him *celebrate* his birthday . . .

Bores

To be a bore is to have halitosis of the mind, as someone should probably have said before me. Bores should not be tolerated but it is frightfully difficult to disengage yourself from them once they have, so to speak, earmarked you. You can try boring them back or forcing them to listen to what you have to say, but the chances are you won't get anywhere. But if you are the sort of person who can find redeeming features in almost anyone, then by all means have a go.

The other person may not be *intrinsically* boring – you may simply be marooned with him or her at a party. In such circumstances, it can be very difficult to detach yourself without making it uncomfortably apparent that you would rather be somewhere else. Making an excuse to go and top up your glass, and then not returning, is quite an acceptable method of breaking away. You could quite legitimately have been hi-jacked by someone else.

Even worse are bores who know they are, and who keep asking, 'Am I boring you?' Even if you said yes, and you won't, it wouldn't help. The poet Browning was once cornered by an admirer who kept on at him for a whole evening. Eventually, with considerable grace,

Browning insisted, 'But, my dear fellow, this is too bad. I am monopolizing you'. It might just work for you, with a little adaptation.

(See also *Talking to left and right* in Chapter 4 GUESTS AND HOSTS.)

First-name terms

Whether you call people by their first name is partly down to where you stand amid the generations. My octogenarian aunt very politely lets it be known that, really, she does not think it right that health visitors, service engineers, cleaning ladies, anybody, should call her by her first name – on first meeting, even – without so much as a by-your-leave. I fear she is waging a losing battle.

First names are now everywhere and the media, understandably, set the pace. Perhaps the difficulty is that we lack an in-between form. To insist on being called 'Mr Stiff' or 'Miss Unbending' is too much of a jump. What one needs is a softer form, the sort of thing family servants (yes, servants) used to say: 'Mr Jonathan', 'Miss Amy', that sort of thing.

In radio broadcasting there is a kind of middle way in any case. In order to keep on identifying who is speaking (something that is done with subtitles in television), the presenter will say, 'Now tell me, Oscar Wilde, why did you do such a silly thing?' But this is an artifical convention that doesn't work in real life.

(See also 'First-name terms' in Chapter 3 FAMILY LIFE and Chapter 15 WORKING LIFE, and 'Dear Sir' in Chapter 16 WRITTEN COMMUNICATION.)

'Larryism'. Another irritating use of first names occurs particularly in show business circles and other small worlds. Here the first name is used to denote the whole person but without any other guide to identification. Fair enough if the talk is of 'Larry' or 'Alec' but infuriating if you are expected to know which 'Margaret' or 'John' the person is talking about. This is a terrible affectation and should not be encouraged. Clarity of meaning and reference should always be important in conversation, even to the point of over explicitness. Interrupt transgressors with, 'Who *are* you talking about?' at every opportunity.

Hospitals. In National Health Service wards, first names are all the rage – with the added risk that a patient will be called *only* by the first name – the first name on the sheet, and not the actual personal name they may known by to their friends and families.

A simple solution. If you really don't know how informal or formal to be on the subject of names, then try not using them at all. This will, of course, prove much more difficult than it sounds. It is a very agreeable thing to keep mentioning a person's name. It provides a kind of bond and shows you haven't forgotten who they are. But when in doubt, you don't have to.

Remembering names and faces

– or rather forgetting them. It is a gift not widely bestowed to be able to remember who someone is when you are not expecting to meet them, to recognize someone you have not met for a while, and to summon up from your memory bank the correct name for people just as you meet them. If you do have the gift, it can be dazzling and very flattering to the people you remember. David Frost is – perhaps was – the master of this. With computer-like facility he could summon up names and facts, even about people he had never met before. Most people feel a temporary glow when subjected to this treatment.

Many jokes are told, however, about people who do

not have the gift and who may try to use some memory prop, particularly to recall a person's name – by using word-association, Pelmanism, or anything they can lay their hands on. If such methods work for you, well and good, but if you can't remember a person's name or recall where you have met before, it is much better to come out and say something like, 'Oh, do remind me where we've met, my mind's gone a complete blank', or, 'Do forgive me, I can never remember names unless I see them written down' – this is particularly useful if you were only introduced to the person five minutes ago and have already forgotten the name – or, 'I'm sorry, I'm quite hopeless when it comes to names'.

What happens if you can't remember the names of people you are introducing? A jolly suggestion that would only work in certain circles is to say, 'Darling, you know darling, don't you?' and scuttle away. Indeed, scuttling quickly away after a fumbled introduction, leaving the two parties to sort it out for themselves, is probably all that you can do ('I'm sure you two know each other . . . ') Otherwise you will just have to come clean – or, rather, you will have to fake amnesia or slight inebriation. Make a joke about it – 'Good God, who are you? I've clean forgotten.' With remote acquaintances you can try such ploys as, 'Remind me what you are called these days' (to a woman who is always changing her married name, for example). Often a degree of hesitation and hand-gesturing on your part will encourage the person with the forgotten name to volunteer it.

In other words, put the blame on yourself, exaggerate your failing. Few people will take offence. The fact that, as host or hostess, you have invited them there in the first place is evidence of your good intentions. If a guest yourself, and should the person be famous (Kings and Queens often figure in anecdotes of name forgetfulness), remember that most people are more likely to be amused than insulted by any shortcomings you may exhibit.

Introducing people

The basic rule here is that you introduce *upwards*. The younger person is introduced to the older person: 'Mrs De Crepit, I'd like you to meet/I'd like to introduce/this is . . . Sharon Gray'. The less important is introduced to the more important, or the junior to the senior (if that is a more polite way of thinking about it): 'Mr Jaguar-Driver, this is Dave Cost-Clerk' (even if Dave is twice the age of the Managing Director). The man is introduced to the woman (if neither of the two previous considerations applies): 'Mrs Gracious, I don't think you've met Gregory New . . .'

It is not too important to get this right and, if you can never remember which way round the process should be, or if you are genuinely uncertain as to which of two people is older or more important, then an equalizing technique is simply to bark out both names while gently gesturing to each person concerned: 'Suzanne Friend . . . Charles Patron', that sort of thing.

You may also disguise the process by combining the introductions with small hints about who the people are and what their function is in life. 'Mrs De Crepit – she's our wonderful next-door neighbour – this is Sharon Gray, David's secretary, you know . . .' This in a sense is introducing in both directions at the same time as well as providing a starting point for any conversation they may then go on to have.

When making an introduction, I think it is always best to give a person's full name – if you can remember it. Calling people simply 'Mary' or 'Trevor' is not much help. After half-an-hour's anguished and possibly foot-putting-in-it conversation, the person they have just met may have to declare, 'Oh, I understand now, you're Mary Morrison . . .'

People still bravely introduce newcomers to a whole room full of people already arrived for a dinner party or other social occasion, knowing that no one is likely to catch or be able to attach any of the names. But it has to be done, even if guests then have to spend the rest of the occasion trying to pin names to people, and even have to ring up next day and ask, 'Who *was* that charming young woman I was sitting next to?' Faint hearts may declare, 'I'll let you introduce yourselves', and run for it.

'It isn't etiquette to cut anyone you've been introduced to. Remove the joint.'
The Rev. C.L. Dodgson (Lewis Carroll) (1832–98)

Above all, even if you make a hash of it, do attempt to introduce people to each other. There is nothing worse for a guest than to be be left hopping from one foot to another waiting for an introduction and not getting one.

Name badges. However useful these are in the business environment – at conferences, especially – they should never be forced upon people at social occasions. Not even at semi-business, semi-informal occasions like charity thrashes.

Whatever the occasion, I always seem to manage to lose mine, irretrievably, at an early stage.

Greetings. When you meet someone, you say, 'How do you do?' The correct reply is, 'How do you do?', not 'Pleased to meet you' or 'Fine, thanks', however, difficult it may be to stop yourself saying these things. There is no real reason why this should be so. On the other hand, there are people I have known who, on being greeted with 'How do you do?', have proceeded to give me an involved medical bulletin on themselves. This is obviously neither welcome nor the done thing.

Introducing yourself

If you have not been introduced, don't hang about, introduce yourself: 'Hello, my name's Tony Modest'. It is such a relief - and by no means pushy – if people take the initiative like this. It may seem rather *American*, and you may think twice about adopting the American custom of following through this sort of approach by calling the person you have just met by first name or surname in almost every sentence from then on. But it is much preferable to the alternative which is the mingy, unresponsive, secretive, reserved, British way. Parties are for being out-going and meeting new people. There is hardly any point in going if you are not prepared to do so.

Difficult situations

A master at Eton told me he once overheard a woman saying this: 'He'd had a long drive down and he asked for the bathroom. And when he was shown into it, he suddenly looked down, and there was his hostess in the bath. He couldn't think what was the correct thing to say, and so he said, "You are looking well!"'

What I find interesting about this anecdote is the notion that there is a 'correct thing' to say when you are faced with your hostess in the nude. I'm sure that in a different decade or century to this one, correct form or etiquette would have dictated precisely what to do or say in such circumstances.

Indeed, it seems to have done. When I consulted Douglas Sutherland, author of the *English Gentlemen* series of books, he advised that the proper comment should have been: 'I beg your pardon, *sir!*' I subsequently found confirmation that this was the correct response when reading a 1932 novel, *Charming Manners* by 'John Michaelhouse'. In the story, a group of Oxford undergraduates happen upon half a dozen naked nymphs dancing in the sunlight on the banks of the River Cherwell. 'We all collapsed in the punt at once, there being no chance of saying "Sorry, gentlemen" in the approved style.' So that must be it, then.

Putting one's foot in it

If you have put your foot in it, it can be argued that the only thing to do is to leave it there. I once told a dyslexia joke to a woman who turned round and assured me that one of her children suffered from it. What should I have done at that point? Mumbled an apology? Maintained a diplomatic silence? Or should I have brazened it out?

If you have just been slagging off some well-known local figure and the pretty but blushing girl in the corner volunteers that she is his daughter, then, if you have the guts, you might say: 'So you know exactly what I mean!' After all, what use would it be, if you just said, 'Oh, I'm sorry, I didn't mean it, of course'?

I have also been told an excellent example of recovery with aplomb. 'All the students at ——— University are either football players or whores', said one man. Another spoke up bravely: 'My wife is a student there!' To which the first man rallied superbly: 'Oh, really? What position does she play?'

I once heard for myself an excellent example of recovery with aplomb. Robert Morley, the thespian, was speaking at the Oxford Union in a debate on private versus state education and started rubbishing his old school, Marlborough. Provoked by this, a member of the audience, and presumably a fellow Old Marlburian, called out, 'Shame!' Morley, quick as a flash, agreed and kept on going: 'Yes, it was the most frightful shame. I don't know how I ever put up with it . . .'

But this sort of riposting is all very Oscar Wilde and beyond the reach of most of us. Still, the basic tenet holds. Don't dig yourself in deeper. Sir John Gielgud who is famous in the acting profession for his dropped bricks, some of which he actually said, illustrates how not to do things in the account of his lunch with Athene Seyler. He fell to bemoaning his lot: 'I spend all my time in the company of these old bags of stage and screen –

Monday, it's lunch with Fay Compton; Tuesday, Sybil Thorndike; Wednesday, Athene Seyler.' Then, realizing what he had said, he quickly added, 'Of course, I don't mean *you*, Athene!'

Putting one's foot in it can, of course, be the cause of graceful behaviour in others. I was with a TV producer once who asked the Chief Rabbi of Manchester, 'Tell me, Dr Goldberg, what is your Christian name?' The Dr Goldberg in question, without batting an eyelid, replied, 'My Christian name is Selwyn.'

Apologies

These should be brief. Whatever the necessity for them, it can only make the matter worse if apologies are overblown or if they appear to be grudgingly given. The person being apologized to should be equally brief in reply, say 'Thank you', and move on or away.

It is sometimes thought that in generational rows, it is incumbent on the older disputants to back down and apologize. This is on the grounds that young people are so inexperienced they cannot be expected to act graciously, so it is up to the older people to act graciously. They have less to lose. An interesting theory.

Making excuses

'No, I can't – I've got a bone in my leg'. There is a difference between making an excuse and giving a reason. The first suggests that an explanation is being manufactured rather than genuinely provided. It has to be said, though, that some people make a life's work out of making excuses for their behaviour. At school, it used to be that you failed to show up because 'you were attending your grandmother's funeral' (this wore a bit thin after the third such). A journalist, late for a radio interview with me, said – unanswerably – 'I've just been to my son's circumcision'. In later life, also, when you are an executive with British Rail, you can devise such high-flown excuses for train stoppages and delays as, 'There were leaves on the line' or 'It was the wrong type of snow'.

None of this will do. Honesty is the best policy. A *reason* is what you should give – not an excuse – and however far-fetched it may sound. When asked to join a woman who had 'got religion' and who said, 'Let's fall to our knees and pray', a woman declined by saying, 'No, I've just Hoovered the carpet.' Excuses come ready-made with an in-built whining noise.

Lame excuses. Or, rather, the consciously lame excuse. This is a sub-division of the genre and can be permissible. It has a precise purpose and therefore should be accepted in the spirit it is intended. The archetypal lame excuse is for a girl to wriggle out of a date because, 'That's the night I wash my hair'. This is palpable nonsense. It is just a coded way of declining a date while letting the inviter down gently. Sometimes decliners may say, 'Can we take a rain-check on that?' This is a delaying tactic, most often used in the hope that the delay will turn into never.

(As I explain in my *Dictionary of Phrase & Allusion*, originally, in the US, a rain-check (or -cheque) was a ticket for re-admission to a sporting event when the event had had to be postponed because of rain. The person to whom it was given would be able to produce it at a later date and claim free admission. Now broadened, the expression is used to mean 'let's put this "on hold"' or 'let's not make any arrangements about this until the time is more opportune'. Obviously, the phrase can be used as a polite way of postponing something indefinitely, but originally there was some kind of commitment to 'renegotiate' at a later date.)

Making an excuse and leaving

There are certain brave souls who are capable of organizing an excuse to get away – from a bore, from an impossible situation, from anything. They manufacture an important job to be dealt with, they arrange for their secretary to phone them with an urgent message that takes them away. Mobile phones make this sort of thing easier to contrive. Only the brave, however, deserve the freedom that this gives them.

Celebrity behaviour

True, this is not a question that every single one of my readers will face, but underlying it are matters of expectation and presumption that even the modestly unknown may encounter in their public lives.

I was once obliged to listen while the wife of a Duke (well known to the media) homed in on an extremely famous visiting American film star (male). 'You *must* come down and spend the week-end with us at ———,' the Duchess barked. The film star muttered something inconsequential. I expect he hadn't a clue who she was. I almost felt sorry for him. Being flavour of the year, I suppose he had to fend off this sort of invitation all the time. As a celebrity, he behaved very well. But it was the Duchess who was at fault. She made the basic error of assuming that just because she had *noblesse* to oblige people with, she had to go around dispensing it. Worse, no doubt considering herself to be the equal of the film star in celebrity, she assumed that he knew who she was.

I have noticed that extreme fame in some people can carry with it a surprisingly touching kind of modesty. Not in all cases, of course, but in some. Your reaction to someone saying, 'Hello, I'm Elizabeth Taylor' or 'We haven't been introduced, I'm Laurence Olivier' may well be, 'Of course you are, you don't have to tell me!' But the lack of assumption or presumption involved is very pleasing. Celebrities, however grand they may be, should never assume that they are known to anyone. If they do, they are more than likely to find they have been mistaken for the wrong person anyway.

The story is told about a certain middle-ranking comedian (now dead) that he once went to a branch of a bank to draw some money out. The bank clerk put on a great show of saying what a great fan of the comedian's he was and then, getting down to the matter in hand, asked if he had any means of identification . . . This was told by the comedian, in outraged tones, as though it reflected badly on the bank clerk. But the bank clerk was only doing his job, correctly, and the comedian, on other occasions, used to complain that he had difficulties on this score even when dealing with people who didn't recognize him.

Treating celebrities like normal people

It cuts both ways. Celebrities should learn how to behave, but the people who deal with them should also remember that even people in the public eye have feelings and may not relish being roughly handled. It is common for people to say when introducing celebrities, particularly minor ones, that they 'Need no introduction'. This leads people to say, 'Well, I've never heard of 'im', so it is an expression best avoided.

Above all, there is a terrible temptation to which members of the public inevitably succumb, to seize the rare opportunity of meeting a celebrity to unload all the resentment built up through years of only being able to shout back at the figure on the TV screen. Even a wonderful man like Eric Morecambe frequently fell victim to these attacks. He knew that, stepping into a bar, there would always be someone who would seize the opportunity to tell him he wasn't very good really, 'I can always tell when a man's not working at full stretch', or similar, offloading some pent-up resentment at his great success.

This sort of put down may be considered unthinking, but it is odd how *often* it happens. It seems to be compulsive on the part of the speakers. Authors have to put up with it a lot: 'Is it my imagination or was your first book a better one?' people will say. 'Do you just do your writing – or have you got a proper job?' 'Do you write under your own name?' 'We usually get a much bigger crowd [for book-signing sessions] if the author's better known than you are'. A rum, and not very pleasant, business.

Autograph-hunting is the bane of any celebrity's life but may not, of course, be totally unwelcome. Most will sign if asked politely but will probably bristle if asked to do so in the middle of a meal or inappropriately at some other event.

$\mathcal{S}$PEAKING

From intimate conversation to public speaking, from saying grace to telephoning – this chapter examines the spoken word in many of its uses.

(See also 'Dinner-party conversation' in Chapter 4 GUESTS AND HOSTS and 'Swearing' in Chapter 7 PUBLIC BEHAVIOUR.)

Opening gambits

The most difficult part of any conversation comes at the very beginning. How to get started? I believe it was Disraeli who suggested you begin with, 'How's the old complaint?' It is suggested, in certain circles, that you ask, 'How's the book coming along?' because everyone there can be expected either to be writing a book or intending to one day.

However, be careful not to try this approach in the company of the noted satirist, Peter Cook. Attempting to start up a dinner-party conversation, he asked someone, 'What are you doing at the moment?' The person replied, 'Writing a book.' To which Cook rejoined, 'Neither am I.'

During that rather testing time when you arrive at a dinner party and simply have to talk to total strangers, the most obvious question to ask is how they know the hosts – in other words, why they are there. 'Where have you had to come from to get here?' may sound a pretty flat inquiry but it gives plenty of scope for tales of traffic jams and other harmless, if less than riveting, tittle-tattle.

Some sensitivity is required when trying to find out how a person you have just been introduced to spends his or her days. To ask 'Do you have a job?' point blank might be upsetting if the person doesn't. You need to employ rather more subtlety to tease out of such a person what they get up to. Even though they may not have a formal job they may lead interesting lives. 'What do you do?' is kinder.

To ask a woman 'Do you have a job?' or 'Do you work?' might suggest you anticipate that she has given up work and is a kept woman (even if by a husband). In this case, it is much less offensive to ask, 'What do you do?' If she is 'only a housewife' and wants to use that regrettably apologetic form, then that is up to her. If she has a job, or had a job, she can tell you. The chief thing is not to make assumptions.

Small talk

If there are two things that people have more nightmares about than any other it is what to say when meeting the Queen and how to make smooth social conversation with almost anybody else. The ability to make instant talk with a complete stranger that we have just met at a party or dinner table is one that most of us do not possess. We tend not to realize, however, that even the fortunate gifted few find it difficult making these 'polite noises'. An ability to keep the conversational ball bouncing backwards and forwards used to be held a social grace. Still there is a belief that if only we can lay our hands on the magical property known as 'small talk', our social difficulties will instantly be at an end, forever. But where is this small talk to be found?

'I have no small talk and Peel has no manners.'
1st Duke of Wellington (1769–1852)

We are all of us fundamentally ill at ease in any social situation that involves speaking. The consequence is that we become tongue-tied, or we become jokey, frivolous or verbose. Yet recourse to the ragbag of off-the-peg phrases, anecdotes and tittle-tattle is one way of establishing contact with other human beings. The glitter and the great thoughts can come later, if they come at all. At the very least, it has to be appreciated that conversation is a two-way medium. It is not enough to transmit, one must also receive.

A good way to do this is to ask questions. My wife insists that the first question I ever asked her was 'How much do you earn?' If indeed I did, then I am very embarrassed. 'Interviewing' people is, though, one approach to conversation. I interview people all the time, at dinner parties, in railway carriages, on planes, wherever I find them. It is almost a compulsion, though I hope it stops short of nosey-parkering. At least I know at the end of an encounter whether the people I have been sitting next to are married or divorced and what jobs they have, if any. The favourite subject of most people is themselves, so asking them questions is always a good way of getting them to open up.

A related problem is what can be done if you are faced with someone who isn't shy or incapable of speech but who can only manage 'big talk', not the small and intimate variety? In the same way that bores often know they are bores (and sometimes apologize for it at excruciating length), big talkers are usually well aware that they are no good at small talk. The giveaway is when they try to join in. TV interviewer David Frost tells of the terrible moment working with Richard Nixon when the ex-President obviously felt he needed to unbend and be 'one of the boys' for a while. He asked Frost, 'Did you do any fornicating over the weekend?'

Consciously trying to upgrade your conversation can lead to similar embarrassments. The Princess of Wales was touring Italy once when she was heard to ask a priest, 'Do you pray a lot?' On the other hand, it may be some consolation that the Royals, for whom making uncontentious small talk is a way of life, sometimes seem to have difficulty, too. They indulge in plonking questions like, 'You must have seen many changes in your time?'

Women, more than men, have something else they can resort to. This is what we might call 'middle talk'. It is a type of chat in which experiences are shared and stories told against oneself. It is possible to do it with total strangers and women can enter into it with the minimum of preamble.

Why is this? It is often said that men are very bad at opening up and showing their feelings. When men talk, they make contact with each other – if at all – using the coded form of jokes and anecdotes. Women rarely tell jokes. They describe what they have observed and experienced. Their instinct is not only to share personal problems with other women but to reciprocate when asked. With a little amplification, this tendency should make it much easier to enter into lighter, party conversation.

Taboo subjects

There are traditional taboos over the subjects you should or should not introduce into conversation when in company – politics, religion and sex topping the list. Money follows close behind and most people are still aware that asking a woman her age is not the done thing. At one time it was even thought impolite to discuss other people (especially those not present) or to comment on *things* (like furniture and decoration, for example.)

But do any of these taboos still operate today? The PAS survey showed that 64% of people thought it unacceptable to ask a friend how much he or she earned, but about the same number thought it was acceptable to ask a friend of the same sex how much had been paid for a new item of clothing. People were more or less equally divided as to whether it was acceptable to talk frankly about sex. But on all these points, the *unacceptability* grew according to the age of the people asked.

All in all, most topics are now fair game in conversation but it is obviously a virtue not to want to upset people with raising contentious issues in a social situation. Talking shop is a terrible affliction especially among media and money folk. It should not be allowed to get out of hand, especially if it excludes others from participating in the conversation.

Guessing people's ages is a harmless enough pastime but people should be allowed to have some areas of vagueness in the fact-filled age we live in. So you may not ask and you may not find out, but there are always other ways . . .

To ask neighbours how much they have sold their house for may be a subject of burning interest to you, but it is certainly impolite to ask them direct. You may want to ask the incoming owners instead, but this, too, should not be done. The chances are that the answer will emerge in due course anyway.

I think the discussion of illness or medical topics at the dinner table is to be discouraged, as should anything unpleasant and likely to put people off their food. I once had to share a table in a small London restaurant with two female students from the Royal Veterinary College who, quite unconsciously, proceeded to have an involved and graphic discussion about the guillotining of rats. I dissuaded them from pursuing the topic.

Strangers are apt to ask, 'Do you have any children?' and, if you are childless, you will have to have some stock response ready, though it is as perfectly understandable an inquiry as, 'Are you married?' To strangers, all one can say is, jokingly, 'Not that I am aware of', or, more seriously, that you 'haven't been blessed'. That then gives them the chance to slide out of the situation by saying that 'being blessed' is not how they would describe having children. On the other hand, if you do not have children, members of your immediate family will *never* raise the subject and you wonder faintly why not.

'When I was a boy it was always considered bad form to talk about food or money. Now no one talks of anything else.'
Harold Macmillan, 1st Earl of Stockton (1894–1986)

'Never ask a question under any circumstances. In the first place, it is too proud; in the second place, it may be very inconvenient or very awkward to give a reply. A lady inquired of what branch of medical practice a certain gentleman was professor. He held the chair of *midwifery!*'
Arthur Martine, *Hand-book of Etiquette and Guide to True Politeness* (New York, 1866)

'The frequent use of the name of God, or the Devil; allusions to passages of Scripture; mocking at anything serious and devout, oaths, vulgar by-words, cant phrases, affected hard words, when familiar terms will do as well; scraps of *Latin*, *Greek* or *French*; quotations from plays spoke in a theatrical manner – all these, much used in conversation, render a person very contemptible to grave and wise men.'
Arthur Martine, *Hand-book of Etiquette and Guide to True Politeness* (New York, 1866)

'The subject of heat is one of extreme delicacy in
Queensland, as indeed it is also in the other
colonies. One does not allude to heat in a host's
house any more than to a bad bottle of wine or an
ill-cooked joint of meat. You may remark that it is
very cool in your friend's verandah . . . and may
hint that the whole of your absent friend's establishment is as hot as a furnace; but though you be
constrained to keep your handkerchief to your
brow, and hardly dare to walk to the garden gate,
you must never complain of the heat then and there.
You may call an inn hot, or a court-house, but not a
gentleman's paddock or a lady's drawing-room. And
you should never own to a musquito.'

Anthony Trollope, *Australia and New Zealand* (1873)

But really these days there are few limits on what can
be talked about. Since the AIDS problem came along, it
is quite stunning how much open talk there is about
condoms. And, as for what used to be known as 'the old
gentleman's operation' – the prostate one – it is really
very hard to stop them talking about it now.

Stop me if you've heard this before . . .

There is nothing worse than having to listen to a joke
you have heard before, particularly a tedious shaggy-dog
story, and with nothing but a frozen smile on your face.
The joke-teller should always give you plenty of get-out
points. 'Have you heard the one about the . . .' is not
much help because it is unlikely that the description will
remind you of the joke. Breaking off to say, 'Are you
sure you haven't heard this before?' is a kindly gesture.
The trouble is, if you say yes, you recognize it, the teller
will still feel abandoned half way up the wall.

But there are many compulsive joke-tellers around and
others should not have to suffer for it.

The joys of gossip

It is hard not to revel in other people's misfortunes, as regaled by gossips. It is one of life's simple pleasures as long as it remains harmless. When, however, it becomes official gossip – by which I mean it is the sort of thing that appears in the papers – one or two rules do apply. People who feature in published gossip should help their friends by showing that they are aware of it. It is a regrettable fact, however, that if people who appear in gossip do not themselves know about it, there are plenty of people who will make sure they do. Anonymously sent envelopes containing a copy of *Private Eye* bearing scandal about an errant husband are not a joy to receive. Close friends can help by getting to the person first – and by not appearing to revel in the fact.

'Oh! gossip is charming! History is merely gossip.
But scandal is gossip made tedious by morality.'
Oscar Wilde, *Lady Windermere's Fan* (1892)

Personal remarks

'You must learn not to make personal remarks,' said Alice to the Hatter, but it didn't stop him and it hasn't stopped anyone else either. It is very difficult not to make remarks about people's fatness, their toupees, or any other distinguishing feature, but it is a kindness not to do this within earshot or in any other way that will make them realize that is what you are doing.

Telephoning

How should you answer the phone? On a personal as opposed to business line, one authority says you should simply say, 'Hello'. If nothing else, this then prompts the caller to do all the work ('May I speak to ——', and so on.) It also means that mischievous callers have been given no information – like what number they have stumbled upon. To give your name straight off may be unwise if the caller is of the wrong type.

It would seem helpful, however, simply to give your number. To give the dialling code and exchange as well would make it rather a mouthful and, besides, the caller may not have had to use the code. I usually just give the number (not the exchange) and, should it be a wrong number, explore the issue from there.

Business telephone operators should give the name of the company – and not rattle it off in a sing-song voice just because they are used to saying the name scores of time each day. Callers may have difficulty knowing what they have got through to.

(See also 'Sins of secretaries', 'Phone manners' and 'Hello, XYZ Ltd . . .' in Chapter 15 WORKING LIFE.)

Unless you know that they would be welcome, it is best not to make personal calls before 9 am and after 10 pm. Even so, you may get people out of the bed or out of the bath. Although clearly haphazard, it is also sensible to avoid mealtimes, and if you suspect that you have brought someone away from the table, ask quickly whether it is convenient for them to talk. If in any doubt about the timeliness of your call, be prepared to say you will call back later. It has been known for callers who are woken up to forget all about the call and anything they may have agreed to do in it. If you don't want to be disturbed, you can leave the phone off the hook, or put on the answering machine, or unplug anything that may ring (despite British Telecom's attempts to insist that a bell will always ring *somewhere* in the house).

If you are calling overseas or being called from overseas, you will know what happens if you don't bother to think what time of day it is at the other end.

The chief problem with the telephone is its intrusiveness. Without warning, a caller can immediately pitchfork you into answering some question or making a decision, when you may have been in the middle of something completely different. In private life just as much as business life, it is important not to be cowed into submission by the demands of a ringing telephone. The ringing may be impossible to ignore, but the content of the call doesn't necessarily have to be dealt with there and then.

'I'll call you back' is a phrase that should be used more often. You should have to make your mind up instantly about very few matters. A decision-postponing technique is not a sign of weakness but of consideration. In business negotiating, it can be an essential tool. It gives you time to think – and in an atmosphere that has not been created by the caller.

(See also 'Telephone negotiating' in Chapter 15 WORKING LIFE.)

Wrong numbers. If you dial a wrong number, all that is necessary is for you to utter a quick apology and replace the receiver. Not to apologize may be to render the wrongly-dialled suscriber nervous. Forget about the James Thurber cartoon with the caption, 'Well, if this is the wrong number, why did you answer the phone . . . ?'

If you are answering a wrong number call, it helps to establish what number the caller was trying to obtain – but without giving away your own number.

Communication. Particularly on business matters, people who are taking information over the phone should acknowledge dictation as it comes over, phrase by phrase. Addresses and spellings should be repeated. Although you may feel as though you are sounding like an airline pilot, the international phonetic alphabet is very useful. It is currently:

ALFA	BRAVO	CHARLIE	DELTA	ECHO	FOXTROT
GOLF	HOTEL	INDIA	JULIETT	KILO	LIMA
MIKE	NOVEMBER	OSCAR	PAPA	QUEBEC	ROMEO
SIERRA	TANGO	UNIFORM	VICTOR	WHISKEY	X-RAY
YANKEE	ZULU				

I have also heard 'N for Nothing' which, given my first name, I feel tempted to use rather a lot.

Answering machines. Rather as with the ancient snobbery over television, reluctance or refusal to speak to answering machines is, with luck, dying out. The heart may sink a little when the message comes on and you know a performance is in order, but the usefulness surely outweighs this. Such machines have been neatly described as the modern form of butler.

Facetious messages, or those containing special music, sound effects and funny voices, may give you an outlet for your sense of humour and frustrated theatrical talents, but just consider that the incoming caller may have some serious news to impart.

If you fear that burglars may assume that because the machine is on, your home is empty, or if there has been any problem with obscene telephone calls, it may be wise not to identify yourself too closely on the message.

'You have reached the —— family. What you hear
is the barking of our killer Doberman pinscher,
Wolf. Please leave a message after the tone.'
                    quoted in *Life*, January 1984

The consequence of not giving your name may be that people will leave messages for you thinking that they are on to someone else. Somebody once left an order on my machine for an immense amount of ice cream, for an (unnamed) restaurant. They must have been very upset when it didn't turn up, but there was nothing I could do about it.

Be warned, it is best not to possess an answering machine if there is any likelihood of your being rung up by clergymen. It is like a red rag to a bull. Tell them 'please speak after the short burst of tone' and they'll go on for hours. Think twice, too, about putting out a message to the effect that 'So-and-so is unable to come to the phone at the moment'. This is equivocal about whether you are at home or not (and may be intentional, given that burglars may be listening in), but evokes images of your being in bed or on holiday 6,000 miles away or stuck in the loo.

Beepers. Although these don't actually talk, they are a form of communication that makes a noise. Needless to say they should never be taken into a restaurant or theatre. There is a type that can alert you by vibrating soundlessly against your body and these are infinitely preferable.

U and Non-U language

In Britain, there is a good deal of snobbery over language lapses. The social divisiveness inherent in choice of words was codified, originally, by Alan S.C. Ross in an article published in a linguistics magazine (1954) and then collected by Nancy Mitford in *Noblesse Oblige* (1956). Ross divided words into 'U' (upper class) and 'Non-U' usage. Examples of the differences in usage which act as an indicator of class and verbal sensitivity, dividing the world into common or genteel, correct or proper, include:

NON-U	U
afters, sweet	pudding
bye-bye	goodbye

comfy	comfortable
couch	sofa
dentures	false teeth
dinner (mid-day)	lunch
horse-riding	riding
intoxicated (etc.)	drunk
kids, kiddies	children
lounge	sitting room, drawing room
pardon?/beg pardon	what?/I'm sorry
passed away (etc.)	died
perfume	scent
preserve	jam
ride (car)	drive
serviette	table napkin
ta/thanks	thank you
toilet	loo

(See also 'Lavatory terms' in Chapter 7 PUBLIC BEHAVIOUR.) I am not going to argue here about the ethics of this game. It should be enough for readers to realize that there are people who notice these things and for them then to do what they see fit.

It is a curiously English madness. Most of the attention paid to it is about as pointless as worrying over the fact that if someone stands on his foot, an Englishman will automatically say 'Sorry' to the person who has done it to him.

Slang

(See Chapter 10 SOCIAL LIFE.)

Pronunciation

'Don't use words you don't understand, for effect,' is obviously good advice. As, too, is 'don't use words of whose pronunciation you are uncertain'. If in doubt, don't be frightened of asking.

Foreign words can be a problem, particularly when one is poring over restaurant menus. I feel fairly strongly that if you are in Britain it is unhelpful for people who speak foreign languages well to pronounce words as they would in the foreign country concerned. If French words are rattled off as they would be in France, the chances are they will not be caught by your average Englishman.

There are some words whose pronunciation has been fully anglicized anyway, like *foyer, cul de sac, champagne, déjà vu,* etc., and this should be maintained. But though Paris is not 'Paree' in English, I think we have happily discarded 'Mar-sales' for Marseilles, or 'Lions' for Lyons. There is inconsistency among those who do insist on the foreign pronunciation, however. 'Florence' and 'Venice' are not English pronunciations, they are English versions (of the Italian 'Firenze' and 'Venezia', respectively). And few would think of not calling those places by their English names.

The point is, though, that an anglicized pronunciation of all foreign words helps the listener to grasp more quickly what is being talked about. It is snobbish to insist otherwise or to accuse people who do anglicize foreign words of being boors. Besides, it is affected to show off your superb foreign accent when you are not in the country of origin.

Pronouncing names. It is a politeness to ascertain how a particular person wishes his or her name to be pronounced. Certain British names are famous for being miniature obstacle courses and solely designed, it might seem, to entrap the unwary. *The BBC Pronouncing Dictionary of British Names* is about the safest guide to use because not only does it point out the several variant pronunciations that there may be of a family name, it also gives some indication of what is appropriate for particular people.

The surname 'Le Mes(s)urier' may be pronounced 'Le muzz-your-ee-ay' or 'Le mezzh-er-uh' – the latter being appropriate for the late comic actor, John Le Mesurier. The surname 'Waldegrave' may be pronounced 'Wawl-grave' or 'Wald-grave' – the first being appropriate for Earl Waldegrave, apparently, the second for the politician, William Waldegrave (though the two men are part of the same family.)

The *Dictionary* is sometimes less than helpful when it comes to place names. It is said that the pronunciation of obscure village names was checked with local vicars who, tending to speak standard English themselves, probably ignored the popular local pronunciation. It is clearly stated, however, that the town of Shrewsbury is called 'Shrows-burry' *and* 'Shrews-burry' in the town itself.

American names (apart from place names of Indian origin which can be quite baffling) tend to be pronounced in the obvious, literal way. Hence, if they are names imported from Britain or are abbreviations of European names, they are not pronounced in any fancy fashion – the singer Dionne Warwick is 'War-wick' rather than 'Warrick' and the late choreographer Bob Fosse was 'Fossee' rather than 'Fosse'. However, the actor Walter Matthau is 'Mathow' (with the 'h' sounded) rather than anything akin to his actual name 'Matasschanskayasky'.

The most notable stumbling blocks among British names include:

Alnwick	annick
Althorp	awltrup
Bethune	beetn *or* bethewn
Broughan	broom
Buccleuch	buckloo
Burgh	burra *or* burg *or* bur

Burghley	burli
Cecil	sessl *or* sissl
Cholmondeley	chumley
Coke	cook *or* cohk
Dalziel	deeyell *or* dalzeel
Devereux	deverooks *or* deverecks *or* deverra *or* deverroo
Douglas-Home	douglas-hume
Featherstonehaugh	fetherston-haw *or* feston-haw *or* feesson-hay *or* feerston-haw
Fiennes	fines
Harewood	harwood
Iveagh	iver
Knollys	noles
Leveson Gower	loosson gore
Mainwaring	mannering *or* maynwaring
Marjoribanks	marchbanks
Menzies	mingiss *or* mengiss (especially in Scotland) *or* menzees
Milnes	mills *or* milnz
Pontefract	pomfret *or* pumfret (though the place is pronounced as it is written)
Ruthven	rivvun *or* ruthven
St John	sunt john *or* sinjun
Strachan	strawn *or* strakkan
Villiers	villers *or* villyerz
Wemyss	weemz

My own surname is properly pronounced 'reez', not in the Welsh way, but I long ago abandoned attempts to ensure that this was what people said, and I no longer pronounce it that way myself. However, there are still some people with exquisite courtesy who inquire what is the correct pronunciation before uttering it.

In the end, the only safe way is to ask the people themselves how they wish their names pronounced.

Unfortunately, people in this position often don't care
and say, 'Any way you like . . .'

Public speaking

The British are not natural speakers or talkers. The
proof of this is often found when they have a micro-
phone stuck under their noses by a broadcaster and all
they can find to say is a mumbled, 'I dunno, really' or –
having regurgitated an opinion first heard on the telly
anyway, say, 'Narmean?'

Americans, on the other hand, have ready opinions on
many subjects and deliver them audibly if not loudly. Is
this because Americans are encouraged from their
schooldays to debate topics in class? Or is it because
their national outlook conditions them to believe that
their point of view is a valid one and that they are
entitled to express it?

Nerves. There is an old observation about speech-making
(in my early days I used to begin speeches with it: about
as original as saying 'Unaccustomed as I am to public
speaking . . .') to the effect that you always end up
making three speeches: the one you make to the
bathroom mirror before setting out, the absolute drivel
you say when you stand up to speak, and the magnificent oration you convince yourself you have made, as
you drive home afterwards.

Your average Britisher quakes at the thought of
having to get up on his hind legs and make a speech –
or make any sort of remarks – before an audience. If it
is the once in a lifetime after-dinner speech to the golf
club dinner, it will probably cast a blight over the
whole of the preceding year, let alone render the
preceding meal all but inedible. Businessmen who have
to make sales presentations break out in sweats, have
panic attacks, and are rendered sleepless, if they are

not actually being physically sick at the prospect of speaking.

Most of this worry is unnecessary. Some of the worry *is* necessary. But it should be harnessed and applied to the cause in the same way as the adrenalin that inevitably flows once you start speaking. The first thing to realize is that even the most hardened public speakers experience some sort of tension before they speak. There will come a time before almost every speech when they will wonder what they putting themselves through the experience for. If they are politicians – who have the added worry that if they say the wrong thing it could seriously harm their political standing – they have even more cause for alarm. Even substantial politicians – Winston Churchill, Harold Macmillan, Margaret Thatcher among them – are known to have been gravely afflicted and sometimes made physically ill by the prospect of delivering a big speech.

The second thing to consider is the simple fact that nobody in your audience is the slightest bit interested in your nerves. They don't want to know about your nerves: they want to hear what you have got to say. If your nerves are apparent then that will get in the way of your message.

Nerves are good for you. It is, indeed, a terrible burden for anyone who *needs* nerves in order to be a good performer. An actor may have to be nervous all day, on and off, if he is appearing on stage in the evening. But, if he is not nervous, the chances are that he will not give a good performance. So it is with speakers.

It is no fun if you can't enjoy a meal before speaking or if you have to keep rushing off to the lavatory (the most common symptom) but if you can appreciate that you are not alone in all this, and that it is necessary, you may learn to come to terms with it. If you remember all these points, what may still seem like an ordeal to you will not appear that way to your audience.

'[Shaw] never wrote or read his speeches, but used a series of cards with lists of subjects. By street-corner practice and phonetic study he had learnt to address an audience "as a man learns to skate or to cycle – by doggedly making a fool of myself until I got used to it" . . . "On the platform you must have the smart appearance of a clerk," he later advised Lady Rhondda, "the articulation of a telephone girl, the address of the shop assistant, and knowledge of your wares and of their talking points of the commercial traveller, all in more than Bond Street perfection . . ."'

Michael Holroyd, *Bernard Shaw* (Vol. 1)(1988)

Notes and alcohol. Two rules often trotted out for would-be speakers are that they shouldn't use notes and they should *never* touch alcohol.

To take the second point first. You will probably have a good idea of the effect alcohol has on you. If it slurs your speech and makes you incline to ramble then, obviously, you would do best to avoid it, even if it does help calm your nerves. And yet, I have a tendency to slur my words even when I am sober and I have also been known to feel that I should not spoil my evening, when everyone else is drinking, just because I'm the one who has to make the speech.

I think I have given perfectly reasonable speeches when I have drunk well and I have no need of the moral superiority that comes from being the only sober person in a room full of drunks. If I have taken to drinking less before speaking than I once did, it is not just because I may be driving home. A lesser-known drawback of alcohol is that it is a drying agent. It can dry your throat out and make speech difficult. Combined with the dryness caused by your nerves – and also, possibly, by speaking without taking enough breaths (because you are thinking on your feet and don't know where your sentences are leading you) – this can create real problems. I know of one speaker who suffered what he called 'panic attacks' and on occasions had to abandon his speeches before they were finished. It turned out that he was literally 'drying up'.

So, alcohol can be a problem and, if you don't think you can control it, it may be best to spurn it all together – until you have finished your speech anyway.

Now, notes. I have often heard it said of a speaker, as a compliment, 'And, you know, he did it all from memory'. But I have never paid this compliment myself. Even if there is something amazing about people who have those wonderful legal brains and can speak without notes, almost as if they had the text on a little screen in their brains, I have never been impressed.

As with an actor doing a one-man show from memory, the audience can be made extremely uncomfortable at any sign of uncertainty. What happens if the speaker does dry up? Nobody will be able to help him. Even fishing out notes from his pocket will cause an agonizing moment. Besides, what's wrong with notes? They show that you have thought about what you are going to say. They also – and this is a small but important point – give the speaker something to do with his hands.

So you should use notes. After all, as Winston Churchill (who knew a thing or two about speaking) once joked, 'Extempore speech isn't worth the paper it's written on . . . ' (It may seem presumptuous to invoke Churchill when all there is in prospect is the golf club annual dinner or opening a bring-and-buy sale, but the basics of all effective speaking are the same.)

What sort of notes? That is the key question. If you are a politician upon whose every word much may depend, there is no real alternative to having every word of the speech in front of you and sticking to it, with a touch of extempore variation and embroidery. The danger of this technique is that it is very difficult to junk material if the speech is going badly or needs to be shortened for any other reason.

For the rest of us, a mixture of headings and key phrases is best. Churchill when he wasn't making a broadcast speech would use detailed notes which were

> laid out in what was known as
> Speech Form
> which meant rather like a hymn-sheet
> or, as someone said,
> like the psalms
> which, if nothing else,
> made them easier to read.

The finished speech would be typed out on many sheets of paper, with plenty of spacing, and then the whole lot was fastened firmly together. Nothing is worse than notes that fall to the floor and get out of order.

Another popular technique, not used by Churchill, is to put the notes on to a stack of postcards. But I believe this is offputting for the audience. They know that the speaker is going to have to wade through that stack before getting to the end. Much better to reduce the material to as few sheets of paper as possible. If all the headings can be fitted on to one sheet, so much the better. This can then be tucked into a menu card – in which case you may even be congratulated on not using notes at all . . .

Preparation. Although you may aim to give an air of naturalness or spontaneity to what you have to say, detailed preparation is the only route to good speech-making. Public speaking is an unnatural act. There is an element of performance about it or, at least, an element of projection – of yourself and your ideas. The most effective communication is fixed.

Decide what you want to say and why you want to say it. In other words, 'engage brain before opening mouth'. Don't just emit words for the sake of it. Decide what sort of people your audience is going to made up of and design your speech with that image in mind. Talk to yourself (even in the mirror) before you talk to other people. Practise phrases, get used to the sound of your own voice – we all do it, so don't be shy. Rehearse in the same position as you will speak in eventually – that is, sitting or standing, as appropriate. Wandering aimlessly around the room, or the garden, will not prepare you for the actual sensation of making a speech from a stationary position.

Ideas for speeches don't come to order, so be ready to pin them down whenever and wherever they occur to you. But ideas on their own are not sufficient to make a good speech. A good speech requires a structure.

On the other hand, don't over-prepare – leave space for inspiration. Be flexible. Never write out a full text – because you will be trapped in it, unable to adapt it or to escape from it as you go along. Mark the cut-able portions of your speech, so that if time runs out on you – or your audience does – you can easily reduce the speech length.

'The composition of a speech was not a task Churchill was prepared to skimp or to hurry; nor, except on some convivial occasion, was he willing to speak impromptu. He might improvise briefly, but only to elaborate or clarify, and he stuck closely to the text he had prepared . . . Quick as was his wit and unfailing his gift for repartee, he was not a man to depart in the heat of the moment from the theme or indeed the words that he had laboriously conceived in set-speech form.'

J.R. Colville, in *Action This Day* (1968)

Timing is utterly important, too. By which I don't mean simply the ability to tell jokes and wait for the response (you probably either have this ability or you don't), but rather an awareness of time passing. Speakers can lose all sense of time. Going on for too long can be fatal. If you need to, put a watch in front of you – or get someone to indicate to you how long you have been boring on for. No speech is too short, in my estimation, but it is quite wrong for the organizers of a function to stipulate a particular minimum length. Speakers must be allowed to decide their own length according to the mood of the occasion and the reception they and any earlier speakers get.

Style. A noted broadcasting executive once came up with the golden rule of all communication: 'Say what you have to say simply, directly and warmly.' I would add that 'simply and directly' usually means 'briefly'. And remember that Churchill said 'Short words are the best.' But not if they are clichés or jargon. Don't be verbose or pompous. Use anecdotes and stories to give colour. Decide what you are *not* going to say just as much as what you are. Apply the underlying principles in all forms of communication – in writing, over the telephone, in meetings. It's better to be over the top than to be a bore. And, remember, you are probably better at it than you think you are.

Body language. Everybody knows this concept now – that the way you stand or look or gesture may, unfortunately for you, be communicating your real feelings about what you are saying or about your audience. Try to perceive how you will appear to your audience. Show your eyes – look around. Use hand gestures sparingly but, whatever you do, try not to repeat just one (the politician's jabbing finger, for example). Be aware of your body – mannerisms can detract from your message. When standing up to speak, it is best to stand behind something – if only a chair.

Modes of address. It is a relief to be able to start a speech simply by saying, 'Ladies and Gentleman' or

'Friends' (if you can make that assumption). Having to
begin a speech, 'Your Royal Highness, My Lord Mayor,
Mr Chairman, Ladies and Gentleman' is a bit of an
obstacle course – though curiously exhilarating once you
have accomplished it. The point, though, is that this
should never become a meaningless ritual. If, as quite
often happens, you are addressing an audience where
there is a token woman or man, it is correct to say,
'Ladies and Gentleman/Sir', or 'Gentlemen and Madam'.
Don't be afraid of drawing attention to the only woman
present at a dinner of the Institute of Concrete Technol-
ogy, for example, as I discovered on one occasion. If
she's courageous enough to go, she won't mind attention
being drawn to her.

(See also Chapter 13 TITLES AND ADDRESSING.)

Introducing the speaker

A good chairman is hard to find, though even a bad one
is preferable to professional toastmasters with their noisy
gavel-banging, and pompous if not incompetent introductions. The chairman should introduce the speaker with
the minimum of words. There is no point in saying that
the 'speaker needs no introduction' if you then plough
through his biography. Nor should you attempt to anticipate the speaker by using any of his jokes – he may have
been planning to use them himself. Above all, whatever
you do say, make sure it is 100% accurate. Check with
the speaker what you are going to say in advance. The
number of speakers who have to begin by correcting
crass errors of fact by chairmen is legion.

Giving a vote of thanks

There should always be something said after a speaker
has sat down, even if it is not a full-blown Ladies'

Luncheon Club type thank-you. Not to have a word from the chairman (or anyone else) after the speaker (or speakers) have finished is anticlimactic and can give an occasion a very flat finish.

Don't say, 'Follow that!' – because everyone always does. Nor give votes of thanks which have too obviously been scripted before you heard what the speaker was going to say. Votes of thanks are usually pretty awful for everyone concerned. Very occasionally you hear a gem. After I had made a speech on the subject of quotations, a woman said, 'When we were at school I could never remember which way up to put my quotation marks – whether to put 66 or 99. Well, today, all the quotation marks have been the right way up.' Perfect. And brief.

Saying Grace

Grace is said before a meal supposedly because Jesus Christ gave a blessing before the Last Supper. There is often awkwardness surrounding the saying of Grace at formal functions these days, but not to have one at all can be equally bad.

At anything other than an informal meal, someone should be deputed to say Grace (and given time to prepare one). If a member of the clergy is present, it is customary to ask that person to say Grace. The shorter it is, the better, and in the rare event of an appropriate grace, the meal gets off to a particularly good start.

At a dinner of parliamentary lobby correpondents, the Grace was: 'Oh God, before whom all are attributable, make us truly thankful'; a speaker's Grace is: 'Lord, fill my mouth with worthwhile stuff and nudge me when I've said enough'; the Rev. Sydney Smith is said to have had alternative graces ready to hand. If he saw that champagne was to be served, he would say, 'Oh, bountiful Jehovah', if not, 'Oh, Lord, we thank thee for even the least of thy benefits.'

'To me it is unintelligible that the full tide of glibbest chatter can be stopped at a moment in the midst of profuse good living, and the Giver thanked becomingly in words of heartfelt praise . . . Clergymen there are – one meets them now and then – who endeavour to give to the dinner-table grace some of the solemnity of a church ritual, and what is the effect? Much the same as though one were to be interrupted for a minute in the midst of one of our church liturgies to hear a drinking-song . . . Let any man ask himself whether, on his own part, they are acts of prayer and thanksgiving – and if not that, what then?'

Anthony Trollope, *Dr Thorne* (1858)

Proposing a toast

At a formal dinner it is customary to drink the Queen's health. Whoever proposes the toast simply says, 'The Queen!' and the guests stand up and say the same. In Lancashire only, the toast is 'The Duke of Lancaster!' Alas, the 'Loyal Toast' is often brought forward during the meal so that it may be coupled with 'Permission to Smoke'. Even if the chairman says something grudging like, 'If you have to, now you may', this is an ungracious coupling.

Other toasts are incorporated into the speechmaking. The speakers will be told what toast, if any, they should propose or respond to. They should try not to forget to do this, but should they forget, or if they wish to end their speeches a different way, they may take their applause, sit down, and then stand up and propose the toast as a kind of coda.

Those drinking the toast rise to do so (except if they are on board ship in the Royal Navy and would bang their heads); those to whom the toast is being drunk, remain seated. Should you be caught with an empty glass, raise it anyway and go through the motions. It is only symbolic, after all.

Taking poison? A tendency we could well do without, and one that occurs increasingly at formal dinners, is for the chairman to stand up and make his remarks and to single out individual diners who are then invited to stand up and 'take wine with me' – that is to say, drink a joint toast with the chairman. This is a slimy habit, to put it mildly. I don't know where it came from but I wish it would go back there.

Weddings

(See 'The reception' in Chapter 5 MARRIAGE AND DIVORCE.)

Opening a garden fête

This is a difficult feat to accomplish well because people may not be able to hear you properly and would rather be off round the stalls and other attractions anyway. Be brief. Extol the virtues of the charity and encourage everyone to spend lots of money. Stride off and set them an example yourself.

Presenting the prizes

If you are presenting the prizes at a school sports day, then nothing more than an 'It gives me great pleasure . . . congratulate the winners . . . everyone did very well' effusion is called for. Prize-giving speech days require an actual speech. It is to be hoped that you can avoid the clichés about schooldays being the happiest days of your life, and all that. A technique which is, in fact, useful in any situation where you are expected to say a few words is to begin by saying how difficult it is. This is particularly true of making prize-giving speeches because you have to appeal to three audiences: the pupils, their parents and the teachers. It will endear you to some if you make a joke about the teachers – if, for example, you say, 'One day in the distant future when you meet them again, and you have grown up meanwhile and they have remained exactly the same, you will find them really quite human' – and then concentrate on the pupils, because they are the real reason for the prize giving.

If you are an old pupil of the school, curiously enough the current crop will be interested to know what it used to be like. Also any news that you can bring from the real world beyond the education system – that it does exist, and that dreams and ambitions may be realized there – may give your younger listeners some hope for the future.

Apart from that, try to raise a laugh or two, and, as always, be brief. Your secret weapon, which is an invaluable way of ending the speech, is being able to grant some sort of half holiday (which, of course you have cleared with the head teacher in advance.) 'Well, the good news is that you are going to get one,' you can say. 'And the bad news is that it's to be on 25 December. No, I'm sure it can be fitted in some time when you will really notice it. And now that I am the most popular person in the hall, I'll sit down.'

Accepting an award

As with compliments, awards and honours should be accepted if offered publicly and only turned down privately. The best and only reason that should be given for turning down an honour or award is 'for personal reasons'. It is always inadvisable to hint at what these might be.

There is one aspect of award-refusing, however, that is not as straightforward as the foregoing might imply. This is in connection with the now highly organized and much-publicized showbusiness and literary awards that nowadays seem to be a mainstay of TV schedules in the early months of each year.

There can be a commercial element here, because an award may keep buyers flocking into bookshops and audiences into shows. Unfortunately, the awards ceremonies have been turned into shows themselves. They are a relatively cheap way of getting star names on to TV and of filling up programme time. But they have been choreographed as gladiatoral displays where those who do not win are expected to put their humiliation or stiff-upper-lipism on display as an entertainment. It is not surprising that some nominees stay away. They run the risk of being thought churlish, but their feelings should be appreciated.

As for those who do turn up to collect awards, and get them, it goes without saying that their speeches of acceptance should be brief, should not attempt to thank everyone who has helped them get to this point in their lives (starting with the obstetrician who brought them into the world), nor facetiously avoid thanking anybody. However, there is no chance that any award winner will heed this advice. It is a process that apparently melts the brain.

Chapter 12

$\mathscr{S}$PECIAL OCCASIONS

In the late 1940s, a Labour minister was dining with King George VI at Buckingham Palace. When asked if he would like a cigar, he declined, saying, 'Oh no, thank you – I only smoke on special occasions . . .'

However he defined 'special occasions', here we examine the manners and etiquette of life's landmarks – births, anniversaries and deaths. For marriage and divorce, see Chapter 5.

(See also 'Surprise parties' in Chapter 4 GUESTS AND HOSTS, and Chapter 11 SPEAKING.)

Births

It is no longer necessary for an expectant mother to hide away until the birth takes place. Quite the contrary: she's going to have a baby, so she flaunts it. Others are not supposed to shrink from recognizing the fact. They must ask, 'When is it due?' with monotonous regularity and may even have the cheek to inquire what sex it is going to be. If the parents know, they should not spoil the surprise by telling. Most working women stay at their posts until positively the last moment.

People should never *assume* that a woman is pregnant just because she looks like it. They should wait to be told.

Arrival. A newspaper announcement of the birth is bald as a baby's bottom:

PARKER. On 27th February, 199–, at St Roger's
Hospital, London, to Clarissa (neé Banks) and
Norman Parker, a son (Derek Clive).

If the parents are not married, a formula may be
attempted that gives both parents' surnames. This is an
excellent opportunity to tell the world at large what
form of surname the child is going to adopt. If the
mother is a single parent, it is quite in order just to give
her name and for readers to draw their own conclusions

The birth must be registered by one or other of the
parents within forty-two days. If the parents are not
married, both parents are required to register in person.

Friends and relatives may be informed of the baby's
arrival, the date, its names and the weight at birth –
through the sending of a card. Usually, these cards are
bought preprinted with the details handwritten in. This
is also a good way to declare how you wish the baby to
be known in terms of parental surnames – and if you
would prefer it that little 'James' didn't have his name
shortened to 'Jim'. It is customary for those who receive
the cards to send a card or letter of congratulation in
return, if they have not already done so. Gifts to the
baby are only expected from close friends.

It is obviously prudent to tread carefully when drawing attention to any likeness thought to be shared by
child and parent. Particularly if the child has been
adopted . . .

Naming the baby. Burdening a child with the names of
your favourite football team (in its entirety) or with that
of some current hero (hence John Winston Lennon in
1940) is a species of long-term cruelty that should not be
inflicted on anybody. The cautious, kindly parent should
also check to make sure that the child's initials do not
knowingly constitute an embarrassment (though the
parents of a woman I know with the initials 'P.M.T.' may
have chosen them before the concept was identified.)

Apart from this, parents usually have the nack of giving appropriate names to their offspring. Or perhaps it is that children grow up to be as their names suggest they should be.

Godparenting

Godparents have a specific function – a religious function – in the upbringing of children, but customarily the job is looked upon as a way of ensuring a supply of birthday presents and gifts for the child over a period of many years. It also may be a way of binding the godparent to the parents by a tie of obligation which loops round the next generation. Under Church of England law, there are three godparents – two women and one man for a girl, two men and one woman for a boy; in the Roman Catholic church, each child has one godmother and one godfather – though there is nothing to stop people having more. It helps if the godparents are of the same religious denomination as the child, but this is not essential, although they will normally have to be baptized, confirmed and practising Christians themselves (though one suspects that vagueness often sets in on these points.) Nor is it necessary for them to be present at the christening, though obviously it is better if they are.

The religious qualifications of few godparents are considered before they are approached (best by letter), although in theory they will find themselves expected to proclaim some sort of allegiance to the particular church and their belief in God, as well as undertaking to see the child brought up according to the Christian religion. Few people who are approached to be a godparent would refuse on the grounds of inadequacy in these areas. Indeed, about the only feasible way to excuse yourself from the task is to declare convincingly, with evidence if necessary, that you already have far too many godchildren and would be unable to perform your function (however minimal) adequately. Edward Heath, the bachelor former Prime Minister, pulled down the shutters only after he had acquired something like twelve godchildren. This will give you some idea of the convincing you may have to do. Gore Vidal when asked to become godparent to the daughter of Kenneth and Kathleen Tynan exclaimed, 'Always a godfather, never the god!' but accepted just the same.

When people do have worries on this score, they probably tell themselves that to decline on grounds of religious belief or lack of it would be more contemptible than simply to acquiesce on social grounds.

Baptism. Even more so than morning prayer and weddings, baptisms are prone to improvisation by the clergyman concerned. He will guide everyone through the service without any rehearsal. With luck, he will make it very informal – a sensible thing to do if the baby is being noisy and troublesome – though this is harder to bring off if the baptism is incorporated, as it frequently is, in regular morning services.

There is no fee for a christening, so it behoves the parents to make a proper, voluntary contribution to the church funds.

Baptismal gifts. Silverware – spoons, napkin rings, and the like – is the traditional type of christening present, though whether the gifts ever really mean much to the actual child is doubtful. Godparents and others taking a long-term view may feel that to lay down wine or port is appropriate, though this may be presumptuous and thought to be nudging the child in a direction in which he or she should not be nudged. Opening a savings account with a gift of money, although it cannot fail to be useful, may smack a little of trade to some parents. Gifts of Bibles and prayer books should wait until the child can read, and normally until confirmation.

Confirmation gifts. If the child chooses to be confirmed, probably, in early teens, the godparents should endeavour to be present at the appropriate service. Indeed, in some versions, a godparent presents the candidate for confirmation to the bishop. It is expected of godparents that they make a gift on this occasion. They should not assume that a Bible or prayer book would be welcome, as the child may already have these, or be getting them from another source. As a godparent myself, who was specifically invited to look after the 'secular' needs of one goddaughter, I have found that gifts of dictionaries or the *Complete Works of Shakespeare* (and other classics) go down well – not least because confirmation tends to occur at an age when an interest in reading really begins.

Duties of godparents – apart from the religious, that is. Prosaic though it may sound, their chief duty is to remember the godchild's birthday, without fail, and to send a present. To a lesser extent, a present may also be expected at Christmas. This may literally be a thankless task (see 'Thank-you notes' in Chapter 16 WRITTEN COMMUNICATION) but has to be done. As the child grows older, outings and meals may also be arranged, coupled with a kindly interest in his or her progress. One godparent I know went so far as to take up the cudgels on behalf of her godchild when she felt that the child's mother had acted unforgivably and neglectfully by leaving home. I believe it had some effect. However unlikely, godparents should see it as their role to protect the child and act as guardians, should the need arise.

Some godparents, alas, find that they develop a marked dislike to their godchildren as they grow older. They simply have to grin and bear it. Similarly, if they fall out with the parents, or move away from the parent's world, they should keep on sending the customary gifts. The whole matter may safely be concluded when the godchild comes of age, though whether this is at the age of eighteen or twenty-one – or frequently both – is a further matter for conjecture.

Coming of age

Now that young people are legally of age and entitled to vote at the age of eighteen, some, though not all, of the significance of the 'twenty-first birthday' has evaporated. For those wishing to make a special present, the only course is to ask the young persons on which anniversary they would prefer to have it. It has not been unknown for someone to say 'eighteen' only to find that at twenty-one they received a second helping.

Bar and Bat Mitzvahs. Thirteen-year-old Jewish children are called to the Torah in religious ceremonies that are customarily followed later on the Sabbath by a lunch or an evening reception. Thus, in a sense, a Bar Mitzvah (for a boy) and a Bat Mitzvah (for a girl) are solemn religious ceremonies like confirmation in the Christian church coupled with a coming-of-age party. Formal invitations are issued and money and presents are bestowed on the young person who has to write thank-you letters and not mind being made a fuss of. However, formal confirmation, in a religious sense, follows a few years later.

Graduation ceremonies

There are few parents who will want to miss the formal conclusion of their offspring's education (if conclusion it is), especially if they (the parents) had a tough time while each successive educational hurdle was being surmounted. They may be a little disappointed therefore when their graduate offspring show rather less interest than them in attending a fancy-dress, 'meaningless' ceremony, simply in order to collect a piece of paper.

Such behaviour is less than gracious and is not to be condoned. However, parents may lighten the burden by not insisting that the offspring wear academic caps on the heads when being photographed in academic robes for the formal photo.

Special birthdays

After the eighteenth or twenty-first birthdays, special celebrations are not usually in order until the fortieth. This anniversary has assumed great symbolic function – a farewell to youth and embarkation upon middle age. In certain professions, a great fuss indeed is made of the fortieth birthday (assuming that the subject is not too deep into the mid-life crisis). 'Life begins at forty' was a slogan invented in the 1930s by an American, William Pitkin, Professor of Journalism at Columbia University. He was dealing with 'adult reorientation' at a time when the problems of extended life and leisure were beginning to be recognized. Based on lectures Pitkin had given, the book was full of uplift: 'Every day brings forth some new thing that adds to the joy of life after forty. Work becomes easy and brief. Play grows richer and longer. Leisure lengthens. Life's afternoon is brighter, warmer, fuller of song; and long before shadows stretch, every fruit grows ripe . . . Life begins at forty. This is the revolutionary outcome of our new era . . . today it is half a truth. Tomorrow it will be an axiom.'

It is certainly a well-established motto. Advertising people, in particular, love to arrange spectacular fortieth birthday parties, possibly as a way of reviewing the life so far. A consequence is that, for everyone, celebrating birthdays thereafter becomes rather more of a thing, though big parties are held only every ten years – for the fiftieth, sixtieth, seventieth birthdays, and so on.

Wedding anniversaries

Most couples make something of the fact that another year has passed since they were married – and woe betide the partner who forgets. Sometimes relatives and friends will send anniversary cards, but this is a practice, rather like Father's Day, that in the mainstream has never quite caught on.

Special celebrations are in order on the Silver Wedding (twenty-five years), Ruby Wedding (forty years), Golden Wedding (fifty years) and Diamond Wedding (sixty years). Few marriages last seventy-five years so the period was reduced to sixty, rather as Queen Victoria's Diamond Jubilee was celebrated sixty years after she came to the throne. If guests are invited to come to a party or dinner, small presents are probably expected, perhaps with something silvery or golden, as relevant, about them.

Other anniversaries, whose names may suggest themes for presents, are, traditionally:

First	Cotton Wedding
Second	Paper Wedding
Third	Leather Wedding
Fourth	Flower/Fruit Wedding
Fifth	Wooden Wedding
Sixth	Iron/Sugar-Candy Wedding
Seventh	Woollen Wedding
Eighth	Bronze/Electrical Appliances Wedding (sic)
Ninth	Copper/Pottery Wedding
Tenth	Tin Wedding
Eleventh	Steel Wedding
Twelfth	Silk/Fine Linen Wedding
Thirteenth	Lace Wedding
Fourteenth	Ivory Wedding
Fifteenth	Crystal Wedding
Twentieth	China Wedding

Thirtieth	Pearl Wedding
Thirty-fifth	Coral Wedding
Forty-fifth	Sapphire Wedding
Fifty-fifth	Emerald Wedding

By writing to the Queen's assistant private secretary and showing a copy of the marriage certificate it is possible to receive a telegram of congratulation on the Diamond (sixtieth) wedding anniversary and at five-year intervals thereafter.

Kissagrams

(See 'Kissagrams' in Chapter 10 SOCIAL LIFE.)

Christmas

– comes but once a year, and the general feeling is that this is quite often enough, thank you. The jaundiced middle-aged tend to wander around in the vain hope of finding of a traditional Christmas 'like it used to be' (i.e. with Morecambe and Wise on the TV), while everyone else wages family warfare at an intensity not seen at any other time of year. Family rows reach their height and sustained ill will towards one's fellow men is commonplace.

The main etiquette problem at Christmas is in connection with greetings cards. It is quite in order to send greetings cards to non-Christians, though it might be judicious to select a picture which is just Christmassy rather than specifically religious. There is, after all, hardly anything wrong with wishing people well, whatever their religion, and 'season's greetings' can be generally applied. On the other hand, one would rather not see the proliferation of 'good wishes for the *holiday*' which tend to emanate from the United States. After all, it is rather more than a 'holiday'.

To send a Hanukkah card to a Jew on the grounds that Hanukkah is a Jewish festival equivalent to Christmas (it merely takes place about the same time) is to make an assumption that might not be well received. Much better to avoid the whole problem by sending a New Year card. No one could possibly object to being wished a happy New Year (even if they are Jewish and will be having their own New Year by and by.)

Christmas cards bearing photographs of the family are not exactly relevant. The late, impossible, magnate Robert Maxwell once sent a Christmas card bearing a picture of his own birthday celebrations earlier in the year. It had to be pointed out, by people at a sufficient distance from him, that Christmas was usually believed to be a celebration of the birth of Jesus Christ.

If you like to have your Christmas cards printed, then on no account should you have your names *and* your address printed. Such an approach would cry out to have some personal touch added. Just your address with a handwritten signature would be a reasonable compromise. The address might help to identify to the doubtful just who 'Jack and Celia' are. To have 'Mr and Mrs E. Scrooge' printed is forbidding indeed and self-consciously to cross this out and write your first names in by hand for your close friends is an uneasy solution. It is best to avoid doing it at all, in my view.

To put a notice in a newspaper saying that 'so-and-so is not sending Christmas cards this year but sends etc.' is – and always has been – unforgivable. If there is good reason why you are not sending cards – a bereavement, say – then your friends and acquaintances will know about it. If they do not, then a card sent early the following December, with a line or two of explanation, will ensure that any desired reciprocity will not be unaffected.

Which brings us to the question of how you reduce the number of cards you send if you feel that you have entered into a meaningless tit-for-tat exchange. There is no doubt that a lot of people feel that too many Christmas cards get sent unnecessarily – often at considerable expense – and that the whole business has become a meaningless one. How can you drop people from your list? If you wait to see whether they are going to drop you first, you will probably find yourself sending off a card hastily at the last moment when *their* card plops on to your doormat two days before Christmas. As a general rule, though, if you do not send a card for a couple of Christmasses, they should get the message.

The growing adoption of the American practice of including with the card a newsletter about the family's doings over the previous twelve months should be treated cautiously. Such newsletters are usually banal and written in a particularly irritating style, with rather too many medical details ('I survived triple-bypass surgery in April') and too many comments in brackets ('And guess who got to do that job!!') Best avoided, I say, or at least only sent out to the known forbearing.

Christmas boxes. The annual tip given to tradesmen and other regular suppliers of services is probably dying out. In some cases – refuse collectors, for example – it may actually be forbidden by the employer, as is the seeking of tips at any other time of year.

Gone are the days when postmen were kindly old souls who seemed to care – so gone, too, are their tips. I can recall the days when mail deliveries were still made on Christmas Day and the postman went on his rounds picking up tips left, right and centre, and becoming more inebriated at every house as he did so. Now postmen dash about in their trainers and don't even give you time to get to the door before stuffing things through the letterbox or leaving you a card saying they were unable to deliver a parcel. Of course, in the light of this, you won't bother to chase after them with a tip.

Newspaper delivery boys and girls seem very organized round about Christmas, even delivering preprinted cards reminding you of their existence. Have I heard the story about a newspaper boy who delivered a note saying, 'Last chance, pay up – or else!'? Oddly, many paper boys don't follow through and knock on your door, but they surely deserve something if they have the guts to do this.

Carol singers. There are few things worse than being asked to listen to a poorly sung carol before a note of it has even been sung. And there are the carol singers who warble two lines and then press the door bell. Then there are the carol singers who, should you decline to contribute because it isn't even December yet, leave you with a most unChristmassy wish ringing in your ears. The only carol singers it is right to support are those who are genuinely collecting for a charity rather than for themselves – if you can determine this.

St Valentine's Day

The supposedly ancient practice of sending a card to one's loved one (or to someone one wishes to advise is being secretly admired) is now a full-scale commercial festival. In recent years, a curiously large number of lovers have shown they are prepared to pay for messages of the 'Wiggly Wiggly Woo loves her Little Sausage' variety, to appear in newspapers on the 14th February.

Although in some cases the identity of the sender will be obvious to the receiver, Valentine's Day cards and messages are much more fun if they baffle the receiver – for they should, in essence, be anonymous.

Leap Year proposals

In a Leap Year, when there is a 29th day of February, it is traditional for a woman to be able to propose to a man, rather than having to wait for him to get round to it. Records are in short supply as to how many women have taken advantage of this somewhat meaningless concession. Originally, however, if the proposal was rejected by the man, the woman could claim a silk gown or a sum of money from him, and in 15th-century Italian states, for example, this claim was legally enforceable.

Hallowe'en

One of the least welcome imports to Britain from the United States in recent years has been the Hallowe'en custom of children, suitably dressed up, knocking on the doors of complete strangers and demanding a 'trick or treat' - i.e. that the house owners should hand over some small present (sweets, money) or have a trick played on them (a message written on the front door in shaving foam, for example). Fairly harmless in essence, the practice soon led to horror stories reaching the UK of children playing 'tricks' which did real damage and of their being given poisoned sweets as 'treats'.

In the North of England, the traditional Mischief Night may have given rise to the same sort of demands, and may also have given rise to the jingle ending:

If you haven't got a penny, a ha-penny will do,
If you haven't got a ha'penny, your door's going
  through.

Parents would do well to ensure that children, especially the very youngest, only attempt to demand treats with menaces from neighbours they know and who will understand what is going on when strange creatures in Hallowe'en disguise come knocking on their doors. All potential victims would do best to arm themselves with small gifts of sweets or small amounts of money in readiness. Unprepared, I have in my time been reduced to giving, variously, a tin of baked beans and one of my books. I'm not sure that this was quite what the trick or treaters had in mind.

Deaths

If weddings are the biggest events most people have to organize in their lives, funerals are the most devastating. On the other hand, it can be a relief to have many practical arrangements to make; the busyness distracts from the sorrow involved. The legal procedures for registering a death and dealing with the body are clearly established and a general practitioner or hospital official will invariably make sure you know what has to be done.

The first thing is to get in touch very quickly with an undertaker or funeral director. With any luck, he will take care of everything – from liaising with a clergyman over the date and time of any religious funeral to inserting an announcement in the press.

If a will has been left, this needs to be consulted very quickly to see whether the deceased has made any stipulations about the form of any funeral and about the disposal of the body (and organs for medical research). Such stipulations are not legally binding. The executors of the will may make their own decisions on this score, though will naturally try to do what the deceased wished, if practical. If there are no executors, the closest relatives must decide among themselves about a burial or cremation and the type of any commemorative service.

Announcing the death. Although 'word of mouth' can work with astonishing speed in a community, it is important for whoever takes charge after a death to inform near relatives and friends (probably by phone) – 'I'm afraid I have some sad news . . .'

If the deceased lived alone, an address book can be most useful in this distressing, but necessary, task.

Word of mouth will not reach everybody and not
everyone scours the 'Deaths' column in newspapers, or
will even read the relevant newspaper.

A typical newspaper announcement would appear in
the 'Deaths' column something like this:

> STEVENS – David Richard Somerset, 4th December 199-, in
> hospital, aged 87 years, beloved husband of the late Jane,
> dear father of Maurice and Sally, loving grandfather of
> Simon, Shirley and Tom. Service at St Peter's Church,
> Portland, Tuesday 12th December at 10am. Family flowers
> only, but donations if desired to The British Heart Founda-
> tion c/o the funeral directors [their name, address and
> telephone number]

The charity or charities selected should be appropriate
to the deceased. Often the choice reflects whatever it
was that person died of but equally may be a cause that
the deceased had shown an interest in when alive.

I have noticed a growing tendency for funeral notices
to contain miniature obituaries. This seems an excellent
idea, especially where the subject may not be going to
merit a full-scale newspaper obituary. Apart from fulfil-
ling the function of an epitaph or memorial, it has the
advantage that it more clearly identifies the deceased.
Close relatives who compose such notices should try to
be as factual as possible and to avoid anything too
maudlin. Here is a paraphrase of what the wife of one of
my contemporaries, who died in his mid-forties, put in a
national newspaper:

> . . . He was the beloved and cherished husband and father
> of . . . . He was a pupil at . . . School; he graduated from
> . . . . College Oxford, in 1966 and was called to the Bar. He
> will be remembered as a colleague of all at . . . . &
> Son and of their associates world-wide. The funeral service
> will be held at . . .

'Flowers if desired' is rare these days, but if flowers are
not specifically ruled out, they should be sent to arrive at

the address given in good time for the funeral. A brief message, 'In loving memory . . .' can be requested from the florist and this will be attached to the wreath or floral arrangement. The flowers are in memory of the dead person and not for the survivors. Accordingly, they should be addressed care of the funeral directors, in the name of the deceased, but not 'the late . . .'. If people bring flowers to the funeral, they may be accepted by the funeral directors and placed in the hearse. After a cremation, the funeral directors will reclaim the flowers and ask the relatives what they wish to be done with them. Usually, they have an arrangement to give them away to hospitals, old folks' homes, or similar.

'No letters please' is a wish that should be respected, but not one that should be made, in my view.

Letters of condolence. The writing and receiving of letters of condolence is one of the ways in which people can come to terms with the fact of death. To deny them this opportunity is to make matters that much harder to bear. Letters of condolence though difficult to write – and to receive – are still wonderful things to have. It does not matter if they are awkwardly expressed or even very short.

Although it appears customary for the families who have received anything more than a few such letters to have formal cards of acknowledgement printed, my own view is that a brief handwritten letter of thanks is preferable. Never mind if writing many such takes a long time to do. It is unlikely that it will make the burden of loss any worse and may even help lighten it.

Another method is to place a notice in the local newspaper:

The family of the late Mrs ——— ——— wish to thank all relatives and friends for the kind expressions of sympathy they received during their recent bereavement.

Mourning. The elaborate Victorian etiquette of mourning has, thankfully, vanished. No longer are blinds drawn in the dead person's house. Black-edged notepaper is seldom thought necessary nowadays. Members of the family no longer have to take turns sitting up all night with the corpse – not least because so many people die in hospital now, or are quickly removed from the place of death. These days it is quite in order to decline an opportunity to 'view the body' – that is to say, the body prepared (if not embalmed) for burial or cremation. Even dark rather than black clothes may be worn for the funeral. People wear mourning clothes hardly at all at other times during any notional 'period of mourning' and nowadays you will almost never see a black armband being worn.

'Mrs Fitz-Adam reappeared in Cranford ("as bold as a lion," Miss Pole said), a well-to-do widow, dressed in black rustling silk, so soon after her husband's death that poor Miss Jenkyns was justified in the remark she made, that "bombazine would have shown a deeper sense of her loss".'

Elizabeth Gaskell, *Cranford* (1851–3)

Funerals

If a full church funeral service or even just a short ceremony at a crematorium is required, the officiating clergyman will probably seek your advice on a choice of hymns and also what to say in his (hopefully short) address. It helps if you ensure that the important aspects of the deceased's life are brought out and that the right people are mentioned. If a cremation follows a full church service held elsewhere, it is customary only for close relatives to go to the crematorium. If others attending the funeral have then been invited to some

form of reception, they can make their way there slowly
and await the arrival of these close relatives.

Even for people who have not practised any religion, a
brief religious ceremony is often thought appropriate,
though not, of course, if any antipathy towards religion
is known in the dead person. Humanist and other non-
religious forms of marking deaths are, apparently,
gaining in popularity. To have no marking of a death is
an utterly bleak way out for anybody.

'It is of no consequence to the dead what his
funeral is; costly obsequies are the affectation of the
living.'
> Euripides, *Troades* (*c* 415 BC)

'The pomp of funerals feeds rather the vanity of the
living than does honour to the dead.'
> La Rochefoucauld, *Maxims* (1665)

'I direct that I be given a modest funeral, either at
sunrise or at sunset, with no pomp, no singing, no
music.'
> Giuseppe Verdi, Last Will, (1900)

(He had his wish, and then they laid on an
enormous memorial service . . .)

Afterwards. What used to be called a 'wake' (because
the family and friends stayed awake all night after the
funeral while the soul of the departed went on its way)
may now be a 'funeral buffet', the hard drink and tipsy
cake replaced by tea and buns. Some people specify in
their wills what sort of shindig they wish to follow their
deaths – though, most likely, these occasions would not
follow immediately after the funeral. Nevertheless, a
belief that the departed would have preferred a party
than a lot of people sitting around with long faces can
mean that that is exactly what is arranged.

Some form of hospitality is almost essential. Arthur

Marshall said once that, 'There is nothing like a morning funeral for quickening the appetite for lunch'. An hour spent in a cold church or by a damp graveside certainly merits a reviving something. Otherwise, the old adage that 'one funeral makes another' may prove only too true.

Helping others in their bereavement. However hard it may seem, the best approach is for the bereaved to confront their loss. Immediately after the death and on the day of the funeral, there is a temptation for well-wishers to try to say something special to the bereaved, yet they may find this unwelcome. Gone are the days when death was unmentionable and the name of the deceased was hardly ever uttered, but in the early stages of bereavement brief, even clichéd, expressions of sorrow, are all that is expected.

A little later, much the best approach is to keep on mentioning the deceased by some affectionate name and to face up to the loss at every opportunity. It takes time, of course, to come to terms with loss, but time is the great healer. The thing about the clichés of death is that they are largely true. At the first funeral I ever attended, as a boy, an elderly mourner did actually say to me, 'There's another page turned in the Book of Life'. People cling to this kind of saying as they might to wreckage and they are not to be mocked.

A continuing irritant for those who are left behind is to receive junk mail addressed to the deceased. It is a good idea to return all such mail to the sender – at their expense, if possible – together with a note explaining the situation and a request that the family be no further troubled.

Memorial services

Few funeral services are anything less than miserable occasions, but memorial services can be wonderful.

Preferably held a good while after the death when the shock or sorrow has begun to go away, a memorial service can be a true celebration of a life rather than a woeful marking of a death. 'Service of thanksgiving' is the better way to refer to these occasions. Dress can range from the formal (for Westminster Abbey and similar venues) to the informal. I believe I attended Arthur Marshall's memorial service at St James's, Piccadilly, London, in a summer suit and white shoes. It was a lovely sunny day and I certainly did not feel out of place.

Such is the importance attached to some of these occasions, that semi-professional organizers may be brought in to bring the elements together.

Wills

Most people do not make a will and, if this is done wilfully, so to speak, it is the last act of bad manners they can perform. Not leaving a will can cause hardship and worry to those who have to clear up after the departed. Even if making a will has been neglected out of spite, the chances are that the spite will not operate in the ways the deceased was hoping.

A formal reading of a will – at which beneficiaries and the disappointed learn of their fate direct from a solicitor – is now a practice close to extinction.

Chapter 13

$\mathscr{T}$ITLES AND ADDRESSING

Spoken communication, mostly by telephone, has largely replaced the written letter and, accordingly, few people would nowadays consider that the way we address other people is one worth losing much sleep over. Yet titles and modes of address are curiously fascinating and there is a certain pleasure to be had in getting things right, whether in speech or writing. But what is right? That is the question. Authorities on this matter quite often give conflicting advice. Usually, indeed, there is more than one way of going about addressing people. Thus, there is often plenty of scope for debate, and I have tried to set out the options as well as the opinions.

Esquire

I would rather not be addressed as 'Nigel Rees, Esq.' That really does seem a pretty pointless affectation these days. I don't even particularly want to addressed, in print, as 'Mr'. 'Mr Nigel Rees' signals to me that my correspondent has decided, of his own accord, that I am not up to 'Esq.' and am thus to be treated like a tradesman.

So, I would rather just be addressed by name alone, without any title whatever. If people wish to put 'Dear Mr Rees' at the start of a letter, then that is fine by me, though 'Dear Nigel Rees' is an increasingly common usage. If they wish to call me 'Mr Rees' in speaking, that is also, of course, quite acceptable. However, I do not mind complete strangers addressing me by first name, or by first and surname either – though I am aware that others view this as a kind of invasion of privacy (see 'First-name terms' in Chapter 10 SOCIAL LIFE.)

Of course, it is easy for me to take this attitude within the easy familiarity of the media, but I wish other people would join me in it. It would help to overcome all sorts of problems. If all such common or garden handles were abolished (I am not suggesting that 'Sirs' and 'Lords' and 'Reverends' should get the chop), there would be much less scope for contention or for offence to being taken.

Women's agonizing over whether to be 'Miss' 'Mrs' or 'Ms' would be finished at a stroke, if they just stuck to their names.

The Msing link

'Ms' (pronounced *miz*) is 'a title substituted for Mrs or Miss before a woman's name to avoid making a distinction between married and unmarried women,' according to the *Collins Dictionary of the English Language* (1979). Thus, it is a compromise designed to solve a problem and sounds like one.

It became popular with feminists in about 1970 at the start of the modern thrust by the Women's Movement. The New York Commission on Human Rights adopted it for use in correspondence at about that time. By 1972, a feminist magazine called *Ms* was being launched.

The idea had been around for some time before it became – in the words of the *Oxford English Dictionary* – 'an increasingly common, but not universally accepted, use.' As early as 1952, the National Office Management Association of Philadelphia was recommending, 'Use the abbreviation Ms for *all women* addressees. This modern style solves an age-old problem.'

But it created new ones. In August 1984, Geraldine Ferraro was the first woman to be selected as an American vice-presidential candidate. In what is known as 'private life', she was, in fact, Mrs John Zaccaro. In public she declined to be known as 'Miss Ferraro', feeling this was inapposite for a woman who was the mother of three children. She asked that she be called either Ms or Mrs Ferraro. The *New York Times* in its traditional way, found this very hard to swallow.

The paper liked to attach honorifics to names but did not permit the use of Ms in its columns and had to call her 'Mrs Ferraro' – despite pleadings from its own word expert, William Safire, who protested that 'Mrs Ferraro' is 'a person she is not . . . It is unacceptable for journalists to dictate to a candidate that she call herself Miss or else use her married name.'

In 1986, the *New York Times* gave way. But one can understand its reluctance. Not for opposing the motives behind the coinage, but on the grounds that it is not an elegant or happy coinage. Do I detect that its use is receding?

Talking to a chair

As with the invention of 'Ms', the attempt at removing gender from 'chairman' has resulted in an oddity – addressing someone as 'chair' – and a ludicrous one. Moreover, it is based on the mistaken premise that the 'man' in 'chairman' denotes masculinity. On the contrary, that merely reflects membership of the human race.

'Chairperson' and similar coinages are equally far-fetched and should be avoided. 'Madam Chairman' would seem to be an acceptable compromise.

'I can't bear being called Chair. Whatever I am, I am not a piece of furniture.'

Baroness Seear, in 1988

'Dear Desk . . .'
Noël Coward, replying to a letter headed 'From the Desk
of . . .'

All this recalls the origin of the title of the musical
Call Me Madam. When Frances Perkins was appointed
Secretary of Labor by President Roosevelt in 1933, she
became the first US woman to hold Cabinet rank. It
popularly supposed that when she had been asked in
Cabinet how she wished to be addressed, she had
replied, 'Call me Madam'. Perkins denied that she had
done this, however. It was *after* her first Cabinet
meeting that reporters asked how they should address
her.

The Speaker-elect of the House of Representatives,
Henry T. Rainey, answered for her. 'When the Secretary
of Labor is a lady, she should be addressed with the
same general formalities as the Secretary of Labor who
is a gentleman. You call him "Mr Secretary". You will
call her "Madam Secretary". You gentlemen know that
when a lady is presiding over a meeting, she is referred
to as "Madam Chairman" when you rise to address the
chair'. Some of the reporters put this ruling into
Perkins's own mouth and that presumably is how the
misquotation occurred, but the logic is as impeccable
as – to my mind – the acceptability of the use, even
today.

Married names

You don't have to be a rabid feminist to appreciate that
some women when they marry do not wish to submerge
their identity in their husband's by becoming known as
'Mrs John Smith'. There is no legal requirement for them
to do such a thing, anyway, though in the days (very
recent) when the Inland Revenue maintained the prehis-
toric practice of dealing with the husband over his

wife's tax affairs, it was impossible to refer to a wife solely by her unmarried name. 'Jane Golightly a.k.a. [also known as] Mrs J.P. Smith' would soon creep in.

It can be very hard work for a married woman to insist on the use of her unmarried name, even if it is already well established, for example, as her professional name. Additionally, in social life, good friends, unthinkingly and for the sake of convenience, will introduce the couple as 'Jane and John Smith'. Possibly, there is, too, a desire in this to make it plain that the two people are genuinely married and not 'living in sin', as it was once thought of.

There is no obvious solution to this problem, where the wife (quite understandably) does not wish to use her married name. The husband, John Smith, will find himself explaining rather often, 'my wife, who goes under her own name, Jane Golightly'. He will also have to deal with telephone calls in which he is asked, 'Is that Mr Golightly?' To which he will find himself replying, 'Yes – after a fashion – it's too complicated to explain.'

How much more sensible is the American fashion for *adding on* the husband's name upon marriage (sometimes with a hyphen, sometimes not). This can give rise to some oddities, of which 'Ariana Stassinopoulos Huffington' is probably the oddest, but it makes what has happened perfectly clear. And then, should the worst happen, and the marriage fail, the husband's surname can simply be lopped off again. (So Farrah Fawcett Majors went back to being Farrah Fawcett. By contrast, how many women in British public life have found fame under their married names and then been condemned to keep them even after divorce?) Alas, the American fashion will not seem to take on in Britain, it appears.

Another way of getting round this problem is – in semi-formal correspondence, anyway – to call a married woman by both names. This has the added advantage of

making absolutely clear what her status is, as well as
hinting that she is not too happy with people who
misunderstand. Thus, 'Mrs David M. Married (Jessica
Single)' or 'Jessica Single (Mrs David M. Married)' or (in
the US) 'Jessica Single (Mrs David M.) Married'.

A curiosity that lingers in certain quarters is that the
wife of the head of a family can just be referred to as,
for example, 'Mrs Brackett' – not 'Mrs Henry Brackett' –
but only if there is no more senior widow living. This
even applies after the husband's death, though not if
there is a mother-in-law still alive or an elder brother
whose wife is still living. All very Jane Austen, but
important to some.

Mrs Thatcher's divorce

You may not have thought that Mrs Thatcher was
divorced, but to say 'Mrs Margaret Thatcher', as she was
known when she was Prime Minister, is to employ the
correct form for addressing a divorced woman. Before
her husband's baronetcy was conferred and before her
own elevation to the peerage complicated matters, her
correct title should have been 'Mrs Denis Thatcher'.

Understandably, of course, the media needed a way of
describing her that would identify her more clearly and
possibly in a way that did not suggest she was merely
an appendage of her husband. So 'Mrs Margaret
Thatcher'.

It could also be argued that to call her so was merely
to use what was already a well-established form for
addressing professional married women. Earlier, in political life, 'Mrs Barbara Castle' was used when, in fact,
she was properly 'Mrs Ted Castle'. And there are
married women who, while not being in business or
public life, unilaterally declare that they wish to be
known by their own first name and their husband's
surname – again to diminish seeming a mere appendage

but also to keep within the proprieties. Theoretically, of course, they cast themselves as divorced women.

These matters may seem of little importance to most people, but they can be a minefield if you are dealing with people to whom they do matter.

Media misleading

Getting such matters right is not exactly a hallmark of the media. More often than not, in society tittle-tattle, titles will be flattened out to the extent that a Countess or Viscountess will just be called 'Lady X' — where it is inappropriate. Wives or widows of knights will be called 'Lady Anne Summers' when they are not the daughters of peers (see below for specific guidance on this).

And then there is the media frolicking with such concoctions as 'Princess Di' for the Princess of Wales. It may be understandable for the press to want to bring her down to the level of the princess next door, but that does not make it any more correct.

The naming of widows

I have just received a postcard from a widow — let me call her 'Deborah Dear'. She is very embarrassed about the postcard, which bears her name and address and was given to her as a present by a friend, because it describes her as 'Mrs Deborah Dear'. For the reasons given above, she is appalled by this because she thinks people will consider her to be a divorcee. She says she also had to berate the solicitor who dealt with her late husband's estate because he also called her 'Mrs Deborah Dear'.

I sympathize with her, but I do not think that people who make this mistake are wholly to blame. They may consider that to put 'Mrs Eric Dear' or 'Mrs E.K. Dear' on an envelope addressed to her is to emphasize her loss, to rub it in that she has lost her husband. True, but another widow tells me she *loves* being reminded of her late husband and thinks it wonderful that the bond can be given such tangible expression even though he has gone.

The young master

In my pre-teens childhood, I can remember receiving letters and cards addressed to 'Master Nigel Rees'. Nowadays, first name and surname alone seem sufficient for the young master.

'Miss Katherine Rees' is still current usage for a girl of any age, though it may wane. Formerly, the unrevealing 'Miss Rees' was used to describe the eldest daughter if there was more than one girl in a family, the younger daughter or daughters being identified by their first names as well as surname.

Letters after the name

Except in the most formal of communications it is probably best to forego letters after a person's name, especially as deciding on the precise order is a very complicated business. Broadly speaking, the order is: decorations (CBE, etc.); appointments (PC, for Privy Counsellor, etc.); legal appointments (QC, JP, etc.); university degrees (MA, etc.); religious orders (SJ, for Society of Jesus), medical qualifications (FRCS, Fellow of the Royal College of Surgeons), membership of learned societies (RA, for Royal Academy); member of parliament (MP); membership of armed forces (RN, etc.)

Getting the title right is the most important thing (Lord, Sir, Rt Hon., Dr, or whatever) and that will probably suffice in most cases. However, if a person does not have a title (other than Esq., Mr, Mrs, Ms), you

should consider whether your remembering their OBE
would make them happy. A label like MP should always
be used. University degrees should not normally be put,
though non-medical doctorates may be brandished in an
academic context. Proud parents will probably ignore
this advice and never fail to mention a doctorate or
other degree (at least until the novelty wears off).

The intricacies of such matters may be more fully
explored in *Debrett's Peerage and Baronetage*. Another
publication, *Debrett's People of Today* solves many
queries on this score as each individual listed is given a
personal 'style' which you can assume is correct, otherwise he or she would not have approved it.

Correct forms of address

The correct way in which you should write or speak to
someone with a title or who occupies a particular
position can be difficult to establish. What follows, in
democratically alphabetical order, is a list – though not
an all-inclusive list – of such people, and guidance – no
more than guidance – on what to do.

As with other forms of etiquette, modes of address are
not set in cement. Usage develops – most notably
towards a more informal style. Hence, in the list, most
formal modes of address have been excluded as these
belong to a bygone age. The chances are that most
people will never even meet or have reason to write to a
Duke, so it would seem pointless to draw attention to
the very formal circumstances in which you would refer
to him as 'His Grace' and call him 'Your Grace'. I have
not been entirely consistent on this score, however.

The point to make, probably, is that though there are
very definite things you should *not* do in this field, there
is choice in what you *may* do. The chief thing is not to
be overawed by it. People don't really mind if you get
things wrong and usually they will be very happy to tell

you what they believe is right or what they expect (which may not be the same).

Another method is to check with *Debrett's People of Today* or with *Who's Who*, especially for those with complicated mixtures of title, rank and honour. It would be impossible to provide a guide which took account of every eventuality. For example, when Robert Runcie was Archbishop of Canterbury, his title was 'The Most Rev. and Rt Hon. the Lord Archbishop of Canterbury' (being an archbishop, a privy councillor and having a bishop's seat in the House of Lords). When he retired he became 'The Rt Rev. and Rt Hon. the Lord Runcie of Cuddesdon' (returning to ordinary lord bishop's rank, though without a bishopric, still being a privy councillor and having being created a life peer). In neither case, apparently, was it possible to squeeze in his doctorate.

Other even more complicated examples could be cited. Discussing these issues can keep interested parties fully occupied for years, if they so desire. For ways of signing off, once you have progressed beyond the opening address on a letter, see 'Yours etc.' in Chapter 16 WRITTEN COMMUNICATION.

'"By the way, you'll think I'm strangely ignorant; but, do you really know, I am puzzled how we ought to address Lady Glenmire. Do you say 'Your Ladyship,' where you would say 'you' to a common person? I have been puzzling all morning; and are we to say 'My Lady,' instead of 'Ma'am'? . . . Will you kindly tell me the most correct way of speaking to the Peerage?"

'"Your ladyship."

'"My dear, if they fix on that way of speaking, you must just let me practise a little on you first, for I shall feel so foolish and hot saying it the first time to Lady Glenmire".'

Elizabeth Gaskell, *Cranford* (1851–3)

ADMIRAL (also for ADMIRAL OF THE FLEET, VICE ADMIRAL, REAR ADMIRAL)

On envelope: 'Admiral of the Fleet/Vice Admiral/ Rear Admiral, (Sir Horatio Fish)'
Starting letter: 'Dear Admiral' or 'Dear Admiral Fish' or 'Dear Sir Horatio', as appropriate
When introducing: 'Admiral (Fish)' or 'Admiral (Sir Horatio Fish)', as appropriate
Refer to as: 'Admiral (Fish)' or 'Sir Horatio' or 'the Admiral'
Addressing in conversation: 'Admiral (Fish)' or 'Admiral' or 'Sir Horatio'

AIR CHIEF MARSHAL

On envelope: 'Air Chief Marshal (Sir David Flight)'
Starting letter: 'Dear (Sir David)'
When introducing: 'Air Chief Marshal (Sir David Flight)' or, as appropriate, 'Sir (David)'
Refer to as: 'Air Chief Marshal (Flight)' or '(Sir David)' or 'the Air Chief Marshal'
Addressing in conversation: 'Air Chief Marshal' or '(Sir David)'

AIR COMMODORE

On envelope: 'Air Commodore (W.A. Heron)'
Starting letter: 'Dear Air Commodore (Heron)'
When introducing: 'Air Commodore (Heron)'
Refer to as: 'Air Commodore (Heron)' or 'the Air Commodore'
Addressing in conversation: 'Air Commodore'

AIR MARSHAL

On envelope: 'Air Marshal (F.O. Ward/Sir Frank Ward)'

Starting letter: 'Dear Air Marshal (Ward)/(Sir Frank)'
When introducing: 'Air Marshal (Ward)/(Sir Frank Ward)'
Refer to as: 'Air Marshal (Ward)' or '(Sir Frank)' or 'the Air Marshal'
Addressing in conversation: 'Air Marshal'

AIR VICE MARSHAL

(As for the above, except that the 'Vice' is always incorporated.)

AMBASSADOR (British or foreign)

On envelope: As appropriate, 'His Excellency, HM Ambassador to ———' [only when in the accredited country] or 'His Excellency, The (British) Ambassador' or 'His Excellency, Sir (Richard Matt), KCMG' or 'His Excellency (Derek Diplo), CMG'
Starting letter: 'Dear (Sir Richard)' or 'Dear Mr (Diplo)' or (formally) 'Sir', or according to rank
When introducing: 'Sir (Richard)' or 'Mr (Diplo)'
Refer to as: 'His Excellency' (formally); 'Sir (Richard)' or 'Mr (Diplo)' or 'The Ambassador' (socially)
Addressing in conversation: 'Sir (Richard) or 'Mr (Diplo)'. 'Your Excellency' only formally
(An Ambassador's wife may be referred to as 'the Ambassadress' and, theoretically, may be addressed as 'Her Excellency (Lady Matt)' etc., but she may prefer simply to keep to her private rank instead.)

ARCHBISHOP

On envelope: 'His Grace The Lord Archbishop of ———' or (less formally) 'The Most Rev. and Rt Hon. The Lord Archbishop of ———'
Starting letter: 'Your Grace', 'Dear Lord Archbishop',

'Dear Archbishop', as occasion demands
When introducing: 'The Archbishop of ——'
Refer to as: 'The Archbishop'
Addressing in conversation: 'Your Grace', then
'Archbishop'
(His wife is ordinarily Mrs, unless she has her own
title.)

ARCHDEACON

On envelope: 'The Venerable The Archdeacon of
——'

Starting letter: 'Dear Archdeacon/Mr Archdeacon' (a
formal letter would begin 'Venerable Sir')
When introducing: 'the Archdeacon of ——'
Refer to as: 'the Archdeacon of ——' or 'the
Archdeacon'
Addressing in conversation: 'Mr Archdeacon'

BARON (see also LIFE PEER)

On envelope: 'The Rt Hon. The Lord ——' (or
socially) 'The Lord ——'
Starting letter: 'Dear Lord ——'
When introducing: 'Lord ——'
Refer to as: 'Lord ——'
Addressing in conversation: 'Lord ——' or 'My Lord'

BARONESS (wife of Baron; see also LIFE PEERESS)

On envelope: 'The Lady ——'
Starting letter: 'Dear Lady ——'
When introducing: 'Lady ——'
Refer to as: 'Lady ——'
Addressing in conversation: 'Lady ——' or 'Madam'

BARONET

On envelope: 'Sir (Richard Heep), Bt.' (sometimes 'Bart.')
Starting letter: 'Dear Sir (Richard)'
When introducing: 'Sir (Richard Heep)'
Refer to as: 'Sir (Richard)' or 'Sir (Richard Heep)'
Addressing in conversation: 'Sir (Richard)'
(His wife is addressed, accordingly, as 'Lady (Heep)'. She is very definitely *not* 'Lady Jane Heep' or 'Jane, Lady Heep'. The first would signify that she was perhaps the daughter of an Earl; the second that she was divorced or widowed. In order to make it clear, say in the media, *which* Lady Heep is being talked about, the first name may be put within brackets as 'Lady (Jane) Heep', though this is not entirely satisfactory.)

BISHOP

On envelope: 'The Rt Rev. The Lord Bishop of
_____'

(The Bishop of London is 'The Rt Rev. and Rt Hon. The Lord Bishop of London'. Not all bishops are lord bishops. And there is another exception: The Bishop of Meath – the Premier Bishop of Ireland – is 'The Most Rev . . . .')
Starting letter: 'Dear Lord Bishop' or 'Dear Bishop'
When introducing: 'The Bishop of ——'
Refer to as: 'His Lordship'
Addressing in conversation: 'My Lord' or (familiarly) 'Bishop'
(His wife is Mrs ——. A retired bishop retains 'The Rt Rev.' and the name of the bishopric is replaced with his personal name, followed by 'DD' (for Doctor of Divinity).

BRIGADIER

On envelope: 'Brigadier (P.O. Popp)'
Starting letter: 'Dear Brigadier (Popp)'
When introducing: 'Brigadier (Popp)'
Refer to as: 'Brigadier (Popp)' or 'the Brigadier'
Addressing in conversation: 'Brigadier (Popp)' or
'Brigadier'

CADET (Royal Navy)

On envelope: '(J.A. Tar) Esq. RN'
Starting letter: 'Dear Mr (Tar)'
When introducing: 'Mr (Tar)'
Refer to as: 'Mr (Tar)'
Addressing in conversation: 'Mr (Tar)'

CANON

On envelope: 'The Rev. Canon ——— '
Starting letter: 'Dear Canon ———' (a very formal
letter would begin 'Reverend Sir')
When introducing: 'Canon ——— '
Refer to as: 'Canon ———'
Addressing in conversation: 'Canon ———' or 'Canon'
(On retirement he does not retain the title unless
made a Canon Emeritus.)

CAPTAIN (Army)

On envelope: 'Captain (V.R. Brave)' followed by
name of regiment
Starting letter: 'Dear Captain (Brave)'
When introducing: 'Captain (Brave)'
Refer to as: 'Captain (Brave)' or 'the Captain'
Addressing in conversation: 'Captain (Brave)' or
'Captain'

CAPTAIN (Royal Navy)

On envelope: 'Captain (J.A. Tar), RN'
Starting letter: 'Dear Captain (Tar)'
When introducing: 'Captain (Tar)'
Refer to as: 'Captain (Tar)' or 'the Captain'
Addressing in conversation: 'Captain' or 'Captain (Tar)'

CHIEF RABBI

On envelope: 'The Chief Rabbi Dr —— ——'
Starting letter: 'Dear Chief Rabbi'
When introducing: 'Chief Rabbi'
Refer to as: 'The Chief Rabbi' or 'Dr ——'
Addressing in conversation: 'Chief Rabbi' or 'Dr ——'

CLERGY (including MINOR CANONS, RURAL DEANS)

On envelope: 'The Rev. (O. Slope)' or 'The Reverend (O. Slope), if you think this looks better
Starting letter: 'Dear Mr (Slope)' (*not* 'Reverend (Slope)') or, where called for, 'Dear Father (Slope)'
When introducing: 'Mr (Slope)' (*not* 'the Reverend (Slope)/the Reverend'), or 'Father (Slope)'
Refer to as: 'Mr (Slope)' (ditto)
Addressing in conversation: 'Mr (Slope)' (ditto)
(A clergyman's wife is simply 'Mrs (Slope)', unless she has a title of her own. Together they would be addressed as 'The Rev. (O.) and Mrs (Slope)'.)

COLONEL

On envelope: 'Colonel (O.T. Lunch)'
Starting letter: 'Dear Colonel (Lunch)'
When introducing: 'Colonel (Lunch)'
Refer to as: 'Colonel (Lunch)' or 'the Colonel'

Addressing in conversation: 'Colonel (Lunch)'

COMMANDER

On envelope: 'Commander (J.A. Tar), RN'
Starting letter: 'Dear Commander (Tar)'
When introducing: 'Commander (Tar)'
Refer to as: 'Commander (Tar)' or 'the Commander'
Addressing in conversation: 'Commander (Tar)'
(A Lieutenant Commander is addressed accordingly
– with his rank abbreviated to 'Lieut-Commander'
on the envelope. A Royal Navy Lieutenant is
addressed similarly.)

COMMODORE

On envelope: 'Commodore (A.B. Parker)'
Starting letter: 'Dear Commodore (Parker)'
When introducing: 'Commodore (Parker)'
Refer to as: 'Commodore (Parker)' or 'the Commo-
dore'
Addressing in conversation: 'Commodore (Parker)' or
'Commodore'

COUNTESS

On envelope: 'The Countess of ——'
Starting letter: 'Dear Countess of ——' or 'Dear
Lady ——'
When introducing: 'Lady ——'
Refer to as: 'Lady ——'
Addressing in conversation: 'Lady ——'

DAME

On envelope: 'Dame (Joan Davis) GBE' (or decoration
as appropriate)
Starting letter: 'Dear Dame (Joan)'

When introducing: 'Dame (Joan)'
Refer to as: 'Dame (Joan)'
Addressing in conversation: 'Dame (Joan)'

DEAN (except RURAL DEAN, for which see CLERGY)

On envelope: 'The Very Rev. The Dean of ——'
Starting letter: 'Very Rev. Sir' or 'Dear Mr Dean' or
'Dear Dean'
When introducing: 'the Dean of ——'
Refer to as: 'the Dean of ——' or 'the Dean' or 'Dean
(Thompson)'
In conversation: 'Mr Dean' or 'Sir' or 'Dean'

DIVORCED WIFE OF PEER OR BARONET

(She is known as, for example, 'Emma, Duchess of
Tewkesbury'. If she remarries, she loses the title
completely.)

DUCHESS (see also under ROYALS for Royal Duchesses)

On envelope: 'Her Grace, The Duchess of ——' or
'The Duchess of ——'
Starting letter: 'Dear Duchess of ——' or 'Dear
Duchess'
When introducing: 'The Duchess of ——'
Refer to as: 'The Duchess of ——' or 'the Duchess'
In conversation: 'Duchess' or, at a pinch, 'Your
Grace'

DUKE (see also under ROYALS for Royal Dukes)

On envelope: 'His Grace, The Duke of ——' or 'The
Duke of ——'
Starting letter: 'Dear Duke of ——' or (familiarly)
'Dear Duke'

When introducing: 'The Duke of ——'
Refer to as: 'The Duke' or 'The Duke of ——'
Addressing in conversation: 'Duke' or, more formally, 'Your Grace'

EARL

On envelope: 'The Earl of ——'
Starting letter: 'Dear Earl of ——' or 'Dear Lord ——'
When introducing: 'Lord ——'
Refer to as: 'Lord ——'
Addressing in conversation: 'Lord ——'

ELDEST GRANDSON
OF DUKE OR MARQUESS

(He takes his grandfather's third title – hence, the grandson of a duke might be an earl. Oddly enough, on an envelope these people should be addressed without the 'the' – hence, 'Earl ————', which distinguishes them from actual holders of these ranks.)

ELDEST SON
OF DUKE, MARQUESS OR EARL

(He takes his father's secondary title: the son of a duke is a marquess, the son of a marquess is an earl, and the son of an earl is a viscount. The envelope rule holds as for the previous entry.)

FIELD-MARSHAL

On envelope: 'Field-Marshal (Lord ——)'
(Otherwise according to rank or title.)

FLIGHT LIEUTENANT

On envelope: 'Flight Lieutenant (R.A. Eff)'
Starting letter: 'Dear Flight Lieutenant (Eff)'
When introducing: 'Flight Lieutenant (Eff)'
Refer to as: 'Flight Lieutenant (Eff)' or 'the Flight
Lieutenant'
Addressing in conversation: 'Flight Lieutenant (Eff)'
or 'Flight Lieutenant'
(For Air Force ranks below this, titles are not used.)

GENERAL, LIEUTENANT-GENERAL, MAJOR GENERAL

On envelope: 'General/Lieut-General/Major General
(Sir Marmaduke Gunn)'
Starting letter: 'Dear General (Gunn)' or 'Dear (Sir
Marmaduke)'
When introducing: 'General (Gunn)' – usually omit-
ting any 'Major' or 'Lieutenant'
Refer to as: 'General (Gunn)' or 'Sir Marmaduke' or
'the General'
Addressing in conversation: 'General (Gunn)' or 'Sir
Marmaduke' or 'General'

GROUP CAPTAIN

On envelope: 'Group Captain (R.A. Eff)'
Starting letter: 'Dear Group Captain (Eff)'
When introducing: 'Group Captain (Eff)'
Refer to as: 'Group Captain (Eff) or 'the Group
Captain'
Addressing in conversation: 'Group Captain (Eff)' or
'Group Captain'

HON. (HONOURABLE)

On envelope: 'The Hon. Mr/Mrs/Miss —— ——'
Starting letter: 'Dear Mr/Mrs/Miss ——'

When introducing: 'Mr/Mrs/Miss ——'
Refer to as: 'Mr/Mrs/Miss ——'
Addressing in conversation: 'Mr/Mrs/Miss ——'
(Note that the word 'Hon.' is never written out in full. Should it have to be spoken – say by a toastmaster – 'the Honourable' is said, but in conversation it is quite normal to refer to someone as 'The Hon. ——', however odd it sounds.)

JUDGE (Circuit)

On envelope: 'His/Her Honour Judge ——' (or, with additional title, e.g. 'His Honour Sir '—— ——')
Starting letter: 'Dear Judge ——' or 'Dear Sir/Madam'
When introducing: 'Judge ——'
Refer to as: 'Judge ——'
Addressing in conversation: 'Judge'
(On the bench, as you might expect, a judge is addressed as 'Your honour' and referred to as 'His/Her Honour'. On retirement, a judge is no longer 'Judge', but 'His/Her Honour —— ——')

JUDGE (High Court)

On envelope: 'The Hon. Mr/Mrs Justice (Probity)' or (privately) 'Sir (Eric Probity)' or 'Dame (Elizabeth Probity)', as appropriate
Starting letter: 'Dear Sir/Madam'
When introducing: 'Mr/Mrs Justice (Probity)' or 'Sir (Eric Probity)' or 'Dame (Elizabeth Probity)'
Refer to as: 'Sir (Eric)'/'Dame (Elizabeth)'
Addressing in conversation: 'Sir'/'Madam'/'Your Lordship/Ladyship', and so on
(In other words, a woman High Court judge is officially introduced as 'Mrs Justice (——)' but socially as a Dame. On the bench, a male High Court judge is 'My Lord' or 'Your Lordship'. Women

judges of the High Court are 'My Lady' or 'Your Ladyship'.)

JUSTICES OF THE PEACE

(Only on the bench would a Justice be addressed as 'Your Worship'. The initials 'JP' would only be put after the name on official business.)

KNIGHT

(As for Baronet, except that if he is a member of an order, this should be put on an envelope – e.g. 'Sir Desmond Gribble KBE, CMG'. The wife of a knight is addressed as for a baronet's wife.

LIEUTENANT, SECOND LIEUTENANT (Army)

On envelope: '(N.O. Action) Esq.' (rank only used on official envelopes)
Starting letter: 'Dear Mr (Action)'
When introducing: 'Mr (Action)'
Refer to as: 'Mr (Action)'
Addressing in conversation: 'Mr (Action)'

LIEUTENANT (Royal Navy) (See COMMANDER)

LIEUTENANT COLONEL

On envelope: 'Lieut-Colonel (De'Ath)' followed by any decorations, followed by the name of the regiment
Starting letter: 'Dear Colonel (De'Ath)'
When introducing: 'Colonel (De'Ath)'
Refer to as: 'Colonel (De'Ath)' or 'the Colonel'
In conversation: 'Colonel (De'Ath)'

LIEUTENANT COMMANDER (See COMMANDER)

LIEUTENANT-GENERAL (See GENERAL)

LIFE PEER (i.e. non-hereditary)

On envelope: 'The Rt Hon. The Lord ——' (or
socially) 'The Lord ——'
Starting letter: 'Dear Lord ——'
When introducing: 'Lord ——'
Refer to as: 'Lord ——'
Addressing in conversation: 'Lord ——'
(NB The full title 'Lord Jones of Smethwick' is never
used. The wife of a male life peer is 'The Lady ——'
and should be addressed similarly, not as a life
peeress.)

LIFE PEERESS (i.e. non-hereditary BARONESS)

On envelope: 'The Rt Hon. The Baroness ——' (or
socially) 'The Baroness ——' or even 'Baroness ——'
Starting letter: 'Dear Lady ——'
When introducing: 'Lady ——'
Refer to as: 'Lady ——'
Addressing in conversation: 'Lady ——'
(NB There is a tendency in the media to refer to
'Baroness ——', with the aim of distinguishing her
as a political figure in her own right from the
appendage of her husband the 'Lady' form might
suggest.
(The husband of a life peeress is not 'Baron ——'.
The children may, if they wish, be called 'Hon.' for
their lifetime.
(Some life peeresses dispute the name, holding that
a peeress is the wife of a peer, which they are not.
Following the introduction of life peerages for
women in 1958, the lavatories in the House of Lords

were originally labelled 'LIFE PEERESSES ONLY', but,
as Lady Wootton pointed out, 'We are very passionate that we are not peeresses: peeresses are the
wives of peers.' Now the lavatories are marked
'PEERS' and 'WOMEN PEERS' (*sic*).
(Women have always been able to inherit peerages
or to be awarded them in their own right –
Baroness Burdett-Coutts, the 19th-century philanthropist, is a case in point – but they were unable
to take their seats in the House of Lords until 1963.)

LORD MAYOR

On envelope: 'The Right Worshipful The Lord
Mayor of ——' – except in special cases (for
example, London, York and Belfast) where it is 'The
Rt Hon. The Lord Mayor of ——'
Starting letter: 'My Lord' or 'Dear Lord Mayor'
When introducing: 'The Lord Mayor'
Refer to: 'The Lord Mayor'
Addressing in conversation: 'Lord Mayor' (but so-
cially according to his private rank). When begin-
ning a speech, say, 'My Lord Mayor'.
(Writing to a Lord Mayor's wife or to a Lady
Mayoress, put 'The Lady Mayoress', otherwise use
private rank.)
(Compare MAYOR – and do not confuse with.)

MAJOR

On envelope: 'Major (T.R. Rex)' followed by name of
regiment
Starting letter: 'Dear Major (Rex)'
When introducing: 'Major (Rex)'
Refer to as: 'Major (Rex)' or 'the Major'
Addresing in conversation: 'Major' (Rex)

MAJOR GENERAL (See GENERAL)

MARCHIONESS

On envelope: 'The Marchioness of ——'
Starting letter: 'Dear Marchioness of ——' or 'Dear Lady ——'
When introducing: 'Lady ——'
Refer to as: 'Lady ——'
Addressing in conversation: 'Lady ——'

MARQUESS

On envelope: 'The Marquess of ——'
Starting letter: 'Dear Marquess of —— ' or 'Dear Lord ——'
When introducing: 'Lord ——'
Refer to as: 'Lord ——'
Addressing in conversation: 'Lord ——'

MARSHAL OF THE ROYAL AIR FORCE

On envelope: 'Marshal of the Royal Air Force (Lord Wing)'
(Otherwise according to rank and title.)

MAYOR

On envelope: 'The Right Worshipful The Mayor of ——' (if of a city) or 'The Worshipful the Mayor of ——' (if of a borough, etc.)
Starting letter: 'Dear Mr Mayor' or 'Dear Mr (Chain)' or 'Dear Mrs (Chain)'
When introducing: 'Your Worship' (if formal) or 'Mr Mayor'
Refer to as: 'His Worship' or 'The Mayor' or according to private rank
Addressing in conversation: 'Mayor'. Beginning a

speech, 'Your worship'.

(His wife his known as 'Mayoress' or by private rank. If the Mayor is a woman, the 'Mayoress' is sometimes called 'The Mayor's Companion' or similar. It should not be assumed that the 'Mayoress' is the Mayor's wife. She might be a sister or mother or no relation at all.)

MIDSHIPMAN

On envelope: 'Midshipman (J.A. Tar) RN' or '(J.A. Tar) Esq. RN'
Starting letter: 'Dear Mr (Tar)'
When introducing: 'Mr (Tar)'
Refer to as: 'Mr (Tar)'
Addressing in conversation: 'Mr (Tar)'

MINOR CANON (See CLERGY.)

PEER, PEERESS (See LIFE PEER, LIFE PEERESS.)

POPE

On envelope: 'His Holiness the Pope'
Starting letter: 'Your Holiness' or 'Most Holy Father'
When introducing: 'His Holiness the Pope'
Refer to as: 'His Holiness'
Addressing in conversation: 'Your Holiness'

PREBENDARY

(Follows the form for CANON.)

PRESIDENT (of the United States)

On envelope: 'The President of the United States'
Starting letter: 'Dear Mr President'

When introducing: 'The President'
Refer to as: 'The President'
Addressing in conversation: 'Mr President' or 'President'
(It has become customary in recent years for ex-Presidents to be referred to in public affairs and in their presence as 'President ———', though properly there is only one 'President of the United States' at any one time. Dwight D. Eisenhower reverted to 'General' when he left office.)

PRIME MINISTER

On envelope: 'The Rt Hon. ——— ———, PC, MP'
Starting letter: 'Dear Prime Minister' or 'Dear Mr/Mrs ———'
When introducing: 'The Prime Minister' (or by name)
Refer to as: 'The Prime Minister'
Addressing in conversation: 'Prime Minister' (or by name)
(Other members of the government follow this pattern, whether 'Chancellor' (of the Exchequer), 'Secretary of State' or 'Minister'.)
(Former Prime Ministers do not retain the title.)

PROFESSOR

On envelope: 'Prof.' or 'Professor ——— ———'
Starting letter: 'Dear Professor'
When introducing: 'Professor ———'
Refer to as: 'Professor ———' or 'the Professor'
Addressing in conversation: 'Professor'
(In some cases, professors may not retain their title on retirement unless they are created Professor Emeritus or Emeritus Professor. In practice, however, it is hard to deny him or her the pleasure. As when calling a distinguished musician or conductor,

'Maestro', it is merely a way of signifying distinction and venerability. However, a past holder of a Visiting Professorship, which is a temporary appointment, does not merit this treatment.)

PROVOST

(Follows the form for DEAN.)

QUEEN, THE

On envelope: 'The Private Secretary to Her Majesty The Queen' – she should rarely be written to direct
Starting letter: Hence 'Dear Sir' (otherwise 'Your Majesty')
When introducing: The Queen is never introduced; people are only presented to her. Hence, 'Your Majesty, I should like to present Mr . . . '
Refer to as: 'Her Majesty' (at a pinch, 'The Queen')
Addressing in conversation: 'Your Majesty' (first time), then 'Ma'am' (to rhyme with 'spam' not 'smarm')
(See also ROYALS below.)

REAR ADMIRAL (See ADMIRAL.)

ROYALS

Generally speaking, the rule to remember is that members of the royal family should neither be addressed or referred to using personal pronouns, so say 'Your Royal Highness' rather than 'you' and 'Her Majesty' or 'The Queen' rather than 'her'. However, the changes may be rung to lessen any tendency to sound pompous and preposterous. Also, relationships are best not rubbed in. So the Queen's grandfather would be referred to as 'King George the Fifth' rather than 'your grandfather'.

If you were talking, say, to the Duke of Edinburgh, you would say 'Your Royal Highness' first time round, and then 'Sir'. If the Royal Highness was female, then you would move on to 'Ma'am' (as when talking to the QUEEN, see above).

You don't have to wait to be asked something before you speak, nor is there any prohibition over asking questions, though few people would have the nerve to be pushy in such circumstances. A gentle 'May I ask . . . ' may ease the putting of a direct question. It always seems much easier at the time than it does in anticipation. The royal family is largely made up of adept conversationalists or by people who, because of their position, seem as if they are.)

People who are a little more familiar with royalty might feel like beginning a letter 'Ma'am' or 'Sir', if they did not want to go the whole hog of 'Your Majesty' or 'Your Royal Highness'. However, signing off is a difficult matter. 'I have the honour to be, Your Majesty's/Your Royal Highness's most humble and obedient servant' may stick in the pen of the most loyal subject and yet there is no real alternative.

Addressing the envelope: the form is quite straightforward, but note (from this incomplete list) where capital letters and commas are put. Ideally, the 'His/ Her Royal Highness' should be written in full:

> Her Majesty, Queen Elizabeth, The Queen Mother
> HRH The Duke of Edinburgh *or* HRH Prince Philip, The Duke of Edinburgh

> (in both the above cases, as with The Queen, letters should properly be addressed to 'The Private Secretary to . . .'

> HRH The Prince of Wales

HRH The Princess of Wales
HRH Prince William of Wales
HRH Prince Henry (Harry) of Wales
HRH The Princess Royal
HRH Princess Alexandra, the Hon. Lady Ogilvy
HRH The Duke of York
HRH Princess Beatrice of York
HRH Princess Eugenie of York
HRH The Prince Edward
HRH Prince Michael of Kent
HRH The Princess Margaret, Countess of Snowdon

Of the princes, only The Prince of Wales and The
Prince Edward have the 'The' after HRH. This is
because they are sons of the sovereign. Prince
Michael of Kent, for this reason, is not 'The Prince
Michael' because he is not a son of the sovereign.
Note that 'HRH The Prince Philip' is less often used
than 'HRH The Duke of Edinburgh', but the 'The' is
in place as he is married to the sovereign.
Of the princesses, note that The Princess Royal has
the 'The' but HRH Princess Alexandra does not –
for the same reason.
Letters to the foregoing, where they are addressed
direct, should begin, 'Your Royal Highness'.

RURAL DEAN (See CLERGY.)

SECOND LIEUTENANT (Army) (See LIEUTENANT.)

SQUADRON LEADER

On envelope: 'Squadron Leader (R.A. Eff)'
Starting letter: 'Dear Squadron Leader (Eff)'
When introducing: 'Squadron Leader (Eff)'
Refer to as: 'Squadron Leader (Eff)' or 'the Squadron
Leader'

Addressing in conversation: 'Squadron Leader (Eff)'
or 'Squadron Leader'

SUB-LIEUTENANT (Royal Navy)

On envelope: 'Sub-Lieutenant (J.A. Tar) RN'
Starting letter: 'Dear Mr (Tar)'
When introducing: 'Mr (Tar)'
Refer to as: 'Mr (Tar)'
Addressing in conversation: 'Mr (Tar)'

UNMARRIED DAUGHTER OF DUKE, MARQUESS OR EARL

(She is known as 'Lady (Laura Stanley)' and is
addressed accordingly.)

VICE ADMIRAL (See ADMIRAL)

VISCOUNT

On envelope: 'The Viscount ——'
Starting letter: 'Dear Viscount ——' or 'Dear Lord
——'
When introducing: 'Lord ——'
Refer to as: 'Lord ——'
Addressing in conversation: 'Lord ——'

VISCOUNTESS

On envelope: 'The Viscountess ——'
Starting letter: 'Dear Viscountess ——' or 'Dear
Lady ——'
When introducing: 'Lady ——'
Refer to as: 'Lady —'
Addressing in conversation: 'Lady ——'

WIDOW OF PEER OR BARONET

(She is addressed as when her husband was alive, except where the present peer is married, in which case her first name is put first – as in '(Alice), Duchess of (Slimbridge)'. Should there be two widowed ladies with the same title, the senior is called 'The Dowager Duchess of (Slimbridge)', or whatever.)

WING COMMANDER

On envelope: 'Wing Commander (R.A. Eff)'
Starting letter: 'Dear Wing Commander (Eff)'
When introducing: 'Wing Commander (Eff)'
Refer to as: 'Wing Commander (Eff)' or 'the Wing Commander'
Addressing in conversation: 'Wing Commander'

YOUNGER SON OF DUKE OR MARQUESS

(He is known as 'Lord ——— ———' (e.g. Lord David Tite) and is addressed as 'Lord (David)' and written to familiarly as 'Lord (David)', the envelope being addressed to 'Lord (David Tite)'. His wife is addressed, accordingly, as 'Lady (David Tite)'.

YOUNGER SON OF EARL, SON OF VISCOUNT OR BARON

On envelope: 'Hon. Stephen Borrow' (the 'the' is properly omitted)
Starting letter: 'Dear Mr Borrow'
When introducing: 'Mr Borrow'
Refer to as: 'Mr Borrow'
Addressing in conversation: 'Mr Borrow'
(Accordingly his wife is: 'Hon. Mrs (Stephen) Borrow'.)

Chapter 14

$\mathscr{T}$RAVEL AND TIPPING

A distinguished man once expressed to another, slightly lesser, person his view of those engaged upon visiting a venerable shrine. 'I am a traveller,' he roundly declared, 'you are a tripper, and they' – here he shook his stick at the rabble – 'are *tourists*'.

Tourists

Tourists do have a bad name but host countries are, on the whole, well-mannered to them for the most obvious of two-faced reasons: they bring in money. If we dislike them, it is only a matter of time before we are behaving like tourists ourselves in someone else's picturesque backyard.

So great are the numbers of human beings now being shuffled about the planet to look at tourist sights that any hope that they can blend into the local culture is a forlorn one. The threat tourists pose range all the way from the physical damage they can inflict – and the spiritual harm they can do to the very way of life they come to inspect – down to the simple irritation they can cause by idly strolling down streets where natives wish to proceed at a more workmanlike pace.

In 1990, the English Tourist Board took the well-intentioned but possibly futile step of issuing '20 Tips for Visitors'. At the same time, the Board's chairman, William Davis, expressed regret at the way visitors to Britain were sometimes depicted. 'There is an anti-tourist feeling in this country,' he said, 'and although it is very limited, we don't want it to get worse. Tourists have been described as hordes, invaders amd even a plague. Few tourists set out to do harm, and these descriptions are both unfair and unhelpful.'

20 Tips for Tourists
Always remember you are the guest: show consideration for residents and their environment. Respect local laws and customs.

Leave beaches, parks and public places as you would like to find them.

Put litter in a bin or take it home: don't expect others to clean up after you.

Keep noise levels down, especially at night or in quiet places like churches and the countryside.

Show respect for nature: keep to proper footpaths, don't feed wildlife and don't pick flowers or shrubs.

Remember that many people find smoking offensive, and careless smokers may cause countryside fires.

Don't carve your initials on trees and historic monuments or spoil them with graffiti.

Complain if you have just cause, but do it politely.

Don't argue with staff who seek to enforce rules: they are only doing their jobs.

Avoid the temptation to touch valuable objects such as paintings, tapestries and vases.

Keep an eye on your children to see they don't indulge in destructive or annoying behaviour.

If you want to photograph other people, ask them first.

Behave towards others as you would wish them to behave towards you: don't push, shove or jump queues.

Good manners are always appreciated: don't forget to say 'please' and 'thank you'.

Dress properly to visit places of worship: remember they are not holiday playgrounds.

Wear suitable footwear to visit historic buildings: high-heeled shoes can cause a lot of damage.

Be enterprising: visit parts of the country off the usual 'tourist trail'.

If you live in Britain, try to visit our popular attractions in off-peak periods; you will enjoy them much more.

Use public transport whenever possible. If you take your car, park in a designated space, not just where you please.

Help the local economy: buy locally grown or made goods wherever possible.

Just to show that this was not just an English nannyish thing to do and that rampant tourism is indeed a global problem, it is worth mentioning that in 1991, the huge growth of visitors to the Himalayan regions of Nepal, India, Pakistan, China and Butan, led to the drawing up of a 'Himalayan Tourist Code' designed to prevent environmental damage. The main points of this code are that litter should be removed, with paper burned or buried. On the other hand, there is a warning that it is dangerous to light open fires (to spare forests). Local water should be kept clean by avoiding the use of pollutants such as detergents in streams or springs.

Plants should not be picked and should be left to flourish in their natural environment. When taking photographs, it is essential to respect privacy. Holy places should be respected but encouragement should not be given to beggars (by giving to children, for example). Otherwise, the key advice is for tourists to observe local customs and respect local etiquette.

Air travel

It may be that a residual fear of flying induces chronically selfish behaviour in some, but I am inclined to see it as a reaction on most passengers' part to the myth that has been studiously built up over the years that flying is a luxury pursuit. It is not. Flying consists of being projected through the air in a packed metal tube with a public lavatory attached. No wonder people behave in a way they probably wouldn't do on earth (or perhaps they would, but you might not have to be sitting behind them there.)

The pushers and shovers of this world come into their own once airborne (and beforehand). They will insist on cramming things under their seats and between their legs, and murdering whatever you have just placed in the overhead luggage compartments. They play with gadgets, suddenly lowering their back-rests so that your in-flight meal meets your chin. They talk – how they talk – and they smell and they want to drink too much. If you want to change your seat to get away from them, a member of the cabin crew will probably make this very easy – provided that there is room elsewhere.

Airport security

They are tiresome, time-consuming and unpleasant, but airport security searches are necessary. As the litany usually ends, 'You know why am I asking you these questions, don't you?' It is quite impossible to avoid searches, so undergo them with as good a grace as you can muster. If you are bad-tempered and show signs of irritability, this only makes matters worse and arouses the suspicion of the security staff.

By all means make sure that your bags are not harmed by being put through X-ray equipment. The procedure for dealing with film is now fairly standard and should not be harmful.

Dealing with customs officers

Passing through Customs is the last unpleasantness reserved for the returning traveller. After the three-hour delay on the flight back from Skiathos and the apparent inability of your luggage to find its way out on to the reclaim carousel – there comes the daunting choice between the red channel and the green.

I know, of course, that many people *do* like to add a final note of pep to their holidays by returning from abroad with dutiable goods tucked away in their socks, unmentioned, but I myself can never be bothered. And yet every time I succeed in getting through the green door at Heathrow unchallenged, unsearched and unscathed, I feel as though I have been put under most unpleasant scrutiny. Why should I be made to run the gauntlet, by walking past the stares of customs officers and made to feel guilty, when in fact I am completely innocent?

I have taken expert advice as to how to avoid being stopped. I don't wear dark glasses. I try to disguise my Middle-Eastern origins. I tell my wife not to wear her fur coat and to stick by my side. But still the discomfort grips me. I don't know where to look. I pretend to whistle nonchalantly while pushing my trolley past the inspectors.

I do not pretend to know the answer. Is there any

other experience in modern life — apart from taking your driving test — when you are so vulnerable to officially approved suspicion? You have nothing to feel uncomfortable about if you are innocent, the Customs would no doubt say, but that rather misses the point.

Hotels

As with air travel, there is something about hotels that can bring out the worst in people. It is not just the hi-jinks with regard to tipping (see below), it is the generally unnatural atmosphere that is generated when one person seeks to make money out of renting a few cubic feet of accommodation to another.

Booking. The elaborate procedure of yesteryear when a hotel reservation made by phone had to be confirmed by letter and then acknowledged by the hotel has now been largely rendered obsolete by the fax machine and the credit card. Giving details of your credit card at the time of booking means that the hotel will keep your room, even should you be delayed beyond your expected arrival time. Naturally, you may still want to have confirmation in writing, by letter or fax, just to have something to wave at the hotel in case of a mistake.

Giving your credit card number does, of course, mean that if you do not show up at all, you will be charged for one night's accommodation and possibly for more if the hotel is unable to let your room to another guest. Should you be unable to take up a booking because you are stuck on an aeroplane, this might be painful. Always try to advise a hotel of any late or non-arrival.

When booking, it is always a good idea to get the hotel to tell you precisely how much you will be charged for the room. They may find this rather tiresome but you should insist and, especially, inquire as to the availability of corporate rates, special schemes, and so on. It is a mistake to think that there is only one price on a hotel room.

Rooms. Advice given to hotel owners and managers from time to time is that they should spend a night in each room in their hotels, just to experience what precise experience they are dishing up to their customers. How would they feel about the kitchen air extractor positioned right outside the window, or the lift clanking away all night opposite the door, or even the ticking of the clock built (irremovably – I've tried) into the bed's headboard?

It is unlikely that the receptionist who checks you into a hotel will be aware of the precise drawbacks of the room that may be selected on a random basis for your use. All you can do is to try to state your preferences at the time of checking in and immediately to request another room if you are dissatisfied with what you are given. Alas, hotel noise is often only apparent at night when the noises of the wider world have died down. There may be nothing for it but to unplug whirring, clanking refrigerators – and never mind the puddle on the carpet next morning.

A number of hotel chains now offer no-smoking bedrooms – in the hope that the clinging cigar-smoke of the previous occupant will not be a problem. They are sometimes coy about revealing that they have these rooms, as they also are about special rooms for the use of women executives. (See also 'Dining out on one's own' in Chapter 2 EATING OUT.)

Another irritant that hotel staff seem to have majored in occurs at the checking-in stage. Of course, they can never find your exact name (probably because they wrote it down wrong when you booked) but they eventually seem happy to let you in anyway (when they can tear themselves away from whatever apparently more important activity they have found to occupy their attention).

Services. It is a simple fact that no two hotels provide exactly the same services – even within those international chains, like Holiday Inns, where the rooms look disconcertingly similar whether you are in Birmingham or Bangkok. You don't know, for example, whether a hairdrier will come as part of the fixtures and fittings or whether you will have to ask for one at reception. (In one large hotel chain when I asked reception for a hairdrier, the receptionist replied, 'I think it (sic) is out.' When 'it' was recovered from the previous user, it didn't work.)

So, ask, demand, and don't be fobbed off. As waiters are trained not to look in your direction, receptionists are trained not to do anything about your problems – presumably in the hope that you will forget that you asked. On the other hand, they do have a tendency to grill you on such matters as whether you want a morning call and newspaper before you've even checked into your room. Don't let them rush you.

Room service can be painfully slow – never more so than in hotels which do not provide you with your own tea- or coffee-making facilities. Forcing guests to make use of room service – when all they may want is just a cup of tea – is a form of blackmail. Doubly so, when the room service is slow, expensive and necessitating a tip from you into the bargain.

Bills. You should always check your bill in detail. Never mind that there is a long queue of checkers-out behind you. Get the checking out person to explain any items you do not understand. The simple fact is that hotels are generally sloppy, if not devious, in preparing bills. There is, of course, plenty of scope for mistakes – other people's bar and restaurant bills being added to yours – and there is an undoubted tendency for managements to assume that you won't be bothered to check or challenge your bill. A certain large Italian hotel chain seems automatically to add in a few international telephone calls to every bill, in the apparent belief that, if you are staying at one of their hotels, then you should have done even if you haven't. Try to bear with their lack of grace when the error is pointed out to them.

Complaints. Don't be reluctant to complain. Hotels have no grounds for making you put up with anything if they are charging you £100 a night, as quite likely they are doing. I have moved rooms at three o'clock in the morning, because of noise. I have insisted on a reduction in the room rate when all sleep was impossible because an exhibition was being constructed overnight in the ballroom of a hotel I was staying at. I have negotiated a reduction in room rate because a strike of hotel-workers meant that I had to make my own bed and breakfast. (This was a new type of strike, in Australia, but the principle remains the same. Even so, I was asked, 'Were you *really* inconvenienced?')

'It is because we put up with bad things that hotel-keepers continue to give them to us.'
Anthony Trollope, *Orley Farm* (1862)

Complainers have their work cut out, because hotels generally have a tendency to see guests as 'accommodation units' rather than human beings. A magnificent tension can arise between customer and management should the customer wish to exercise his will in a way that disturbs a management's calm repose.

This prompts me to expound one of my theories about hotel owner/proprietors in the remoter parts of Britain. They are rather like the owners of small bookshops in market towns. In their previous careers, they have usually worked for large organizations, or been in the services, and now they want to start a business which has as little as possible to do with other stupid human beings. So they open up hotels in out-of-the-way places and the really annoying thing is that people *will* keep bothering them. *Really* stupid people!

Taxi drivers

As is made clear under 'Tipping', below, a certain caution is needed in dealing with these people. A good deal of aggression is worked up by their being situated in a driver's cab for several hours a day. The thing about London cab drivers, in particular, is that they are exactly as portrayed in fiction. I know, I had one in the front of my cab last week. They do want to lecture you on the right wing of politics. They do say things about who they've had in the backs of their cabs. "Ere, I 'ad that Meryl Streep in the back once. She had terrible skin. Nar-wot-I-mean?'

Particularly if you are travelling alone, closing the glass partition can act as a pointed indication that you do not wish to be entertained with all that kind of chat. However, if the glass is already closed, this may not prevent the driver from opening it when he feels like it and launching into a tirade. You may need to busy yourself with papers (not newspapers) so that you can claim to have work to do. You may even have to adopt this method, even if what you really want to do is daydream and stare into space.

Tipping

In few areas of modern life is more dread involved than in the business of bestowing tips. But however outmoded a custom it may be, it shows no sign of going away. And as we shall see, in America for example, it is organized and codified to a forbidding extent.

Cloakrooms, hat-checks. There is something very unlovable about the tipping sought by cloakroom attendants.

For a start, there is usually a saucer full of large denomination coins indicating that a contribution will not go amiss. Secondly, there is basic confusion as to whether you tip when you leave your coat or when you pick it up. Anyone who fishes to this degree deserves not to catch anything. My inclination is to give as little as possible, in 'silver' rather than 'gold'. Where I have been *required* to leave coats, bags etc. in a cloakroom (at an art gallery, say, and for security reasons), I see no great need to tip. I often feel in restaurants, too, that the cloakroom side of things is covered by whatever general service charge has been levied.

Hairdressers. Tipping is rather a worrying aspect of a visit here, especially when more than one tippee is apparent. Does the hair-washer, -stylist, -colourist, rate a tip as much as the hair-cutter? Should you feel obliged to seek out the hair-washer at the end of your treatment in order to hand over a tip? No, to the latter – but if the hair-washer presents herself or is visible (perhaps attending to another customer) then by all means. 50p or £1, according to the establishment. For the hairdresser, think in terms of 10% plus – rounding up from the cost of the haircut. That could mean £10 on the sort of bill easily run up in a fashionable London salon.

And yet . . . if you still have worries on this score, it would not be amiss if you were to sound out the main practitioner who deals with you as to what her/his expectations are in this matter (they are often very forthcoming). Or, you could give a handsome tip to the main person and suggest that he/she divides it up among the underlings. Or, you could give nothing at all, if your bill is stratospherically high anyway. Nobody is going to hold it against you or bear a grudge, you will not bear the mark of Cain for the rest of your life, provided the people to whom you deny a tip are reasonably well-paid anyway. Frankly, the expectation of a tip is an imposition, it has got out of hand, and until the unlikely day when someone gets to sort out the whole business, you should not let it worry you.

It is *not* necessary to tip if your hair is being done by the proprietor of an establishment – though a person's precise status may not be apparent. In which case, tip anyway. Or cut and run.

Hotels. After many years trekking in and out of hotels, my heart still leaps when I am given the *option* of coping with my own bags. I would love to be one of those suave men one sees in the movies who know exactly how to stand while the porter goes through his rigmarole and then know precisely the moment to press exactly the right amount of money into a grateful hand.

Instead, if I do have a porter, I spend the journey up in the lift trying to sort out the money in my pocket (which, of course, I have been organizing for days for just this moment). Then I hop from one foot to the other while he demonstrates how the telly and the fridge work. And then I give him his tip just as he goes on to describe the bathroom – or don't manage to get it out at all until he has left the room with a slight air of someone who may (but you don't know for sure) have been programmed not to hang about fishing for tips. In New York, of course, I have handed over a consignment of the lean green only to have it stared at and pronounced, verbally and otherwise, as being insufficient. It is a business, like I said, and no amount of campaigning by hotel guides and the like has really lessened the problem or enabled one to detect which particular system of remuneration is being operated in any particular establishment. Is tipping discouraged? Does a service charge on the bill cover porterage and such like? Why can't someone sort out this terrible mess?

The only way to feel remotely comfortable is to be prepared to verge on the unnecessarily generous. According to how you perceive the swankiness of the hotel, work on the basis of 50p or £1 per substantial item of luggage. Think in terms of whole pounds rather than divisions from then on. If there is more than one porter, give to the senior of the two in the expectation that he will share the tip. If, as in some country house hotels, you are shown to your room by the receptionist or even the manager, do not tip. However, they may accompany you to your room and the bags are left to be brought up separately. Then you tip the porter who brings them.

On going out of the hotel, the procedure is repeated. The tip should go to the porter who has performed the service rather than to the head porter who has called a cab or arranged for your car to be brought from the garage. Everyone who has performed a recognizable service during this process should be tipped. A tip for calling a cab is only necessary when this has involved a good deal of trouble – not if one is just waiting to have its door opened.

Should you tip the chambermaid especially as, or in spite of, the little note she has put in your room telling you her name? I think not – unless she has peformed some special service. This may be tough, but one has to draw the line somewhere. There are plenty of other 'unseen' operatives in a hotel who work just as much as chambermaids to make your stay pleasant. This is where a percentage service charge added to your bill is fairer to all and more sensible. The ideal of simply getting what you pay for without the 'service' element being separated out is still a long way off.

Some hotels make a point of not allowing their staff to expect tips, and close scrutiny of hotel guidebooks may tell you which these are. But few people have ever been known to refuse a tip, and if you do tip unnecessarily, it hardly matters.

Celebrities and others who tip lavishly to get some imaginary rating for generosity are best left to waste their own money, unmourned by the rest of us.

On board ship. The mysteries of tipping aboard cruise ships and ocean-going liners in the grand old days of sailing were pretty impenetrable. Nowadays, you are still very definitely expected to tip your cabin steward and others, in proportion to the length of the voyage and the grandeur of the ship. Take advice. A travel courier will tell you what the going rate is. If in doubt, think in terms of 10% of the total cost of the cruise to be divided between all concerned. Yes, that will be quite a lot, but about right.

On a Nile cruise, we were told by the courier more or less what was expected of us. We put the money in an envelope with our cabin number on it and we were assured, and did not doubt, that the tips would be shared out among *all* the crew, the seen and the unseen. The method was a shade organized and impersonal but it was very painless.

Taxi drivers. A remarkable change brought about by the most recent recession was that taxis became a passengers' market. Taxis for hire were not only easier to come by, their drivers – often a byword for rudeness and cavalier behaviour – seemed positively grateful for your custom and amazed at your tips.

About 10% is about right. Rather than fumble around with the change to hand out the tip, I have taken to handing over a note and saying, 'Call it . . . ', rounding up the fare from, say, £8.20 to £9. If the fare was £8.50, then I would find a way of adding on the extra 30p or 50p to make up the 10%.

If a taxi driver could not be bothered to help me out with major luggage or open the door if I was old or handicapped, I would nevertheless think twice about registering a protest by not tipping. Although the chances of your having the same taxi twice are infinitesimal (I'm talking about London here, obviously), I think discretion would be the better part of valour. There is an incredible amount of pent-up frustration inside a driver's cab (as one knows from the standard of driving) and no one wants to be on the receiving end of that.

Mini-cabs are outside my experience, though I would merely make the comment that it seems odd to think of tipping anyone who has to be shown which route to take, probably turns up late, and may be half-asleep anyway. People say they are cheaper than licensed cabs, but I'm not prepared to take the chance, frankly.

If a car has been sent for you, chauffeur-driven, do you tip the driver? Probably not, as almost certainly the bill is being paid by an account-holder and a tip element is included in the charge.

(See also 'Service charges' in Chapter 2 EATING OUT.)

There are times when I feel that too much fuss is made about tipping. The best option is just to accept it as a way of life.

Chapter 15

*W*ORKING LIFE

Why do people behave differently in the workplace? The extraordinary thing is that a perfectly normal human being, who might be caring and considerate in an everyday environment, willing to hold open doors for the elderly, happy to help pregnant mothers, generally courteous towards all women, can turn into an unfeeling, unhelpful, sexist monster when at work.

This is something of a mystery. And why should 'customer care' and 'inter-personal skills' training be necessary at all in companies and organizations? Surely, getting on with people and appreciating the importance of being well-mannered to clients and colleagues should be something that occurs naturally?

People can spend more of their lives at work than at home, and I suppose it must be that they feel they are in a different world when they are at work – a world where normal human responses such as those expected in home and social life, do not count. Work is an artificial environment and is, for the most part, one for which people are never sufficiently prepared. They just slide into it.

It is also an area in which people find themselves working with colleagues they would not choose as friends in the outside world. People are thrown together, solely for professional reasons, and there is bound to be some incompatability.

Something odd happens when people walk through the door into an office or workplace. They stop being human. Another reason, particularly in big business, may be the role models they adopt for the workplace. As one customer care expert puts it, 'They think of Arnold Schwarzenegger and J.R. Ewing rather than Mother Teresa.'

Sins of managers

Bosses are bad-mannered if they treat employees as little better than slaves – if, in pursuing some macho image of management:
1) they expect too much of their staff
2) they work longer hours than necessary and then expect their staff to do the same
3) they hand out work just as people are finishing for the day
4) they expect tasks to be completed within an unrealistic time.

Male bosses are bad-mannered if they try and claim *droit de seigneur* over female colleagues and (especially) secretaries, but then overlook simpler matters like remembering their birthdays or fail to familiarize themselves with the domestic situation of their staff and any difficulties arising therefrom. There is a scene in the film *The Seduction of Joe Tynan* in which Alan Alda, as an American Senator in pursuit of power, beckons his secretary to bring him an index card whenever he is speaking to someone on the phone. The card contains the caller's personal details, name of wife, children, hobbies, etc. This enables the Senator to ask personal questions and make personal references, aimed at buttering up the other person. In the context, it is a calculating, unlovable technique, but there is a lot to be said for it, and not just in dealing with the world outside the organization. The standing of many bosses would be improved if they could remember details of their colleagues' lives, if they could remember their assistant's birthday – if they could even remember his or her name properly.

Bosses can be very bad at introducing new staff and at helping them to find their feet. New staff should be told very clearly what their duties are and exactly what is expected of them.

When bosses receive visitors from outside the company, they tend to operate as though the secretary isn't there (except to fetch the tea) and never think of introducing the secretary to the visitor when they may well have spoken on the phone together already fixing up arrangements for the meeting.

Bosses don't say thank you often enough or recognize good work adequately. They are usually extremely good, however, at bawling out people for bad work.

Bosses are often inaccessible. They do not leave the office door ajar. This prevents casual dropping in and superficially aimless conversation – the sort that often results in good ideas. The closed door also inhibits employees from expressing worries and dissatisfaction which then gets bottled up.

Often allied with this sin is a foolish reliance on impersonal memos. One boss I encountered issued so many memos that we suggested they all be bound together in a fat volume and handed back to him, just so that he knew. Shouting by memo is a sign of insecurity. Electronic mail may make this kind of megaphone memoing a little less objectionable in practice – but some senders make sure there is a hard copy as well, which only makes matters worse.

Bosses strive too much towards running a streamlined, impersonal system that just hums along. The most creative and productive outfits are not always the tidiest.

Assumptions about women. The patronizing way in which women can be treated by men at the workplace is without doubt also a question of manners. I recall returning from honeymoon with my wife, who was then and is still a working woman, and hearing a certain politician, who ought to have known better, say to her, on being introduced, 'And what did you use to do?' This was an assumption he should not have made.

Men can also too readily assume when they encounter a woman in the workplace, maybe just because she happens to be the person who has answered the phone, that she is a secretary rather than a manager. (Contrast this with the general view that secretaries are invariably female. These days they are not.)

It is also completely unacceptable to use the woman's femininity as a stick to beat her with. To inquire, 'Time of the month, dear?' as a way of challenging irrational or irrascible behaviour – as is often done – is unforgivable.

Women in business and industry, even those in senior jobs, may find that men simply do not take them seriously. Both sides then find it difficult to establish a good working relationship and, with the woman usually in a minority, if not actually on her own, she has to shout that little bit louder, work noticeably harder, to win her male colleagues over. She should think twice, however, about adopting the role of The Bearded Lady, as it has been described – that is to say, she should not 'become' a man in terms of behaviour and attitude on the foolish assumption that meeting men on their own terms is the only way to get on.

Standing up. Should men stand up when a female colleague enters the room at work – as it is to be hoped they might in the social world? Certainly they should if the situation is in any way social – in restaurant or canteen, or at a work-related function. But in an open-plan office, obviously not – otherwise the men would be up and down like yo-yos. If a woman arrived at a meeting and her male colleagues were all seated, and the meeting had not yet begun, it would be pleasant if the men did get to their feet, but the woman should very quickly ask them to sit down. If the meeting had already begun, the woman would slip into her place with the normal, brief apology, and no one need stand up.

(See also Chapter 8 RELATIONSHIPS AND SEX.)

Sins of employees

It is commonplace for employees of any company or organization to 'make use of the facilities' – to pinch office materials, from humble paperclips to substantial electrical equipment, to carry out personal tasks on the office photocopier and, of course, to run up substantial bills on the office telephone.

Were you to confront people with this behaviour, they might argue that they were not being paid properly anyway, so they think it perfectly legitimate for them to pick up these perks. If they weren't allowed to do so, they would certainly have to ask for a higher salary . . .

One sympathizes with this justification, but the method of protest is undoubtedly bad manners of a kind. That such petty theft is considered harmless does not make it other than what it is. In consequence, many organizations have banned the making of personal telephone calls, or other than local calls, and mobilized snoopers and itemized telephone bills to stamp out the menace. This creates a bad atmosphere – and considerable inconvenience – if important personal calls genuinely have to be made.

Too often, though, people misuse office phones even in that grey area between professional and personal calls. They hold very long conversations, often not on work-related matters. They hold loud conversations in shared offices which do not allow the other occupants to concentrate on their work. It is obviously bad business if a lengthy telephone call devoted to the secretary's private life prevents a work call getting through to the boss.

Sins of secretaries

Chief among these is obstructiveness over the phone —
not only to people outside the company, who may be
trying to speak to the boss — but to colleagues within.
The secretaries may see this as part of the job —
protecting their bosses from unnecessary and time-
wasting callers, but it can easily be perceived as high-
handedness.

Telephone callers know the sort of routine they put
you through. First they ask you, 'Which company are
you from?', even though you may well not be from a
company at all. 'May I ask what it is about?' is in order
if it means that a wrongly directed enquiry is speedily
re-directed, but if it suggests that the secretary thinks
they know best, then it is again obstructive. 'Does he
know you?' is never in order.

Again, being over-protective of the boss can be
infuriating if the secretary uses phraseology that suggests vagueness over the boss's whereabouts. To say,
'He is not available today' or 'he is not by his phone'
(which could mean anything or nothing) or 'I'm afraid
he's tied up in a meeting' (giving a curious insight to the
company's *modus operandi*), without *immediately* offering to help the caller, is not good business practice. At
any sign of unhelpfulness, callers are entitled to ask
who can then deal with their call properly, whether it be
someone more senior, or junior, or anyone.

For a secretary to say, 'Hold on, I'll see if he's in', risks
making the caller feel very small indeed as, quite
palpably, it probably means the secretary knows 'he' is
in but wants to give him the opportunity of pretending
that he isn't. 'Just one moment, please' gives no such
hint of deviousness, though presumably because the
caller is not being put straight through, it is plain that
their credentials are being examined.

Equally sinful is the habit of secretaries calling you
and saying, 'I've got Mr Terribly Important to speak to

you' – then leaving you hanging in the air while trying to locate Mr Terribly Important, sometimes not managing to do so. If there is one thing that would win friends for bosses and managers all over the world, it would be to abandon this technique completely. Dialling one's own calls is simple and straightforward these days. Even terribly important people now do it themselves and know that it is a very winning thing to do.

It is tempting for secretaries, once they have been with a particular boss for a while, to project the feeling that they see themselves as a unit. Indeed, they may do, and this is obviously good for the secretary's personal esteem, but it is quite wrong for the secretary then to speak to others in the same organization or to outsiders as though the boss. It is all too easy for secretaries to become proprietorial and to start saying things like, 'Well, we haven't made our minds up on that one yet . . .' As soon as colleagues or outsiders sense that secretaries think they are running the show, or are in fact taking the decisions, they will become resentful, and with justification.

Going for manners

What can a company do to create a well-mannered environment for its employees and its customers? There *are* companies which have apparently been refurbished from top to bottom to keep their staffs happy, which operate on an almost breathtaking level of courtesy to the outside world, and which are almost squeakily clean in their approach to business behaviour. The managements of such companies and organizations presumably believe that by creating a working environment where people are happy and where good manners can flourish, they will be able to conduct business more easily and more profitably.

Regular appraisals of every member of an organization can give employees an opportunity to reveal weaknesses in colleagues both above and below them on the ladder. Managers are assessed by their own managers as well as by their teams. It is a two-way process. If a manager is not good at delegating, or poor at explaining, or prone to groping colleagues, there is every chance that these points will emerge through appraisal procedures. Then the employee concerned can be advised, re-trained or cautioned, as appropriate.

And if a firm doesn't have these appraisal and training methods, what can happen to it? Frustration will mount, it may lead to a crisis, and, if nothing else, the leaving-rate of personnel will shoot up.

First-name terms. Is it a good thing for bosses and employees to call each other by their first names? In the PAS survey, people were asked, initially, if there was someone who could be described as their boss in the context of paid employment. Of these, a massive 94% said that the boss called them by their first names. Almost as high a number − 80% − said they called their boss by the boss's first name. Hardly what you'd call a Dickensian picture of master and slave working relationships.

It is worth noting, also, that first-name manners do not just apply within the workplace, but also in relations with customers and clients. There is a terrible temptation these days for salespersons, in particular, to assume familiarity with potential customers. But, by slipping in a first name every few seconds, they invade that person's space. They try to exert an insidious hold, over their victim − for how, after all, is the customer expected to complain effectively about, say, faulty goods or services, if he and the seller or provider are locked into amiable first-name terms?

A businessman should not assume that it is in order to call a customer or client by the first name. If the other person does want it, he can always say, 'Call me "John"'', or whatever. Similarly, if someone is present at a meeting

with his boss and an outside client, he shouldn't assume
that the boss will necessarily want to be called by his
first name there and then, in front of the client.

(See also 'First-name terms' in Chapter 3 FAMILY LIFE.)

Personal organizers. A well-known television weather
forecaster once held up a copy of the Bible and, such
was the trendiness of his audience, he had to explain
that it was not a Filofax – though he did add, amusingly, that the Bible could indeed be construed, in its way,
as a form of personal organizer . . .

Yet to some people, Filofaeces and other similar devices
have become as important as Life Itself. They brandish
them every bit as much as an evangelist does his Bible.
When they get left behind somewhere, bereavement can
be total. It strikes me, in fact, that when men carry them,
they are the equivalent of women's handbags. Everything
that is most dear to the person, everything most worth
not losing, most valuable, is concentrated in ideal form
for being stolen or lost.

Personal organizers should not be carried into *social*
situations – least of all deposited on the restaurant
table, along with the car keys and the cigarette packet.
Fortunately, if not actually on the wane, they seem much
less apparent than they were at the boom-time of the
economy.

Phone manners. It is usually impossible to ignore someone else's phone ringing, so you are tempted to answer it.
But then you may get involved in a long exchange that
you resent, even if you are simply taking a message for
someone else. If you are unable or unwilling to take on a
little responsibility for others, by all means don't answer
the phone. If you do happen to answer the phone, and
don't want to get involved, ask the caller to try again –
making it clear from the very start that you were only
passing the phone at the time you picked it up.

It is the height of bad manners (and bad business) to

leave a phone unmanned for any length of time. If you do this, you will never know what opportunities may have passed you by nor the irritation caused to people who have fought their way through the switchboard to your extension only to get no reply at all. Always make arrangements to have calls transferred to someone who has been well-briefed how to field them. Even putting an answering machine on your extension is better than giving no answer at all. Unfortunately, it is seldom done.

If switchboard operators ask you whether you would like to hold, they should come back to you very frequently – not just to check that you are still holding on (that should be apparent to them from their equipment) but to cope with any requests you may have to be re-routed to another extension or to leave a message. Some PBX systems do not have any kind of tone and, although you may be told that, 'The number's ringing for you', you may not believe it. There is nothing worse than being left in silent limbo with no way of getting out other than putting down the phone and redialling.

Well, there *is* something worse, and that is being put on hold and being force-fed with an 'appropriate' piece of 'hold music', perhaps the managing director's favourite, usually played on what sounds like a toy synthesizer. It can drive you mad. There is also a new development called a 'hold jockey', in other words a disc jockey who plays music, gives out announcements and keeps you informed as to how long you are likely to have to wait for an answer (no, I am not making this up). Again, this is not interactive, so you may still be left mouthing your frustration to yourself.

A simple rhythmic device or tone is much preferable, if this kind of system is necessary at all. It is better still if companies have a policy of not stacking calls but of promising to ring back. One large company I know of not only aims to answer any call within five rings, it has a policy of never forcing the caller to ring back. If the right person is not immediately available, rather than

pass the caller from pillar to post, the company under-
takes to take care of the inquiry and to return the call.

A small point: if you return a phone call and find
yourself having to say who you are, the correct thing is
to say, 'This is Clive Sandwich', not 'It's Mr Sandwich
here'. 'Mr' is a title that can only be bestowed by others.
It is bad form to apply it to yourself. (See also 'Self-
addressed envelopes' in Chapter 16 WRITTEN
COMMUNICATION.)

As for, 'Hello, Spongeyfoam PLC, this is Sharon
speaking, how can I help you?' If this sort of greeting
makes you want to throw up, it may be some comfort to
know that the people who do it aren't always completely
at ease with it either. It is very much an answering
policy that is imposed from above, by management
which believes it is what the world wants. There is also
the justification that if a telephone receptionist or
salesperson identifies herself or himself, then at least the
customer has a reference point in case of further inquiry
or complaint.

But if a practice is so universally loathed, why do
companies persist with such a freeze-dried ritual from
which all spontaneity and genuine personal contact have
been removed? It is presumably because, ironically, they
see the telephone link with the outside world as being of
prime importance. So, indeed, it is. It is probably the
first point of contact between customer and consumer.
Even so, nothing can make the ritual of name identification and greeting, all done in a singsongy voice from
which all humanity has been removed, worthwhile
persisting with.

Any suggestions for countermeasures, falling just short
of terrorist attacks, will be warmly welcomed.

(See also 'Mobile telephones' in Chapter 6 NEIGH-
BOURLINESS.)

Telephone negotiating. The phone is a tyrant just as
much in the office as in the home. Few can resist

answering it when it rings, not least because they believe it may be bringing them good news. But it is pernicious, for example, because it can enable callers to engage you in decision-making when you are least prepared for it.

The only way in which you can get back to a position of strength, to regain the upper hand, is to remember this: no decision has to be made just because someone rings you up and implies that this is so. It is almost always better, if you have the any doubts about a course of action that is being proposed to you, not to give your decision there and then, but to say you will ring back with your decision in a little while. This takes the heat out of the decision-making process, gives you pause for reflection and, possibly, will enable you to take up an offensive position. By ringing the other person back, with the randomness of time and circumstance that this entails, you will be reasserting yourself. It is *always* best to buy yourself time for reflection. The telephone should make this easier. You don't (yet) have to look someone in the eye while you are saying something on the telephone. Your ability to cut off a call abruptly should not be forgotten.

(See also 'Telephoning' in Chapter 11 SPEAKING.)

Giving references

It can be embarrassing to be asked to speak up for someone who is undeserving of a 'good' reference, particularly if what you write is likely to be seen by that person. If you have any doubts, you should excuse yourself with some such statement as, 'I make it a rule not to – it's nothing personal', even though this may not get you off the hook with some people. If you do have to go through with it, then it is most important to say in your letter only what you believe to be true. After all, you might find yourself in a court of law if you don't.

Rather than trying to communicate your true feelings (if they are unfavourable, that is) by coded hints, it is safer simply to be brief and only say what you can say, that which is truthful. Praise what you think is worth praising about a person's character or performance. Hope that the receiver of the reference will deduce from whatever you leave out, that those are the areas where the candidate may be wanting. It is best not to volunteer information that you consider the person dishonest, for example. If this is an important question for the future employer, they can always 'take up the reference' and ask you the question direct.

Similar considerations apply when friends apply to you for work or when they ask you to find a job for their offspring. If you are happy to oblige, well and good, but if you genuinely can't help, or do not wish to, make it clear that company policy is that recruitment is by group decision and not by you individually. Try not to give precise reasons for turning down applicants, as this may lead to prolonged arguments. 'We do not have an opening *at this time*' is a well-worn phrase of rejection because it is suitably vague and does not suggest that there is anything wrong with the candidate.

Being interviewed for a job

A survey of employers recently made the point that, particularly among school-leavers and other young people, a great many people failed to get jobs because of a complete lack of basic manners on the part of applicants. However incredible it may seem, a lack of punctuality, a lack of attention to appearance, a surly manner and a lack of curiosity about the job at stake are all that many candidates for jobs offer potential employers.

In days of widespread unemployment, even turning these negatives into positives provides the starting point for possible acceptance by an employer. The chief thing then is for the candidate to mark himself or herself out from the other applicants. When the employer comes to consider who will get the job, the memory of most of the candidates will be a blur. If you can be remembered for something – an off-beat inquiry about some aspect of the work involved (*not* the pension fund), the revelation of some quirky hobby (playing the saxophone) – you are much more likely to be remembered favourably.

Office life

What of social life, in the office, once you have sought and won employment?

Office kissing. Is it correct, or even advisable, to kiss colleagues at the office or in the workplace? If there is something serious going on between you, definitely not. Wait until you get home. If, on the other hand, it is meant merely as a pleasant, social gesture . . . it is probably best not to either.

Perhaps an exception might be made on a birthday, or some such occasion, but this kind of thing can so easily get out of hand. It is but a short step to having the sexual harassment police knocking on your door. If you still have to do it, wait until you are out of the workplace – in a pub or bar. Even the most innocent of gestures can cause problems at work and is best avoided.

Sexual harassment. It does seem at times that after more than twenty years of the Womens' Movement and after an equal number of years spent in consciousness raising directed at the male chauvinist classes, next to no difference has been achieved. Even outside the work-place, women are still subject to sexist remarks and behaviour, as though all the effort had been wasted. The wolf whistle from the building site, the ingrained assumption that women drivers are worse than men, the smutty joke told when it will cause maximum offence – nothing has changed. It is simply bad manners – because it is discourteous to the woman, whatever the motive. About all one can say is that at least some men are now, however dimly, aware of what they might be doing wrong.

The basic trouble is that men are not sure how to deal with women they encounter at work. They may only be used to dealing with women as friends or sexual partners and they have no frame of reference for this other type. No wonder that they can behave to their female colleagues in a way they would never behave to their wives or girlfriends.

Sexual harassment is a problem, certainly, but what is meant by it? Sexist banter can be offensive, but it is more the sexual advance that is at issue here. This can include everything from pestering for a date, through touching up, to promising promotion in return for sex.

The worst way of dealing with it is to allow it to continue and then have to deal with it as a major confrontation. In the early stages, a gentle, good-humoured putting down of the office groper by the victim may well have an effect. Men do not like their approaches – however half-hearted they may appear – to be rejected. Even just a hint that the victim considers the approach ridiculous or inappropriate may well nip the problem in the bud, so to speak.

Indeed, humour is the key. It can deflect all kinds of problem. So much better to employ it early on than allow an unwanted dispute to fester. Victims should always take other people – male and female – into their confidence. The personnel officer should have received training in how to deal with complaints like this and may well be able to defuse the situation by a quick word in the right ear. It can be much easier for people other than the victim to dissuade the harasser from his habits. Merely knowing that other people are aware of what is going may make him shrivel up and stop.

If the trouble still won't go away, it is important to keep a note of when incidents occur. If the harasser has ever put down anything on paper, keep the evidence. But it is an unedifying spectacle for everybody when this type of allegation has to be aired in court and the verdict can often appear as humiliating for the complainer as is the harassment complained of. It is so much better if the problem can be headed off at an early stage.

The office party. Or licensed sexual harassment. Usually more to be anticipated expectantly than enjoyed, office parties are notorious occasions of subsequent anguish. Just how often sex occurs behind the photocopier between the sales manager who has lusted after the secretary for the past twelve months and the secretary who has fancied the boss similarly, is anybody's guess. Terrible tales have often been told, too, of careers that have been blighted when a junior blurted out some terrible opinion of his boss, *in vino veritas*.

The chances of any of these things happening is immediately lessened if the party is held off the firm's territory. A sit-down lunch or dinner is much less likely to end in fireworks, and if spouses and partners are invited they can finally get to see the terrible colleagues they are always hearing about.

It is said that the taxman now concerns himself increasingly with this kind of business entertaining, in which case the writing may be on the wall for it anyway. In origin, it is a very agreeable thing for everyone to socialize once a year, but – rather like Father's Day – the Office Party has become a formalized, commercialized event and much of the original spirit has gone out of it.

The office whip round. A feature of office life is the frequent request to contribute to a colleague's wedding/

leaving/retirement present. You should only be invited to contribute if you genuinely know the person concerned. The organizer of the fund should suggest a minimum donation and invite you to sign a card almost as though you were getting something for your trouble. The frequency with which these requests come round, particularly given the turnover in employment of some offices, may be annoying. And sometimes the organizers do tend to be officious. In one large organization I know, each contributor signs a ready-cut piece of paper (and perhaps adds a personal message). Then all these pieces of paper are bound together in a leaving book.

Bear in mind that one day the recipient might be you and give selflessly.

Chapter 16

WRITTEN COMMUNICATION

To put it rather grandly, the letters that you send are an expression of your personality. They signify to the world how you wish to be considered . . . even before you have finished the first sentence. There is also real pleasure and satisfaction to be gained from writing a letter that is not only well-expressed but also well presented and legible.

Give us the tools

When it comes to choosing writing materials, it is best to avoid:

> paper that is too thin (thickness is not a luxury)
> coloured paper
> lined paper (cranks use it)
> 'borrowed' hotel notepaper
> personalized paper that has cute little designs, pictures or logos on it
> stick-on labels rather than printed addresses
> inks other than navy blue or black (cranks use a different colour on alternate lines)
> biro, ball-point or felt-tip (for personal correspondence, at any rate)
> envelopes that are brown (except for business purposes)
> envelopes that have been put through the office franking machine

None of these attributes is entirely sinful, or plain wrong in itself, but each is questionable if you want to put over a favourable image. The degree of sinfulness in each case is, of course, debatable.

'Evil communications corrupt good manners'
1 Corinthians, 15:33

For example: should you type or not type a personal note? It is still considered impersonal, too business-like, to type a letter of thanks or of congratulation, let alone a letter of condolence. And yet, I have an uncle who has the most appallingly illegible handwriting in the world; he knows this, and has always typed everything. This, to my mind, is perfectly considerate and courteous to the recipients of his missives. So I am very glad that he does. Unfortunately, no man's handwriting is illegible to himself. It was remarked of the indecipherable hand of Sybil Colefax, that the only way to tell what it said was to pin her notes to the wall and run past them.

Should you use or not use the word-processor? It is not snobbish to say that a properly printed, let alone embossed, letterhead is preferable to one that the writer has manufactured using a word processor. It is just that this last type can project a lacklustre image, look samey, and – if done on a dot-matrix printer – be vague and grey and hard to read.

'Remember that Charles Kingsley once received a letter from Dean Stanley, the illegibility of whose hand was notorious, at a time when Mrs Kingsley lay very ill. Kingsley examined the letter for many minutes in vain. At last he said: "I have every reason to believe this is a very kind letter of sympathy from Stanley – I feel sure it is. Yet the only two words I can even guess at are 'heartless

devil'. But I pause – I pause to accept that suggestion as a likely one under the circumstances."'
quoted in *The Week-End Book* (1955)

Notepaper. Good thick notepaper and envelopes are delicious things to receive and handle and, yes, to keep. The plainness and simplicity of your writing materials speaks volumes. Who would ever wish to treasure a fax, whatever information it contained?

At one time it was not thought to be the done thing to have your address and telephone number printed on personal notepaper. Engraved, handwritten, or applied by yourself with a presser, yes, but not printed. Again, there was no reason for this. Unfortunately, nowadays people are perhaps a little too creative with their personal printed notepaper, almost producing for themselves the equivalent of a personal logo in coats of many colours. A certain starkness, however, is to be favoured. Black ink on white paper is still the best.

Addresses. Using small pre-printed stick-on address labels is so widespread as almost not worth complaining about, but it only shows that the user is not prepared to pay for printed notepaper or is not prepared to write the address by hand.

To put the name of a house within inverted commas – e.g. 'Dunroamin' – is still considered incorrect. It is also unnecessary. (Indeed, anybody who 'writes' with too frequent 'use' of 'inverted commas', if you 'know what I mean', is to be discouraged, if not referred for a medical opinion. As for people (!) who never miss an opportunity to put in exclamation marks (!!), well, frankly, words fail me (!!!!)

The Post Office encourages the use of full addresses, including counties, where even a PO Box number is being used and a Postal Code. This is because not all sorting offices are capable of handling Postal Codes which, theoretically, contain all the information to target an area, though not always a precise letter-box. I should think it might also have something to do with the fact that many people write the letters in Postal Codes illegibly – which would not have occurred if an all-numbers zip-code system had been chosen, as in the United States.

So, however tedious it may be, full addresses are advisable. I prefer writing out the county name in full rather than use the traditional odd abbreviations – 'Herts' for 'Hertfordshire', 'Oxon' for 'Oxfordshire', and so on. The Postal Code should be put on a separate line and not underlined.

Punctuation in addresses is a science in itself. I once worked for a company which instructed secretaries to omit *all* punctuation from addresses. It was rumoured that this was to make a saving on the cost of typewriter ribbons. I agree with it up to a point as it gives a cleaner appearance, though a comma after a house number can make it clearer. Hence, what I would recommend is something like this:

Horace Gentleman
The Larches
22, Fortescue Road
Townsville
Countyshire
AA1 XY2

As regards pre-printed addresses, I have a personal dislike for the use of the italic typeface often used in engraving, where the letters and numbers of the Postal Code are almost unfathomable.

Phone numbers. It is not just people with ex-directory telephone numbers who might do well to consider leaving their numbers off their notepaper – or even of having two sets of notepaper, one with, one without. Telephone selling – cold calling, or what you will – is

rampant and you may like to ensure that as many
people as possible have to write to you instead of calling
you up out of the blue.

Dear Sir/Yours etc.

As has already been stated (in Chapter 13 TITLES AND
ADDRESSING), I advise a simple approach to titles: ignore
most of them. Only use them where it would be
outstandingly rude not to do so, or when the person
addressed is perceived as being the kind who likes
them. In other words, you should address people as they
would like to be addressed.

For the vast majority of people one is likely to have
to deal with in correspondence, ignoring titles in these
democratic days is a wonderfully refreshing thing to
do and overcomes any number of niggling associated
problems. Similarly, if you start a letter in what used
to be thought of as 'BBC' form, 'Dear Nigel Rees', it
obviates having to worry whether it should be Miss,
Mrs or Ms. This approach also lessens the likelihood
of annoyingly wrongly-sexed mail. There is something
particularly unwinning about a mailshot addressed to
a woman beginning 'Dear Sir', or indeed addressed to
a man beginning 'Dear Sir or Madam'. Indeed, 'Dear
Sir or Madam' is a curiously ungracious opening at
the best of times and should be avoided at all costs.

Now it should be said that there are some etiquette
gurus who deplore the omission of titles, honorifics and
designations of all kinds – it reduces everyone to the
level of schoolchildren, so they say – but I do not find
that this is so. What I do find is that addressing
someone in a letter, as 'Mr —— ——', instead of '——
——, Esq.' is, in a way I can't explain, not very
complimentary.

But what if you are writing to someone whose name
you may not know (like the bank manager) or if you are

writing to an institution? Simple. If you begin, 'Dear Manager' or 'Dear Midland Bank' (even if you are not in the habit of addressing bricks and mortar) you can end with 'Yours sincerely' rather than the 'Yours faithfully' that should end a letter beginning 'Dear Sir'.

Which brings us to:

Yours etc. Do you end a letter by writing 'Yours faithfully' or 'Yours sincerely'? Frankly, I dislike 'Yours faithfully'. It speaks from a different age – of knights in armour and blood oaths and all that paraphernalia – and yet Correct Form dictates that if you begin a letter 'Dear Sir/Madam', you must end 'Yours faithfully'. By beginning 'Dear Person's Name', however, you avoid this necessity and can sign off 'Yours sincerely'.

Personally, I would seldom end with any of the variants like 'Yours truly', 'Yours cordially' (Beachcomber recommended the response 'Dear Limejuice' to this one), 'Yours ever' (all right between very old acquaintances, but a bit wet with it), or 'Yours aye' (surely the province of Scots only). 'Yours' on its own, while conveniently non-commital, is a pretty tepid way out.

A servant of George IV who wrote him a letter beginning 'My dearest sir' ended it 'Invariably yours' (but joking with the sovereign is best avoided except by those who know exactly how it will be received). You can even avoid the matter entirely, by signing off with 'Best wishes' or 'All good wishes' and eschewing a 'Yours' of any kind.

These days, almost anybody will attempt to get away with 'Love from . . . ' or 'With Love'. This does not bear thinking about and, of course, should not but will be done.

Writing to newspapers for publication. An exception to the foregoing: depending on the paper, you will find that whatever you write will get rewritten to suit the paper's house style, or dispensed with completely. For example, should you follow the above advice and write 'Dear Editor' or 'Dear *Newspaper*' when writing to *The Newspaper*, you will find your copy replaced with 'Dear Sir' and 'Yours etc.', as a matter of course. If you write to the London *Evening Standard* and other tabloids your 'Dear' and 'Yours' will be excised completely.

Signing on and off. Like me, you may feel that 'Yours Etc.' is not much of a way to end even the most mediocre epistle, but there it is. Only *The Independent* seems to allow letters to start with a Dr Johnson 'Sir:', but it does permit its correspondents to depart from Correct Form by ending 'Yours sincerely', 'Yours truly', 'Yours etc.', as they will. Likewise, *The Times* disciplines everyone to an initial 'Sir' while allowing whatever ending the correspondent requires – even such baroque variants such as, 'I remain, dear sir, bemused' or 'Yours in stunned disbelief'.

Yours . . . (Mrs). There is something slightly effortful about adding after your signature 'Celia Molestrangler (Mrs)', but any attempt at (a) making clear what your signature is saying, and (b) letting your correspondent know how you wish to be addressed (Miss/Mrs/Ms), is surely to be encouraged.

Dear Couple. At a time when many people live together as couples and are not married, it is rather slack to address a card or invitation to them as 'Bob Bloke and Jane' or, for that matter, 'Grizelda Mate and Dick' and 'Hermione Mate and Liz'. You are probably doing this because you have never quite caught the partner's surname. So find out what it is. Putting only the name of the person you do know on the envelope and 'Bob and Jane' inside is artful but still sleight of hand.

Signing 'p.p.' And since we've got going on these rather arcane matters: how should one feel if one receives a typed letter signed not by the sender but, 'p.p.', by the sender's secretary? It stands for *per procurationem*, which is Latin for 'by proxy', not 'on behalf of', and so, in theory, it should precede the secretary's name rather than that of the person the letter is being sent on behalf of.

I think it is a wretched practice. It quite often appears to be used even when the dictator of the letter is still around the office and quite capable of signing it. I suppose if waiting for the dictator's own signature meant that a letter was unduly delayed, there might be something to be said for 'p.p.', but it is pretty ungracious even so.

Once I received a letter of congratulation about something I had done from a sort-of friend who obviously saw it as an occasion to keep in with me on a professional basis. It was signed by his secretary, 'p.p.' – thus completely negating any kindness of thought, and indeed demolishing any reciprocal feelings on my part.

Self-addressed envelopes

When you are writing to another person, soliciting information, when should you enclose a self-addressed and stamped envelope, and when not? Well, obviously if such a thing was requested, you would, but otherwise I do not think you should automatically send one. If, for example, the person you are writing to is a professional or business person, then he or she may well be able to claim the expense of any such correspondence off tax. If you are writing to a private individual, however, it might well be the case – though not necessarily – that sending an s.a.e. will encourage if not ensure a reply.

Incidentally, it is not correct to write 'J.N. Inquirer, Esq.' on a self-addressed envelope. However, although normally 'Mr/Mrs/Miss/Ms' are titles that can normally only be bestowed upon you by another, in this context, it is correct to put one of them on your s.a.e. before sending it off. Presumably the logic is that you are doing the addressing on the sender's behalf. (See also 'Phone manners' in Chapter 15 WORKING LIFE.)

Postcards

Postcards, whether blank or printed with your name and address (also called 'correspondence cards'), are an ideal way of dealing with small matters – not least briefly acknowledging something or simply saying thank you, without having to write a full-blown letter. As these do not require a 'Dear ——' at the start of the message, nor a 'Yours' anything at the end, they are also a good way of sidestepping the problems of just how to address your correspondent.

If you are sending a picture postcard with a thank-you message, it is not necessary to put your address on it, though if the postcard is of a foreign place or not of a place at all, it might be as well to write 'London', or the name of your home town, to make it clear where you are writing from.

If a printed postcard already bears your name, this is sufficient indication and you can safely just use your initial or initials to sign off with.

It might be thought that a postcard was too casual for some types of thank-you message – those requiring the full treatment. Putting the postcard within an envelope may lessen this charge, also because it means that you can write over the space where the address would have gone on the postcard and thus give what appears to be a more substantial message.

Theatricals are great senders of little messages – of good luck on first nights, of thanks for almost anything, of congratulations – and it is one of their most agreeable traits. The use of a postcard or correspondence card makes this ever so much easier to do than writing a formal letter.

Holiday postcards are a curious ritual and it is hard for even the most inspired senders not to fall into the 'Wish you were here/hope you are keeping well/the x shows our hotel bedroom' mode. The main thing, though, is that you have remembered to send a card and nobody is very interested to know whether you are enjoying yourself in the sun, or not.

Terribly well-organized people who set off on holiday intending to buy postcards and then use pre-printed stickers with their friends' addresses on them run the risk of turning what should be a kind thought into an industrial process.

Should you be nervous of dealing with foreign post offices and trusting your cards to the international mail, and should you rather not have your postcards arrive home three weeks after you do, it might be an idea to post them at home, as soon as you arrive there (with some such line as 'this is the PC I would have sent you if . . . ') But this should not become your usual mode of operation.

Christmas cards

(See under 'Christmas comes but once a year' in Chapter 12 SPECIAL OCCASIONS.)

Visiting cards

Once upon a time, these were a key element in the etiquette of visiting. Leaving a card at someone's house, with or without a corner turned over, was of the utmost significance. The card gave no more information than the name of the person who called – and this was long before a card bearing a clearly printed address, postal code and long and involved telephone number would actually have been of some use. Now, almost nobody uses visiting cards – except in business, where, if anything, they are proliferating.

Invitations

(See 'Issuing invitations' and 'Replying to invitations' in Chapter 4 GUESTS AND HOSTS, and 'Planning' in Chapter 5 MARRIAGE AND DIVORCE.)

To fax or not to fax

Another modern communications dilemma: should you or shouldn't you use the fax machine for personal rather than business purposes? Has the etiquette industry produced a set of rules to govern the use of that interesting piece of machinery which enables you to send letters, as it were by telephone?

The short answer is yes, you may. The sending of personal messages by fax is one of the most welcome of recent communications developments. It can be a discreet and speedy way of conveying information without having to engage in a telephone conversation. If you are sending instructions, say, the recipient has something tangible to hold on to. Above all, faxing has an agreeable informality to it, not least when it has encouraged people to return to handwriting their notes.

I think one can assume that if other people have fax machines, then they will be happy to receive personal messages on them. It has been known for love letters to be faxed, but on the whole the machine should not be used for thank-you letters or for replying to invitations or for letters of a sensitive nature – unless, of course, the exchange has been initiated by the other person via fax.

Whether for personal or business use, it is important

that some form of standard cover note is included with the message to make it very clear who the sender is, who the fax is intended for, and how many pages are being sent. It is important to remember that faxes may well be received in an open office and not just by the people they are addressed to. The confidentiality of any information contained is therefore always at risk.

Junk mail sent by fax is totally unacceptable. It is intrusive and, what is more, it uses up your paper into the bargain. Senders should be requested to remove your name from their lists.

Thank-you notes

People complain generally about a lack of 'pleases' and 'thank yous' in modern life, but what about that formalized communication, the written thank-you letter? Sometimes when I send presents off to my nephews and godchildren, and the months go by without my hearing anything, I wonder whether they still exist. Yet others describe a different experience. One woman wrote to me to say that the young friends to whom she dispensed gifts on birthdays and at Christmas were 'absolute angels' when it came to writing thank-you letters. It was their parents who had never yet thanked her for her wedding present who were the problem . . .

Few, if any, young people actually like writing thank-you letters – not least because presents may only have been given out of some misplaced obligation rather than genuine generosity. I can remember virtually copying out the same note to everyone when writing thank-yous for the umpteenth diary or box of handkerchiefs or postal order (in those days) sent at Christmas. There was the ritual hint of what I meant to spend the money on; the ritual mention of the trip to the pantomime (lots of exclamation marks); and the ritual concluding remark, 'Hope you are well'.

I look forward to the day when I can reasonably withhold presents from my young friends to save them the embarrassment and labour of writing to thank me. Occasionally, the odd gem is produced, of course. A relative, who shall be nameless, as he is now very grown up and responsible, once wrote to me from his prep school:

Dear Nigel,
    'Thank you very much for your card and 3 pound postal order I am not sure what I am going to spend it on yet. I might get some more tuck or another book. On Wednesday part of the playing [field] was under water I hope you are well love
    —— xxxxxxxx'

In adult life, and in the wider world, the PAS survey revealed that about four in every ten people *never* actually write a thank-you letter for a present, and almost seven out of every ten people *never* write to thank for a meal. There is no doubt that most people are very shaky, not to say inconsistent, on the subject of thank-you policy.

I am not inclined to be prescriptive on these questions of manners but surely, when it comes to thank-yous, the rule is: when in doubt, do it. You can't really thank people *too much* – even though I do have a wonderful aunt, who when I write to thank her for something, automatically writes back to thank me for my thank-you. And so it goes on.

But the forcing of innocent young children to write thank-you letters does draw attention to the difference between manners which are doing the done thing and manners which spring from genuine feelings. It also raises uncomfortable questions about the way in which manners can be cunningly employed to advance your own interests. The bestower of the gift gives because it enables him or her to exercise some kind of hold over the recipient (even if only a momentary hold over the attention). The recipient may say thank you, not from real gratitude, but in order to ensure that the bestowal of gifts will continue.

A murky business, then, but one worth persevering with. Some people do have a *gift* for saying thank you, and to hear from them is really worthwhile. There are signs, too, that thanking is coming back into vogue. Sometimes staying for a weekend merits an immediate telephone call *and* a subsequent letter. If the speed of your written thanks is hastened by using the office franking machine, think again. The genuineness of your appreciation will be lessened by treating your kind hosts as a mere cog in the modern communication chain. Thanks by fax is never permitted, except among jokey friends. The message may be handwritten, which is good, but it is not the real thing.

(See 'To fax or not to fax', above, and also 'Present giving' and 'Saying thank you for having me' in Chapter 3 FAMILY LIFE, 'The morning after' in Chapter 4 GUESTS AND HOSTS, and 'Planning' in Chapter 5 MARRIAGE AND DIVORCE.)

Business letters

The fustian of business correspondence – 're yours of the 5th ult', and so on – is no longer necessary. Indeed, it is actively to be discouraged. The only thing to be encouraged in business correspondence is that writers remember to put any reference number or designation that will enable the company or organization to deal with their letter swiftly. It is also vital that writers should keep copies of any correspondence so that they know what has been said, and when it was written.

Messrs and Ltd

At one time it was considered incorrect to put both 'Messrs' and 'Ltd' on the same envelope. However, 'Messrs' (plural of 'Mr' and an abbreviation of French *messieurs*) has now almost completely disappeared from use, and a limited company is now quite likely to be a public limited company (written 'plc' or 'PLC'), anyway.

Unsolicited correspondence

When does unsolicited correspondence have to be answered? Only when you feel like it and *if* you feel like it. Commercial junk mail never has to be answered, of course, but there is a certain type of mail that may detain you for a little longer. People however loosely in the public eye receive requests for help and information, even autographs and photographs, which may cost a good deal in terms of time and money.

I have seen certain public figures tip unsolicited correspondence straight into the wastepaper basket, the contents barely read and certainly unanswered. Others painstakingly reply to every letter, either with a view to winning popularity or votes, or because they feel that if someone is sufficiently willing to spend money on a stamp and an envelope (even to be rude) then they deserve a reply.

Some requests – to read attempts at fiction or to help someone with their campaigns – can be extremely tedious. If no postage is enclosed for the return of the manuscript, it deserves not to be returned. Veterans of this kind of harassment often devise all-purpose printed cards which they can send off with the minimum of thought:

Thank you for your inquiry but XXXX regrets that it is impossible for him/her to: read manuscripts/

judge literary contests/answer questionnaires/donate
copies of his/her books to libraries/give advice on
how to start a literary career/etc.

George Bernard Shaw, Edmund Wilson and A.J.P. Taylor
were practitioners of this art. They may have been
driven to it, but it seems a little less than gracious. A
scribbled note on a compliments slip – even one not
bearing the sender's address and telephone number, to
discourage further correspondence – will probably do
the trick.

The only correct response to mad correspondents was
formulated a number of years ago by H.L. Mencken,
when editor of *American Mercury*. Senders of unsolicited
manuscripts were advised:

> **Mr Mencken has just entered a Trappist monastery in
> Kentucky and left strict instructions that no mail was to be
> forwarded. The enclosed is returned, therefore, for your
> archives.**

Opinion-sharers were sent a postcard bearing the sym-
pathetic but correspondence-concluding message:

> Dear Reader,
> You may be right.

As to dealing with unsolicited mailing-shots, junk
mail, and so on – even telephone selling – there is a
contradiction here. Rather as with men shaving, if they
were offered the option of never having to bother with
shaving again, they would probably turn it down. If we
were told that we would never receive any unsolicited
brochures and advertisements ever again, we might well
feel a little disappointed. After all, it does occasionally
bring us something that is useful to know about. It is
possible to have your name and address removed from
mailing lists, officially, and sometimes organizations with

membership lists, like charities and credit companies, and which sell mailing lists on to advertisers, give you the option to have your name and address withheld. But no one can guarantee that your name and address will be removed from every existing list, everywhere.

Anti-junk mail campaigners return the material to sender without using any postage and enclose a duplicated request for their names to be removed from any lists. Or they make use of any prepaid envelopes and cards to convey this message back to the sender. How far this works I am not sure, but, if nothing else, it helps the anti-junk mail campaigners get things off their chests.

$\mathcal{I}$NDEX

address, modes of 247–8, 274–305
addresses (correspondence) 340
afternoon tea 22
AIDS 178
air travel 309–311
alarms, burglar and car 136
alcohol 129–131, 204, 243
alphabet, phonetic 234–5
amends, making 188
anniversaries, wedding 261–2
announcement (wedding) 113;
    (marriage) 97; (death) 267
answering (telephone) 233, 235, 326–
    7, 329–332
apologizing 187–8, 220
applause 157–8
artichokes 9
asparagus 9
At Homes 64–76
au pairs 51
audiences 155–161
Austen, Jane 58, 199
avocados 9
awards, accepting 252–3

babies 254–5
backstage 201
bad breath 46
bananas 9
banks 194–5
baptism 257
Bar/Bat Mitzvahs 259
Beaton, Sir Cecil 44
bedroom manners 179–181
bedroom, sharing 61–2
Beecham, Sir Thomas 128
beepers 236

begging 121–124, 309
belching 43, 44
bereavement 272
Beresford, Lord Charles 71
best man (wedding) 100, 111
bill (restaurant) 27, 38–9; (hotel)
    313–4
bill paying (on dates) 173
birthdays 260
births 254–5
black tie 67, 144
B.O. 43
body language 247
Bogart, Humphrey viii
bones (in food) 10
bores 212
borrowing 119
bosses 322–5
'Boston Switch' 89
bottle, taking a (for party) 75
bottles (drinking from) 4
boxes, Christmas 264
bread 10
breastfeeding 150
breath, bad 46
bridegrooms 99, 110
brides 107
bridesmaids 100
Burgess, Gelett 3
Burke, Edmund xi
burping 43, 44
business letters 344–5, 351–2
Butler, Samuel 128
buttons 144

cake (wedding) 112
callers, uninvited 117–119

Calman, Mel 26
candles 4
car phones 140–1
cards (Christmas-, post-, visiting)
263, 346–7
carol singers 265
Carreras, José 159
Carroll, Lewis 217
Carter, Jimmy 211
Carter, Lady Violet Bonham 169
Castle, Mrs Ted 279
cats 56
caviare 10
Cecil, Lord David xviii
celebrities 222–4
chairman 276
champagne 18–21, 31, 60
charities 120–121
cheese 10
Chesterfield, 4th Earl of 27
Chesterton, G.K. viii
children 47–50
Christmas 262–5
Churchill, Sir Winston 244–7
cigars 86
cinemas 155–161
clangers 219–220
cloakrooms 315–6
clothes 143, 149, 161; (evening dress)
67; (wedding) 103
clothing disorders 44
Clough, Arthur Hugh xvii
coasters 5
cocktail parties 64–93
coffee 86
Colefax, Sybil 339
coming of age 259
complaining (in restaurants) 34–5
complaints 185, 314–5
compliments 85, 199–202
condiments 5
condolence, letters of 269
condoms 178–9
confetti 112
confirmation 258
congratulations (marriage) 98
Congreve, William 168
consumerism 183
conversation 164, 225–232; (dinner
party) 87–91; (restaurant) 36–37
corn on the cob 10
corporate entertaining 156
correspondence see letters

couples (invitations to) 72–3;
(addressing) 344
courses (order of) 7
courtesies, meaningless 198
Coward, Sir Nöel 277
Cowper, William xiv
crashes, motoring 139–140
cruise ships 319
Curzon, Lord xiii
customer care training 184–5
customers 182–195
customs officers 310–311
cutlery 5

dances 94
dating 173
deaths 267–273
debts 191
degree ceremonies 259–260
Dempster, Nigel 172
diners 27
dining alone 26, 32
dinner parties 64–93
dinner jackets 67
dinner party books 79
disordered clothing 44
display, sexual 149
divorce 115–6
divorcees, addressing 279–281
doggie bags 41
dogs 56
doors (opening) 167–9; (revolving)
162
dress (fancy) 74; (when eating) 16, 28
drinking 4, 6, 129–131
drinks parties 64–93
drugs 203
drunks 91

eating (in street) 166
eavesdropping 37, 164
Edward VII, King 71
elbows 1, 17
Elizabeth the Queen Mother, Queen
211
Elizabeth II, Queen 44; see also
Queen, The
embarrassments 43–7
Emerson, Ralph Waldo xiv, xxi
endearments 198
endorsing products 201
engagement (marriage) 94–7;
(breaking off) 114–5

envelopes, self-addressed 345
Ephron, Delia 14
'esquire' 274
etiquette, definition of xiii
Eton 90
Euripides 271
evening dress 67
excuses 220–2

families 43–63
fancy dress 74
farting 43, 45–6
faux pas 219–220
fax machines 348–9
feminism 171
Ferraro, Geraldine 276
fête, garden 251
Filofax 329
finger-bowls 6
fingering (plates) 17
first-name terms 53–4, 213, 328–9
fish 11
flirting 177–8
flowers 61, 63; (funeral) 268–9
food (ordering) 28–30; (inedible) 33;
    (party) 74; (tasting) 34
forks 8
forthcoming marriages 97
four-letter words 154
Franklin, Benjamin xv
Frost, David 214, 227
fruit 11
Fuller, Thomas xv
funerals 268–272

Gallico, Paul 141
Gaskell, Elizabeth 9, 14, 26, 283
gatecrashing 75–6
George VI, King 254
Gielgud, Sir John 156
gifts 105–6 (and see presents);
    (baptism) 257; (Christmas) 264–
    265; (confirmation) 258
Giles, Frank 176
glasses, drinking 6
godparenting 256–7
going away (wedding) 112
gossip 232
Gowon, President 44
grace, saying (before meal) 7, 249
graduation ceremonies 259–260
grapefruit 11
gravy 12

greetings 217
Gregory, Rev. Ian xviii
guests 60, 62–3, 156–7; (wedding)
    109
Guinness, Sir Alec 155
Gulbenkian, Nubar 90

hairdressers 194, 316–7
halitosis 46
Hallowe'en 266
handbags 145
handicapped people 141–2
handkerchiefs 147
handshakes 196–8
handwriting 339
Hanukkah 263
Harding, Gilbert 171
hats 145
Hawkins, Francis 3
Hawthorne, Nathaniel 124
Heath, Sir Edward 257
heels, stiletto 210
hen parties 106
homosexuality 179
honeymoons 114
hotels 311–5
Hunt, Leigh 89

illnesses, 'sharing' 128–9
inedible food 33
interviews (job) 333
introducing people 215–7
introducing speakers 248
invitations (party) 64–73; (wedding)
    102–3; (weekend) 58–9
inviting back 93
irritating mannerisms 205

jacuzzis 151
jelly 12
Johnson, Samuel x
jokes 231; (practical) 113
junk mail 352–4

kebabs 12
Kingsley, Henry 146
kissagrams 211
kissing 210–11; (office) 334
knives 8

labels, address 338
Laboulaye, Edouard 59
language, U and Non-U 236–7

'Larryism' 213
lateness 82, 207–8
lavatory, terms for 151
Leap Year proposals 265
lending 119
Lerner, Alan Jay 3
letterheads 338–9
letters 342–5; (condolence) 269–270; (thank-you) 57, 93, 106, 349–350
letters (after name) 281
litter 166
Little, Mary Wilson xvi
lobster 12
locations, party 73–4
lonely-hearts columns 174
loo 152
lovers (terms for) 175–6; (unmarried) 61–2
Luce, Clare Boothe 162

Macmillan, Harold 230
madam 277
managers 322–5
mannerisms, irritating 205
marriage 95–115
Marshall, Arthur 272–3
Martine, Arthur xv, 38, 128, 130, 168, 197, 230
Marx, Groucho 201
'Master' 281
match-making 175
Maugham, Somerset 91
Maxwell, Robert 263
Melly, George 146
melon 12
memorial services 272–3
Mikes, George 3
mistakes 219–220
Mitford, Nancy 236
mobile telephones 135, 140–1
modes of address 247–8, 274–305
modesty, false 203
Montagu, Lady Mary Wortley xvi
Morecambe, Eric 223
Mosley, Diana 104
motoring 137–141
mourning 270
Ms. 275
muggers 165–6
Muir, Frank 199
Mulock, Dinah Maria xiv
mussels 12

name badges 217
name-dropping 202
names 213–5; (babies) 255; (first-) 53–4, 328–9; (married) 277–281
napkins 6, 80
negotiating, telephone 331–2
neighbours 117–137
Nelson, Horatio 208
nerves, speaking 241–3
Newman, Cardinal xii
newsletters, Christmas 264
Nixon, Richard M. 227
noise 131, 140, 159–160
non-smokers 127
notepaper 338–340
notes, using (when speaking) 243
nudity 150
number plates 141

office parties 336
old people 55
opening garden fête 251
ordering food 28–30
ovations, standing 158
oysters 13

paper, writing 338–340
parents, doting 49–50
Parker, Dorothy 162
parties 64–93; (hen & stag) 106–7; (office) 336; (surprise) 78
party-hopping 75
passes, making 177
passing the port 87
paté 13
peaches 14
peas 1, 13
pens 338
Perelman, S.J. 201
Perkins, Frances 277
personal organizers 329
personal remarks 232
personal stereos 134
personalized number plates 141
pets 55
phones 135, 140–1; (answering) 233; (office) 325; (numbers) 341
phonetic alphabet 234–5
photography 108; 163–4
planes 309–311
plate-fingering 17
plates, car number 141
pocket handkerchiefs 147

pockets 147
police 192
Polite Society, The xvii
politeness vii
port 87
portion control 17
postcards 346–7
practical jokes 113
prawns 14
presents 56, 257–8 (and see gifts); (dinner party) 80; (leaving/ retirement) 336–7; (wedding) 104–6, 107, 113, 115; (when staying) 60, 62–3
prizes, presenting 251–2
Prochnow, Herbert V. xvi
pronunciation 237–241
proposal, marriage 96, 265
proposing a toast 110–111, 250
Proust, Marcel 71
punctuality 82, 207–8
put downs 88

Queen, The 44, 90, 301
queuing 153

reception, wedding 99, 109–113
Reed, Thomas B. xii
references, giving 332–3
refusing invitations 71–2
regrets only 70–1
rejection (affairs) 181
relationships 167–181
remarks, personal 232
replying to invitations 67–71
restaurant 23–42; (bill splitting) 38–9; (conversation) 36–7; (service charges, tipping) 39–41; (smoking in) 35–6
restaurateurs 23–4
return visits 93
revolving doors 162
ribs, spare 16
rings (engagement) 96, 115; (wedding) 106–7
road manners 137–141
Ross, Alan S.C. 236
royalty 301–303
rudeness, responding to vii, 165
Runcie, Archbishop 283

sales people 189–190
salmon, smoked 15

sardines 14
sauce 15
saunas 151
Schopenhauer, Arthur xi
seafood 15
seating plans 83
seats, men giving up 169–170
secretaries 326–7
security, airport 309–310
Seear, Baroness 276
self-addressed envelopes 345
selling, telephone 190–1
servants 54
service charges 39
service (marriage) 101
service providers 182–195
serviettes 6
serving food 31–2
serving yourself 18
sex 61–2, 167–181
sexual display 149
sexual dressing 149
sexual harassment 334–6
shaking hands 196–8
Shaw, George Bernard xvi, 50, 209, 243
ships (cruise) 319
shoes 147
singing telegram 211–2
skips 136–7
slang 209–210
sleepiness 92–3
small talk 226–228
smells 161
Smith, Rev. Sydney xvi, 177, 197, 249
smoked salmon 15
smoking 205–6; (at dinner parties) 84; (in company) 125; (in restaurants) 35–6
snails 15
snobbery 206–7; (wine) 18, 30
snoring 93
social kissing 210–11
socks 148
soup 15
spaghetti 15
spare ribs 16
speaking, public 225–253; (wedding) 110
Spenser, Edmund x
spillages 77
St Valentine's Day 265
stacking plates 84

staff (for party) 75
stag parties 106
staircases 209
standing ovations 158
standing up 170
stay, going to 58–63
stepfamilies 52
stereos, personal 134
stiletto heels 210
stutterers 142
subjects, taboo 87
supermarket checkouts vii
surprise parties 78
swearing 154
Swift, Jonathan x, 13

table laying 4–7
table manners 1–42
table talk 87–91
taboo subjects (in conversation) 87,
    228–231
tasting (food, mutual) 34
taxi drivers 315, 319–320
tea (afternoon) 22
telegrams 262; (singing) 211–2;
    (wedding) 110
telephone selling 190–1
telephones 232–6, 326–7, 329–332;
    (numbers) 341; (mobile) 135
television 3, 206–7
thank-you letters 57, 93, 349–50,
    (wedding) 106
thank-yous (sex) 180
thanks, vote of 248–9
thanksgiving services 272–3
Thatcher, Mrs Denis 279
theatres 155–161, 201
theft, office 325
themes (party) 74
tipping 315–20, (restaurants) 39–41;
    (weekends away) 60
titles 274–305
toast, proposing a 110–111, 250
Tolstoy, Leo N. 50
tourists 306–9
travel 306–320, 346–7

'trick or treat' 266
Trollope, Anthony 231, 250
twenty-first birthday 259
Tynan, Kenneth 257
typing 339

U and Non-U language 236–7
unmarried lovers 61
unsolicited correspondence 352–4
unwanted food 33

Valentine's Day, St 265
vegetarians 80
Verdi, Giuseppe 271
Vidal, Gore 179, 257
videos 108, 163–4
visiting 58–63; (cards) 347
vote of thanks 248–9

waiters 24–7, 40–41
wakes (funeral) 271
Wales, Prince of Wales 71, 109, 154
Wales, Princess of 109, 228, 280
walkers (companions) 176–7
walking on the outside 171
Waugh, Evelyn xiv
wedding anniversaries 261–2
weddings see marriage
Wellington, 1st Duke of 227
white tie 67
whitebait 16
Whitehorn, Katharine 44, 84, 92
widows, addressing 280
Wilde, Oscar xii, xxi, 199, 232
wills (death) 273
Windsor, Duke of 148
wine 18–21, 30–31; (snobbery) 18, 30
withdrawing (at dinner parties) 86
Wodehouse, P.G. 14
Wollstonecraft, Mary xi
women (at work) 323–5; (dining
    alone) 26, 32
work (conversation topic) 88;
    (manners at) 321–337
writing 338–354
Wyld, Henry Cecil xii